GARDENING
with Trees and Shrubs

IN ONTARIO, QUEBEC, AND THE NORTHEASTERN U.S.

TREVOR COLE

D1399756

GARDENING
with Trees and Shrubs

IN ONTARIO, QUEBEC, AND THE NORTHEASTERN U.S.

To Muir

TREVOR COLE

Plant a Tree

Trevor Cole

Whitecap Books
Vancouver / Toronto

Copyright © 1996 by Trevor Cole
Whitecap Books
Vancouver/Toronto

All rights reserved. No part of this publication may be reproduced, stored in a retrieval system,
or transmitted in any form or by any means, electronic, mechanical, photocopying, recording or
otherwise, without prior written permission of the publisher.

The information in this book is true and complete to the best of our knowledge. All
recommendations are made without guarantee on the part of the author or Whitecap Books Ltd.
The author and publisher disclaim any liability in connection with the use of this information.
For additional information please contact Whitecap Books Ltd., 351 Lynn Avenue, North
Vancouver, BC, V7J 2C4.

Edited by Elaine Jones
Proofread by Elizabeth McLean
Cover design by DesignGeist
Cover photograph by T. Bonderud/First Light
Interior photographs by Trevor Cole
Illustrations by Brenda Cole
Interior design by Warren Clark
Typeset by Warren Clark

Printed and bound in Canada.

Canadian Cataloguing in Publication Data

Cole, Trevor J.
  Gardening with trees and shrubs in Ontario, Quebec and the northeastern U.S.

  Includes bibliographical references and index.
  ISBN 1-55110-400-8
  1. Ornamental trees—Canada. 2. Ornamental trees—United States.
3. Ornamental shrubs—Canada. 4. Ornamental shrubs—United States.
5. Gardening—Canada. 6. Gardening—United States. I. Title.
SB435.6.C2C64 1996   635.9'76   C95-911140-9

Contents

Introduction

In my many years as curator of the Dominion Arboretum in Ottawa, I received hundreds of enquiries from members of the public about which trees and shrubs to grow and how to take care of the plants they had growing already. I wrote this book to try and provide this information for gardeners in colder climates.

I have tried to supply the information on how to grow plants in a simple, non-technical way, taking readers through the process of buying, planting and taking care of their woody plants. Similarly, I have tried to distill the selection process down to the essential facts readers need to know to make a decision on which plants to grow in their own garden.

Living in a cold climate, I have focused on plants that will grow where winters are cold and generally long. In Canada this covers hardiness zones 1 to 6 and in the U.S. zones 1 to 5 and takes in the northern U.S. and Canada east of the Rockies.

I am indebted to my wife, Brenda, who suffered through my grumpy times when the words wouldn't flow, who criticized my rough draft (politely), and who did the line drawings that help make sense of the words.

I also acknowledge my debt to Carolyn Jones of VanDusen Botanical Gardens in Vancouver, B.C.; to Roger Vick, Curator Emeritus, The Devonian Botanic Gardens, Edmonton, Alberta; and to Bernard Jackson, Curator Emeritus, Memorial Botanical Garden, St. John's, Newfoundland, for reading my rough manuscript and putting me wise to gardening practices across the country. Thanks are also due to Heather Graham of the West Carleton Garden Club, a keen but neophyte gardener, who read the manuscript and told me what she didn't understand.

Back to Basics

Trees and shrubs are wonderful things. You buy them in a nursery or garden center, take them home and plant them. Lo and behold, a few days later little green leaves start to appear, the plant flowers and it starts to put on new growth. Before you know it, the young tree you planted is a mature specimen shading the house, or the shrub has grown to provide a floral screen. If only it were so simple.

In real life, the place you wanted to plant is like concrete; the plant falls over in the car and the main shoot breaks; it takes forever to leaf out and then is covered in bugs; and, come the first winter, you find it was never hardy where you live in the first place. Read on to learn how to identify and deal with these potential problems.

The basics of soil

Plants are not dependent on soil for growth; in fact hydroponic culture uses no soil. Plants must have something to give mechanical support and act as a reservoir of water and a source of dissolved minerals. Soil provides all of these things.

Soil consists of a mixture of different-sized particles of broken rock plus some plant and animal (mostly insect) remains. The proportion of the different-sized particles in the soil determines the type of soil: sandy, silty, or clay.

Sand particles are finely ground rock, like a very fine gravel, but are still comparatively large.

The particles have large spaces between them, allowing water to drain rapidly. If you think of the difference in the spaces between a bowl of oranges and a jar of small ball bearings you can get the idea. Sand is also an inert material and has little ability to retain any manure or fertilizer you apply.

Silt is much finer, about ten times as small as sand—more like grapes on our size scale. It drains comparatively slowly and can pack down to give an almost impervious soil. It also retains little of the plant foods, allowing them to drain through.

Clay particles are ten times smaller still and are the tiny ball bearings of our analogy. They pack very closely and, if badly treated, form a waterproof soil. After all, clay is the basic material for making pottery. Conversely, clay is a very rich soil and forms a chemical bond with the nutrients, holding them in a solution that makes them available to plants.

A simple test will determine which soil type you have. To get an average sample, take a small trowelful of soil from various parts of your garden and mix them together. On a large property, where soils may differ considerably, take a separate sample from each different location. Allow the samples to dry until you can crumble them with your fingers. If you are doing this in summer and the soil is baked hard, place the samples in plastic bags, add a few drops of water and leave them overnight.

Put about half a cupful of crumbled soil into a straight-sided glass jar, such as a peanut butter jar, and fill it almost to the top with water. Screw on the lid and shake it well so that all the soil is in suspension. Place the jar on a level surface and allow the contents to settle out. A windowsill works well because the back-lighting makes it easy to see the layers that will form.

The sand, having the largest particles, will settle quickly. Silt, with intermediate particles, will settle on top of the sand. The fine particles of clay may take several days to settle enough for the water to be clear. The humus—plant remains—will float on the top. In some muck soils, this can be the largest amount, but generally it is less than 10 percent.

Now you can measure the relative amounts and decide which type of soil you have: sandy, loamy or clayey (Figure 1.1). While there is no hard and fast dividing line between the soil types, and different books will give slightly varying proportions, a soil with more than 50 percent sand

Figure 1.1
A simple method to tell your soil type.

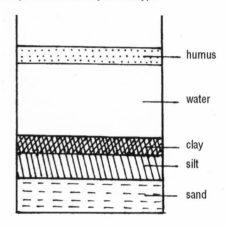

and less than 15 percent clay is very open and sandy. Silty soils contain about 50 percent silt and 15-25 percent clay. They are good soils that can be improved by the addition of coarse sand to increase the drainage.

A soil containing more than 50 percent silt and more than 25 percent clay is a clay loam, and the higher the proportion of clay, the more difficult it becomes to work. Indeed, they are the most difficult of all soils in which to garden, sticky when wet, poorly drained and slow to warm up in spring. They bake as hard as bricks in summer and frost-heave badly in late winter.

Because of their chemical bonding, they tend to crack deeply as they dry, so even when it rains, the water runs into the cracks, rather than soaking in all over the surface. Such soils can be improved by the addition of small gravel or coarse sand, plus all the humus you can possibly add. Soil improvement is worth every effort, but it is a slow process and it may take years to develop a good soil.

In chapter 11 you will find lists of trees and shrubs for specific soil types. In part, this is a measure of how well or poorly these plants react to the presence of water in the soil. Heavy clay soils are often waterlogged and when that happens, there is little air left in the spaces between the particles. Plant roots do not grow in soil, but in the spaces between the soil particles, where they find dissolved minerals and oxygen.

All living plants need oxygen, just as we do, and for the same purpose: to oxidize stored sugars to provide energy. In plants, the energy is needed to make new stems and leaves (grow), extend the root system (hunt), produce flowers and set seed (reproduce), and store energy to survive the winter (fill the pantry).

Since plants don't have a heart and blood system to take oxygen to all parts, the roots must get the oxygen they need from the air in the soil structure. Their ability to extract dissolved oxygen from the water in the soil determines their soil preference.

Sweet and sour: the pH scale

Years ago, gardeners found that some plants grew better in a soil where the underlying rock was limestone, and languished or died in a soil with a high peat content. With time, it was realized that the limestone soil was alkaline while the peaty soil was acid; they were *sweet* and *sour* in gardening terms.

The pH scale measures the relative alkalinity or acidity of a soil. It runs from zero (pure acid) to 14 (pure alkaline), with 7 being the neutral point. Each number is 10 times as strong as the one below it—working out from neutral. Thus a pH of 5.5 is 10 times as acid as 6.5, while 4.5 is 100 times as acid as 6.5. The range that most plants prefer is 6.5 to 7.2, but some (for instance, blueberries) like a really acid soil with a pH of 4.5. In general, more plants seem to tolerate a slightly acid soil than a slightly alkaline one.

The most commonly grown shrubs with a specific preference are members of the rhododen-

dron and azalea family. They like a pH of 4.5 to 5.0 and if most of your neighbors have a rhodo in their front garden, your soil may be so acidic it will limit what other plants you can grow. See the list in chapter 11 for trees and shrubs that prefer an acid soil. Most plants are not too fussy, and by looking around your neighborhood you will soon find what grows well in your region.

Within reason, you should try to grow the plants that do well in your soil type, but it is possible to modify soils to a degree. Acid soils are comparatively easy to make more alkaline by the addition of lime. The amount needed depends on the soil type. Adding 25 pounds (10 kg) of lime to 1000 square feet (100 sq m) of a sandy soil will raise the pH by one point. Use twice this amount on loams and three times this on clay soils for the same degree of change.

Alkaline soils are more difficult to make acid. Sulphur and sulphate of iron are the best acidifiers, but the amount to add can vary and they are slow-acting. Use one of the soil-test kits (available at larger garden centers) to find the pH of your soil, then add half a cup (125 ml) of powdered sulphur to a square yard (metre) and retest after a few weeks. This will give you a basic reference on how much to add in future. To create an acid soil bed in an alkaline region, it is best to make a raised bed so the ground water does not affect the pH.

The effect of pH is quite complicated, but it helps if you understand a little about it. The acidity or alkalinity of a soil affects the availability to the plant of some of the minerals dissolved in the soil moisture. There seems to be a kind of blocking action; for example, while there may be plenty of iron in a soil, if the pH is high, it may not be available to the plant. Plants themselves differ in the amount of iron they need. What is plenty for a hydrangea is slow death for a rhododendron when planted in an alkaline soil.

What do the numbers mean?

The topic of soil nutrients and the chemicals a plant requires for growth is a complex subject that that can't be detailed here, but knowing what role the various elements play in plant growth will help you understand why you use certain fertilizers.

Three numbers are printed somewhere on every packet of fertilizer sold. On some houseplant fertilizers the numbers are in very small type, but they are there. The three numbers represent the percentages of the three major plant nutrients in the fertilizer: nitrogen, phosphorus, and potassium.

Nitrogen is the major building block for plant cells. Without nitrogen the plant becomes stunted and sick-looking, new growth stops, and the plant eventually dies. Nitrogen is soluble and continually leaches out of the soil with the soil moisture. Luckily, it is a part of every plant and animal cell, so the breakdown of organic matter in the soil releases more nitrogen. An overdose has the opposite effect, causing lush growth, large leaves and elongated, spindly stems, usually at the expense of flowering and fruiting.

Nitrogen is available in many forms, both organic (from natural sources, such as blood meal) and inorganic (from artificial—manmade—sources, such as petrochemicals). It may be instantly available, as in soluble fertilizers, or available over a period of time, as in slow-release formulations. From the plant's point of view, whatever the origin, it has to be converted to a dissolved nitrite before it can pass through the root cell wall and be usable by the plant.

Phosphorus is not soluble and so does not leach out of the soil, but it doesn't move through the soil either and must be placed in the root zone to be effective. The phosphorus in liquid fertilizers soon becomes tied up by the soil and then can move no further. Phosphorus is essential for growing tips of roots and shoots, and for flower and fruit production. Because they stimulate root growth, fertilizers with a large middle number (equalling a high phosphoric acid content) are sold as plant starters. Phosphorus can be found in bone meal and superphosphate.

Potassium is essential for the formation of starch and sugars and for the movement of chemicals within the plant. It is commonly known as potash and is essential for healthy growth. It is moderately soluble, but most soils contain sufficient for normal plant growth. As a landscaper friend of mine puts it: nitrogen for tops, phosphorus for bottoms, and potash for all-round good health.

Trace elements is the name given to the many other chemicals plants require in varying amounts. Carbon is a large part of cells but is obtained from the carbon dioxide in the air. Calcium and magnesium are also needed in relatively large quantities for cell formation and photosynthesis respectively. Then there are a host of other chemicals that are required in very small amounts, sometimes minute amounts, but without which the plant cannot grow properly. These trace elements are usually only of concern if you are trying to grow plants in soil that is unsuitable.

Plant names

When gardeners get talking, they often talk about plants. Unfortunately, they may not be talking about the same plant, even though they think they are. One common name can apply to several different plants, while botanists, with their love for reclassifying plants, can give a new name to a plant we have known for years. Fortunately, botanical changes are usually slow to be adopted by garden centers so the names given in this book should locate the plant you want.

All the plants in this book have two names. One, the common name, is not fixed and can vary from region to region. There have been efforts in the past to standardize common names, but they have not been very successful.

The other name is the botanical, or scientific, name. This is the specific name given to a particular plant and is recognized world-wide. When you go to a garden center or nursery, it is helpful to have the botanical name written down, so you are sure of getting the plant you want.

Botanical names are in two parts, the genus and the species. The genus (the plural is genera) is the group to which the plant belongs—for example, *Acer*, the maples, or *Malus*, the apples and crab apples. The species name is the specific plant within that genus and may refer to the color of some part of the plant—such as *rubra* (red), *rosea* (pink), or *alba* (white). It may denote the plant shape, as in *pendula* (weeping) or *fastigiata* (upright); where the plant came from, as in *chinensis* (Chinese); or refer to some botanical attribute, such as *dentata* (with toothed leaves). In written works, botanical names are printed in italics and the genus name starts with a capital letter.

A species is a plant that you could find growing in the wild somewhere in the world. For example, green ash grows wild from Quebec to Saskatchewan and as far south as Texas. It will come true from seed, although there will be some slight variation in shape or final height. The word species can be abbreviated to sp.; more than one species within a genus is abbreviated to spp., as in *Fraxinus* spp.—several individual species of ash.

Within a native population, there may be a group of plants that is significantly different, and these are known as a variety. For example, the native honeylocust *(Gleditsia triacanthos)* has long, sharp thorns, but there are also almost identical plants without thorns growing in the wild. These are a natural variety, known as var. *inermis* (Latin for unarmed), and will, like the species, come true from seed. Variety names also start with a lower-case letter and, like the species name, are printed in italics.

A hybrid is a cross between two closely related plants. It may have occurred in the wild or be the result of controlled plant breeding in a nursery. The species name is preceded by a multiplication sign to indicate this, as in the purple-leaved sand cherry *Prunus* x *cistena*.

A cultivar (short for CULTIvated VARiety and abbreviated to cv.) is either a selected hybrid that arose in a garden or nursery—such as 'Peace' rose—or was chosen for some outstanding attribute from a group of wild plants. For example, the green ash cultivar 'Patmore' was selected at Vegreville, Alberta, by Richard Patmore for its superior shape and lack of seeds. The majority of cultivars are propagated by cuttings or grafting so that all the plants are identical. Cultivar names are usually enclosed in single quotation marks, begin with a capital letter, and are in regular type.

CHAPTER 2

Decisions, Decisions

Trees are usually planted in lawns, while shrubs are planted in beds. Some large shrubs are useful as specimen plants in the lawn (these are identified in chapter 10), but in the main, shrubs are planted in company with plants other than grass. There is no reason, however, why trees cannot be planted in a border. They will add height and textural contrast, as well as providing shade, which will enable you to grow a wider range of plants.

Impulse buying can lead to very costly mistakes. Before you rush out to your local garden center, stop and think about the plants you are going to buy. If you go without any sort of ideas in mind as to their characteristics, you could well end up with a totally unsuitable plant. It is rather like going to the pound to choose a puppy. They all look so cute, how do you decide? With trees and shrubs, a little homework before-hand will prevent you bringing home a St. Bernard when you really wanted a spaniel.

Size

Trees and shrubs have a maximum size at maturity. This may vary somewhat depending on where you live, and a tree that grows 40 feet high (12 m) in the north may reach 50 feet (15 m) in mid-New York State. But the sizes given in the plant listings are the average maximum. This is particularly important with shrubs, where the same species may have cultivars that differ greatly in height. Generally, tree cultivars do not vary to as large a degree.

When buying a shrub to plant in front of your living-room window, you need one that will grow no higher than the sill, rather than one that covers half the window. Having read the descriptions in chapter 10, you can make an informed choice rather than relying on guesswork. Should the plant grow a lot larger than its cultivar description, you have a legitimate beef with the nursery for selling you a mislabelled plant.

Knowing the final size of a plant is especially important with trees, particularly if they are planted close to utility lines or if your property is small. The shape of your home can also affect the type of tree you select. A low, ranch-style bungalow needs a tree with a spreading shape; a slim, columnar shape would complement a narrow townhouse better.

Select a plant suitable for the type of soil you have and for the amount of sun or shade it will receive. Some plants, such as viburnum and dogwood, are happy in either sun or shade, but the majority will not grow well if planted in the wrong light conditions.

Make a list of the features you require in the plants you intend to buy, in order of preference. This will not be the same for every plant—the specifications for a specimen tree could differ greatly from those of a shrub screen—but it will help you to make up your mind and decide what is most important.

Shape

This can vary greatly in trees and shrubs, but in both cases there is a shape to fit every location. **Columnar** plants have branches growing parallel to the main stem; it is more pronounced in trees, probably because they are larger, but also occurs in a few shrubs. **Conical** plants taper from the base to the top; many upright junipers have this shape. **Pyramidal** plants also taper, but are much wider at the base. This is a common shape, particularly in shrubs. **Vase-shaped** plants arch from the base outwards. Good examples are bridal-wreath spirea and American elm. **Mop-headed** plants are those that don't really have a definite form; they defy description. **Prostrate** and **mound** shapes are both

very low. Prostrate plants follow the contours of the ground while mound plants form a little hummock; they are restricted to shrubs. **Globe-headed** trees are natural forms that make an almost circular head without clipping. Topping a bare stem, they look like a giant lollipop. **Weeping** trees trail their branches down to the ground. They can be large, like a weeping birch, or quite small, like some of the weeping peashrubs. Last are the shapes made by a pruner in the nursery, often referred to as **topiary**. They must be pruned regularly to retain their shape, and these manicured plants do not fit into every landscape design.

Foliage

Color is an important aspect of your choice. The basic color of plants is green, but some cultivars are available with leaves of different hues. They may be solid colors or variegated patterns of green with a second color. These colors may be present all the time, as in the purple-leaved sand cherry, or the new growth may unfurl one color and slowly change to green as the summer progresses, as in Deborah Norway maple. Fall color can be quite dramatic in deciduous (leaf-losing) plants and is often the main reason for growing a particular plant. We do not think of evergreens as having fall color but many do undergo a subtle, but still noteworthy, color shift as colder weather starts. Look at some of the junipers or 'PJM' rhododendron.

Color also plays other roles in the garden. Trees and shrubs with pale or light-colored foliage appear closer than they are and can visually shorten a long garden. The opposite is true for dark-leaved plants. Also keep in mind the background seen from the normal viewing area. A red-leaved shrub will be lost against a red brick garage, for example.

Think about the **density** of the foliage. Although you plant some trees to give shade, the density of the shade depends on the type, size, and shape of the leaves. Plants with large leaves cast a much denser shade than those with fine leaves made up of individual leaflets, or those with small leaves. This can also affect what you will be able to plant in and around shrubs, or as a ground cover under a tree. Even the ability to grow a good lawn under a tree depends to a large extent on the depth of shade the tree casts. On a practical note, large leaves are easier to rake than small ones, but small ones break down faster in a compost pile.

Trees and shrubs leaf out at different times. Some are among the first to show green in spring, while others wait almost until summer before they take the plunge. Late leafing allows the soil under the tree to warm up and gives bulbs a better chance.

Flowers and fruit

For most people, the main thing to consider when choosing woody plants is the **flowering**. This can be broken down into **season** and **color**. The majority of trees and shrubs flower in spring and early summer. This allows the maximum time to set and ripen seed, and for the resulting seedlings to become established before winter. Seed that ripens late in the season often has a built-in delay mechanism to prevent it germinating until the following spring when it will have a full season to become established.

White, pink and red are the predominant colors for tree blooms, but shrubs come in just about every shade you can imagine (except black). The warmer the climate, the greater the range of colors available. While most people think of the showy blooms of forsythia, crab apples or rhododendrons, many trees we don't normally associate with flowering have attractive blooms. Next spring, look at the flowers on maples or oaks, and see how colorful and intricate they are.

There are fewer trees and shrubs that flower after early July (especially trees), and they are possibly more desirable because of this, since they attract hummingbirds and butterflies into the garden. However, the early-flowering plants often have an advantage from the gardener's point of view, as they have attractive **fruit**. Fruit can add color to an otherwise drab winter garden. If chosen with care it can be a source of food for wildlife, which again adds interest.

Fruit does have some drawbacks. Berries and small fruit not eaten by birds have to be cleaned up in spring. It also acts as a source of food for mice and voles, which then stay around to nibble on other goodies, such as the bark on newly planted shrubs (see chapter 4 for prevention).

Winter effect

Winters in our region tend to be long and, in many places, cold. Our gardens may be covered with a blanket of snow for months on end, and the weather does not tempt one into the garden. We spend our time indoors, looking out. Plants that add interest to this winter scene are a bonus.

As well as fruit, consider also the textural quality of the plants, both the shape of the tree and its bark. The shape of a tree is revealed when the leaves fall and may be very beautiful. The peeling bark of paper birches is probably the best-known example of interesting bark, but many trees and shrubs are equally attractive. Bark may be patterned with marks, either vertically or horizontally; it may be flaking, revealing a different color beneath. The bark on some cherries seems to glow from within when lit by sunlight; and the winged bark of euonymus is well known for its winter beauty. Add to this the effect of bright bark on the new growth of dogwoods, willows and kerria, and you have a whole new color palette to play with.

Hardiness

I have left till the end the most important criterion you should use when deciding on what to plant—**hardiness**. If a plant is definitely not hardy in your area, it is a waste of time (and money) to plant it.

North America has two major ways to measure hardiness: the United States Department of Agriculture plant hardiness map and the Agriculture Canada plant hardiness map. They are not interchangeable. Be sure which the author was using when reading about a plant. Many books give only the U.S.D.A zones, even those written by Canadian authors. The U.S.D.A. map has eleven zones to cover a climate ranging from frigid Alaska to tropical Hawaii. The Agriculture Canada map uses nine zones from frigid Yukon to temperate B.C. The U.S. zone 4 covers the Canadian zone 5 with some southern zone 4 and northern zone 6. See pages 214 and 215 for the correct map for you.

Having said that, hardiness zones are only a guide, an indication of what will normally grow in an area. Two adjacent gardens, one sheltered by hedges, the other swept by winter winds, could grow entirely different plants. This is especially true close to the edge of a hardiness zone. Microclimates, small local variations in the overall pattern, are everywhere. A garage wall that deflects winter winds down a narrow path could make the end of this wind tunnel several degrees colder than the norm. Mountainous regions are especially difficult. A bend in the road can change the exposure from southerly to northeasterly and may alter the hardiness by two zones.

Do not be afraid to experiment. Use the zones as a guide to what should grow in your area, but do try plants that you think may be on the borderline of hardiness for you. Join your local horticultural society or garden club. There you will meet with others who have been through all this already. They can advise you on what is impossi-

ble (for them at least). Don't spend a lot of money on these dubious plants. The smaller the plant, within reason, the better it will transplant and the easier it is to protect while young. Plants can adapt to some degree to harsh conditions and may surprise you. I am not trying to say you could ever grow palm trees outdoors in Toronto, but it is sometimes surprising what will survive.

Study your garden for a winter or two before you start experimenting. Snow is a great insulation, so plant iffy plants (if they survive it will be wonderful) where they will get the best snow cover. It doesn't hurt to mollycoddle these plants for a year or two; protect them in late fall to help them along. In warmer regions, where snow is rare or fleeting, plant dubious plants on the south side, close to the house, where they will receive the maximum benefit of reflected heat.

At the garden center

You now realize there is more to buying a tree or shrub than just slipping down to the local nursery to grab the first plant that takes your fancy. I am constantly amazed by people who will cheerfully pay out large sums of money for plants that are totally unsuitable for the location they have in mind.

You, the informed shopper, having done your homework and studied this book (and I hope similar ones, for each writer describes things differently), will have decided on the perfect plant for that specific place. Now all you have to do is find it.

When you enter the nursery or garden center, your resolve starts to crumble. How can you ever hold to your choice when surrounded by such a multitude of plants? Take a deep breath, count to ten and relax. Be single-minded: keep your original plant list firmly in mind and ignore all the rest.

Even if you stick to this rule, you could be

faced with several choices for the same plant. Shrubs may be bare-root, prepackaged, potted, or balled and burlapped (B & B). Trees could be bare-root, potted, or B & B. Sometimes large trees are in wire baskets or dug with a tree spade (a hydraulic spade). These are probably not actually on view in a nursery, but are often available if you ask. The choice varies across the continent.

Bare-root plants are just that—plants that have been dug from the nursery row and are offered for sale without any soil on their roots. As long as the plants are dormant and are kept cool, this is a good way to buy them. Bare-root plants are found chiefly at local nurseries that grow their own plants. Plants may be heeled-in, that is, the roots are covered in soil to keep them from drying out, but they are not properly planted.

Prepackaged shrubs have been dug bare-root, have had their roots wrapped in a moist packing material, such as wood fibers or sphagnum moss, then have been put into a plastic bag and stored cool until sales time. This is an inexpensive way to buy small plants, which usually thrive if they have been stored correctly.

Basic, popular shrubs are often sold in prepackaged bags. If you are lucky, you might find some unusual plants among them. Good garden centers keep prepackaged plants outdoors in a cool environment. If you buy a prepackaged shrub with shoots an inch (2.5 cm) or more long it could indicate future problems. The plant has drawn on food reserves in the stem to make new growth and there may not be sufficient reserves to make a strong root system. Moreover, the tender new growth will probably be killed when put out in the garden. Prepackaged shrubs are not a bad buy, but be sure to get them while they are still dormant, before they are forced into premature growth.

Many large wholesale nurseries are now growing some of their plants exclusively in containers. It's a more efficient way to control watering, feeding and weed competition, and the plants are easier to sort and pack when making deliveries. Providing they are looked after properly in your local garden center after delivery, these plants are the equal of bare-root plants grown locally. As a bonus, they can be planted at any time the soil is not frozen, although I would not advise planting during a heat wave.

Some potted trees and shrubs are similar to prepackaged plants except that when they are dug in fall, they are potted individually. This has advantages and drawbacks. If you buy them early, before growth starts, they will not have made any roots to hold the soil together. When you remove them from the pot, in all probability all the soil will drop off. As long as the plants have not made any growth, this does not matter. It is just the same as buying a bare-root plant from the nursery. Occasionally, roots are chopped off more than is advisable to fit the plant in the pot, which can result in slow establishment.

From the retailer's point of view, having woody plants in pots means that sales are not restricted to a few hectic weeks in spring. Containerized trees and shrubs can continue to be sold long after the normal planting season. The drawback for buyers is that if plants are grown in a small container for too long, the roots start to curl round inside the pot. If this is not corrected at planting time (see "Planting potted or B & B plants," chapter 3) it can shorten the life of the plant considerably.

B & B plants are dug from the field with a large ball of soil, which is then wrapped in burlap. This is done chiefly with conifers (which are also available potted) that need the minimum of root disturbance, and a few shrubs, such as magnolia, that have a fleshy root system.

Trees that are too large to pot are put into a wire basket which may be up to three feet (1 m) across. This type of tree is generally sold to land-scapers and municipalities who have the equipment to handle them: a three-foot (1-m) rootball is more than the average home owner can manage, and Superman doesn't make house calls.

If you have a landscape contractor plant this type of tree for you, make sure the basket is cut off once the tree is in place and before the hole is filled. Problems are beginning to show up on trees that were planted several years ago. It was assumed the basket would rust away before there was any danger of roots being girdled, but this is not proving to be the case. In some soils, the baskets rust very slowly and roots growing close to a wire are constricted by it, which shows up later as problems in the crown.

Even larger trees are available. They are dug with a tree spade that takes out a rootball several feet across and lifts the entire tree onto a cradle over the cab of the truck. I must admit I am not a lover of the "instant garden" school of thought. Trees put their roots out on either side, approximately as far as they are tall. If you move a twenty-foot (6-m) tree, you are chopping off most of these roots, even with a five-foot (1.5-m) rootball. If nursery-grown, they will have been root pruned to reduce trauma, but even so trees can take several years to recover from such treatment, if at all. You may have a one-year guarantee, but the tree can linger on for four or five years, putting on less and less growth each year, before finally dying. Even trees sold in wire baskets suffer tip kill and premature leaf fall for two or three years before growing normally.

In comparative plantings, I have seen a normal-sized tree, such as you would buy and take home on the roof of your car, that has caught up in size with a large tree in about ten years. The larger tree was still putting on little new growth, while the smaller tree was growing several inches per year.

The perfect plant

When buying shrubs, look for plants with a few sturdy branches from the base, rather than a thicket of thin stems, although this does depend to some degree on the species involved. Inspect the branches for injury, scraped bark, and broken twigs. The pots are often packed one on top of the other during transport from the wholesaler, and a little damage is normal, but avoid the badly mauled plants.

Trees can be roughly divided into two groups, those which grow upwards, like oaks and lindens, and have a definite leader, and those, like crab apples, that form an ever-expanding crown. The leader is the main shoot of a tree that continues to grow upwards and, in time, forms the main trunk.

With the first group, trees that grow upwards, you are looking for a well-balanced branch system, with the branches evenly spaced round the tree. They should form a rough circle when seen from the top. The leader is all-important to this type of tree and should be undamaged (Figure 2.1). If the trees were not given adequate space in the nursery, they could have grown more towards

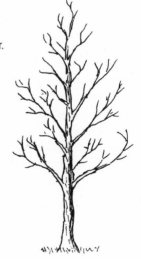

Figure 2.1
A tree with a
central leader.

the spaces between the rows because of competition from neighboring plants. This can result in a tree with an oval crown, which may be desirable for planting in some garden designs or in an enclosed space. Next, inspect the tree for general damage. As with shrubs, a few broken twigs are not a major problem, but steer clear of trees with a broken main branch or areas with badly skinned bark.

Although the trees in the second group often have a leader when young, it is the branch structure that is most important here (Figure 2.2). A tree with a large gap in the branches on one side will need very skilful pruning to bring it back

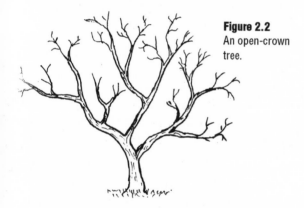

Figure 2.2
An open-crown tree.

to the correct shape. If you are that good at pruning, you probably don't need this book.

Again, look for broken branches and missing bark. Remember, if you don't like the plants in the first nursery you visit, there is another down the road, or in the next town. Be choosy: a tree or shrub will be in place for a long time and is a major component of the landscape.

Once shrubs and trees have started to leaf out, you can still plant them, but be a little more cautious before you buy. Look at shrubs very carefully for wilting shoot tips or a rootball pulling away from the pot (both signs the plant has been allowed to get extremely dry). Feel the soil and

push your fingers deep into the rootball. Is it wet only on top (a sign of poor watering) or right through? The burlap surrounding B & B plants may be treated to slow down evaporation from the rootball as the plants wait for their new owners; this also makes it difficult to water them, so check plants carefully before you buy. Poke around on top of the rootball and find an opening in the burlap. Again, push your fingers into the roots and feel for moisture content. On conifers, look at the needles: there will always be some dead ones, but a general yellow tinge denotes poor storage or dryness. Be a good customer, be careful, and handle plants carefully. Replace any burlap you pull aside and never leave a plant worse than you found it.

As mentioned, shrubs and trees are often dug in the fall, put into containers, and stored over winter for sale next spring. While in storage, they do not make roots, so when you remove them from the container, much of the soil will fall off. This does not matter while the plants are dormant, but once the leaves start to appear you need the minimum root disturbance possible.

Shrubs will take more root disturbance than trees, probably because they do not lose as many roots when dug. Providing you plant them with care (as described in the next chapter) you can move them even when in full leaf. In fact, if they were properly cared for in the nursery, you may be better to wait a while. As well as making top growth, the shrubs are also putting out roots which help hold the soil in the container together.

Trees in containers should always have been potted for a year before they are sold, but unfortunately this does not always happen. To test for root formation, ask the nursery staff to unpot a plant for you so you can look at the roots. Keep your eye on the soil. If the tree pulls out of the soil, it is not well rooted; if no soil movement is seen, the tree is well rooted, and if the entire rootball lifts out of the pot, you know for sure it is well rooted.

It is possible for the tree to be too well rooted; this is known as being rootbound. If it has been growing in the same container for several years, the roots may have circled inside the pot several times. If planted out as is, this type of root system can kill the tree several years down the road. As the roots expand, they gradually strangle each other where they crossed on their circular path. Researchers are trying to devise a type of pot with slits or ridges inside that will prevent this from happening.

As the season progresses and the plants come fully into leaf, it is still possible to plant them, although I would avoid planting during the heat of summer. You can often get some good bargains at this time of year—but examine the plants in the garden center very carefully before you buy. Because they are growing in a very limited amount of soil, they need feeding regularly. Failure to do so results in plants that are pale-looking and have very little new growth. If it is not too pronounced, the plant will recover, but I wouldn't buy these plants late in the season. Strange streaks in the leaves, especially along the veins or round the margins, are symptoms of a trace element deficiency. This is not usually serious and will generally clear itself once the plant is growing in the open ground. Wilting tips, along with burnt margins on the leaves, indicate an overdose of fertilizer or burn caused by fertilizing while the plant was in need of water. These plants should be avoided.

Survival of the fittest

I like to buy plants from a local nursery that is growing them in the area. Woody plants grow much faster if they are transplanted into the same kind of soil. Trees and shrubs grown on heavy clay soil take a long time to start growing properly if moved to a light sandy soil, and vice versa.

The majority of nurseries and garden centers grow very few of the plants they are selling. It is so easy to ship plants across the country, or across the border, that the plant you buy in London, Ontario, is as likely to have started life in Oregon as in New Jersey. It is almost impossible to tell the origin of a given plant, but it is important, especially when trying to grow plants close to their hardiness limit. This is particularly true for species, less so for cultivars.

There is a noticeable difference in the hardiness of species, depending on their origins. Plants propagated from northern-grown stock will tolerate lower temperatures than the same species grown from more southerly stock. (This doesn't apply to cultivars, which are propagated by methods other than seed and are genetically identical.) It is worth asking about the origins of borderline-hardy plants before you buy, but don't be too surprised if you cannot get a clear answer: a plant may change hands several times between the original grower and the final point of sale.

First winter survival can also be influenced by the time of planting. If you plant in spring, the tree or shrub has all summer to adjust its internal clock to local conditions, even if it came from a more southerly source on the other side of the continent, and it will harden itself off at the correct time for your location. If, on the other hand, you plant this tree in the fall, it may still be on the rhythm of where it was grown and may not drop its leaves in time and go dormant soon enough, suffering serious winter kill or even death. The harsher the winter climate in your region, the more important this is. Locally grown plants can be planted with confidence in the fall, since they are in tune with local conditions.

CHAPTER 3

On Planting and Aftercare

One of the many laws attributed to Mr. Murphy states that before you can do any job, there are three other jobs that must be done first. This is especially true in gardening. No matter how much you plan, it always seems that before you can do the task you set out to complete, something else takes precedence.

This chapter looks at the immediate care of plants when you get them home, at things that have to be done when planting trees and shrubs, and at the tasks to be done once the plants are in the ground. I will try to organize them in a logical sequence so that Mr. Murphy's law has minimal effect.

Impulse buying

It may occasionally happen that, while you are in the garden center looking for an item, you suddenly spot a tree or shrub you had been reading about, and at a very good price. As you unload it from the car, you realize that the garden is still frozen solid, you need to research this plant a lot more to know where to place it, you have a dozen other things to do this weekend and can't possibly find time to plant it, workmen are coming on Monday to start excavating for the extension to your house, or all of the above.

Apart from taking the plant back to the store and trying to get your money back, there are several things you can do. If you live in an area where the ground is frozen, there is little need to worry. Put the plant, still in its wrapping or container, in the corner of an unheated garage or in a sheltered alcove outside the house until the ground thaws.

If the ground is still frozen but the weather is warming up, you know spring is on its way. If the plant is a prepackaged shrub, a bare-root tree, or B & B, keep it in a shady, cool place, in an upright position, and plant as soon as possible. If the plant is in a container, you can leave it in full light as long as you remember to water it occasionally.

Remember, dormant deciduous plants don't lose moisture through their leaves, because they haven't got any. While the roots should be kept moist, they do not need a daily watering. How much and when to water depends on the temperature, wind, soil type, what the container is made of, size of the rootball and whether the plant is fully dormant or just starting to grow. Use your finger to feel for moisture in the soil a little under the surface, and water if it feels dry. Water until it runs out the drainage holes at the base of the container. This way you are sure you are wetting the entire rootball, not just the surface.

Evergreens, because they keep their leaves or needles all winter, need watering more often than deciduous plants. Even though they are dormant, they still lose some moisture from their leaves, especially once the temperature starts to get above freezing. Again, use the finger test to determine dryness. Moisture probes, sold as an aid to watering houseplants, can also be used to gauge when watering is needed. Allow the needle to indicate a need for water for two or three days before you water.

In situations where there is workable soil but you aren't ready to plant yet, the plant should be heeled-in until a more convenient time. Dig a trench with an almost upright back. Unpack the plants or remove the packing, but do not disturb B & B plants. Lay the plant against the back of the trench and shovel the soil over the roots (Figure 3.1), making sure you don't leave large air pockets. Lightly firm the soil over the plant and water once to soak the root area. It is not absolutely necessary to get the plants to the correct planting depth, as long as the roots are covered with soil. Remember, this is a temporary measure, to hold plants for a short time only.

In an emergency, plants can be left in this sort of situation until the new shoots start to show green, at which time they must be planted. This

Figure 3.1
Heeling-in will hold plants until you can put them in their permanent location.

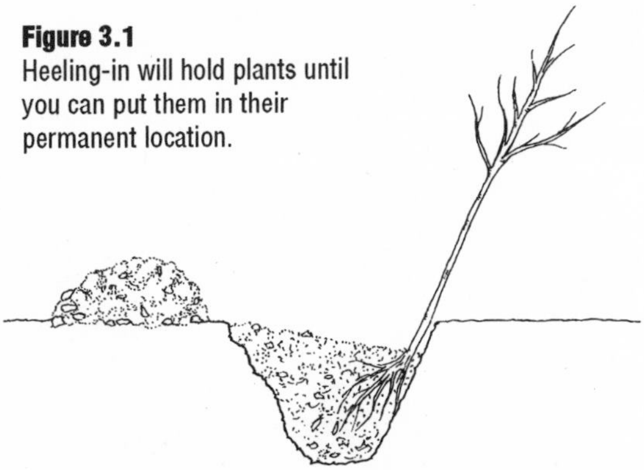

method works equally well for one plant or many. When I was managing a nursery, this is how we handled whole shipments of young stock that we wanted to grow to salable size. It held the plants in a moist, dormant state and kept the roots from drying out while we started planting.

The best time to plant

While trees and shrubs in pots can be planted whenever the soil is suitable, some times are better than others. As a general guide, conifers, such as pines, spruce, cedar, yew, hemlock and larch, should be planted in early fall—about the time the early deciduous plants start to turn color—or late spring, after the buds have broken on deciduous trees. Fall plantings need time to make new roots before winter and spring planting should wait until the soil has warmed up. If you are fall-planting conifers in areas where the soil freezes for several weeks in winter, it is a good idea either to wrap them in burlap for the first winter or spray them after planting with an anti-desiccant. This helps reduce moisture loss from the needles during winter, but it does slow growth for a year or so. These precautions are not needed on needle-losing species such as larch (a.k.a. tamarack).

Delay planting bare-root deciduous trees and shrubs until most of the leaves have dropped in fall. In spring, plant them before the buds start to break, if possible, and certainly no later than just a glimmer of green showing in the buds.

While most plants can be moved equally successfully in spring or fall, you will have better luck with the following if you plant them in spring: magnolia, red maple, birch, dogwood, beech, mountain ash, tulip tree, yellowwood, white oak, hemlock, larch and Austrian pine.

Preparing the plant

Examine the shrub or tree carefully and trim off any broken twigs or small branches. Use a pair of sharp pruning shears (secateurs) and cut just above a bud. If possible, choose an outward-facing bud, as this will give the plant a better shape when it grows. If the next outward-facing bud is a long way below the point of injury, then cut just above the next bud, regardless of where it faces. Small areas of damaged bark can be ignored, but any branchlets with large patches should also be removed.

If you are dealing with a potted plant, stand it in a larger container filled with water, deep enough to cover the pot. When bubbles stop rising to the surface, you know that the rootball is soaked right through.

Balled and burlapped plants are a bit more difficult to water thoroughly. They are often too heavy to soak, although this is the best method if possible. Failing this, tuck the end of a hose pipe that is turned on to just a trickle under the burlap, and let it run. The water will slowly soak into the rootball and wet it right through.

Examine the roots of bare-root plants carefully and remove any that are damaged. There are no buds on roots, so it doesn't matter where you cut them. It is also a good practice to cut about half an inch (1 cm) off the end of all the main roots, and then stand the plant in water for at least 15 minutes. This enables the plant to absorb water through the freshly cut root ends and it will have less stress when planted.

Preparing the planting site

Digging holes is hard work. There is a great tendency to stop when the hole is just big enough to take the roots. I know, I've done it myself, but it is false economy. The hole should be big enough to hold the roots without any of them touching either the sides or the base when the tree or shrub is at the correct planting depth.

To determine the correct depth, examine the stem of your plant, just above the roots, for a change in color. The part that was in the soil will be mud-colored, while the exposed part was washed clean by the rain. This is your best guide. Make the new hole deep enough for this color change to be at soil level. The easiest way to judge the soil level is to lay a thin stick across the hole with the ends at ground level—not on the pile of soil you dug out (Figure 3.2).

It is most important that the depth of planting is correct. Recent research suggests that planting too deep is responsible in part for sunscald, frost cracks and cankers. Planting too deep stresses the plant because the roots cannot absorb oxygen properly, and plants under stress are

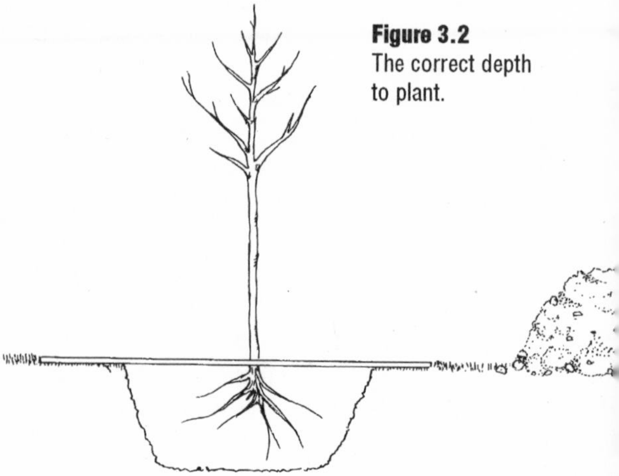

Figure 3.2
The correct depth to plant.

more prone to attacks by pests and diseases. Deep planting can also cause sidewalk and driveway heaving as the roots grow upwards to their correct level.

With some potted shrubs and trees, the level they are planted in the pot is not necessarily the correct planting depth. If a plant had extra long roots, it may have been potted high, rather than being put into a larger pot which needs more soil and doesn't fit in the holding area as well. Look for the color change on the stems of potted plants; don't assume the pot soil level is right.

In the past, all gardening books recommended adding compost or peat moss to the soil you removed from the hole even if it was good soil to start with. It has now been established that this is not such a good idea. When the roots start to grow, they do fine while they are in this nice rich soil, but then they enter the real world—the natural soil that makes up most of your garden. There is a tendency for the roots to stop growing at the tip and start putting out side roots that stay in the good stuff. Eventually, the plant becomes rootbound, which may result in the roots strangling themselves. It also means the plant has poor support and is more likely to blow down in a gale.

You only need to add organic matter to planting soil if it is very light and sandy. In this case use something poor in nutrients, such as old compost, leaf mold or peat moss; you are only adding it to improve the moisture retention of the soil and want the roots to grow out and search for food.

For the same reason, do not add granular fertilizer to the soil. Of course, there must be enough nutrients present to keep the plant alive, but if you are planting in what was previously lawn and the grass lived, so will a woody plant. Bone meal can be added to the planting soil, but it is not essential. Bone meal is very slow-acting and has to be broken down by bacteria in the soil before it becomes available to the plant. By the time it is usable, the new roots are already growing well.

Those gardening on heavy clay have to take special care. Holes dug in clay can end up as sinks filled with water. It is difficult not to glaze the clay as you dig, forming an almost waterproof surface inside the hole. Then when you firm the plant in place, you end up with a bowl from which the water cannot drain away. Using a garden fork, loosen up the base of the hole and drag the points of the fork up the sides of the hole to break the glaze. In very heavy soils, you should even add some gravel to the base, but be sure to mix it into the soil at the bottom of the hole. A layer of gravel on its own just acts as a collecting point for the water as it drains through the planting hole.

On low-lying heavy sites, where drainage is very poor, it is worth considering planting above the surrounding grade. For this you will need extra soil to cover the roots. Dig a very shallow hole and position the plant in it. Pile soil round the roots, spreading it out to form a gradual mound (Figure 3.3). The plant will need some support for the first couple of years, unless it is very small. It will root out into the added soil and slowly push roots down into the clay to anchor

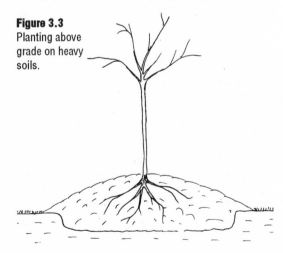

Figure 3.3
Planting above grade on heavy soils.

itself. This method should only be used where the soil is pure clay that is very difficult to dig in the normal way.

Now, which way up do the roots go?

It is not always easy to tell with bare-root plants. I was once asked about some Virginia creeper that was showing no signs of growth several weeks after planting. When I examined it, I found it had been planted upside down, as the tops and roots are so similar. In spite of spending all that time with its roots exposed to every passing breeze, when replanted the right way up, it burst into growth—a testament to the toughness of the plant!

Holding the plant in place, look at the roots. Are they spread out evenly and, most important, are any curled up by the sides of the hole? Roots seldom grow evenly spread around the plant. If there are more on one side than the other, you can turn this to your advantage. Place the side with the fewest roots towards an area that will give poor nutrition to the tree. If you are planting in front of the house, point the side rich in roots towards the area with the greatest root space, away from the house, driveway or road. On windy sites, face the majority of the roots into the wind, as this gives the best anchorage.

Of course, you have to take into account the top part of the plant as well, and it may be that there is a good reason to plant a tree or shrub in a certain direction. Maybe it is one of those oval trees discussed in chapter 2 and you selected it to go close to a fence so you could train it as an espalier. With a specimen tree—one that will be standing by itself in the lawn—turn the tree so that the best side is facing the direction from which it will be viewed most often. In other words, turn the good side towards your windows and the scratty side towards the neighbors. If it will not be seen from the house, turn the side with most

branches towards the north. This way, the side with least branches will get most light, rather than being shaded, and will grow just that little bit better. After a few years this will even up the shape of the crown.

Staking

Depending on what you are planting, it may or may not need staking. Most shrubs, conifers and B & B plants don't need to be staked if planted in spring. If fall-planted, it is a good idea to give them some support for the first winter until they make new roots. Trees may or may not need staking. Container-grown plants almost always do: they have such a small root system at planting time that they need something to hold them up. Bare-root trees planted in spring may also need support for at least the first year. If they are very young, with flexible stems, they should be staked high enough that the top of the stem will not bend over when left unsupported. This is well below the height at which trees were commonly staked in the past.

Recent research has shown that trees that are tied to a stake just below the crown do not develop a gradual taper to their trunks as they grow. When the stake is eventually removed, these trees are more likely to snap off in a high wind, usually close to the ground. Trees that are staked just high enough to keep them upright flex in the wind and grow with a tapered trunk which doesn't break as easily.

Using this short staking system, you can either put in one stake upwind of the tree, or, better still, two stakes placed across the prevailing wind. If the trunk is not very flexible and can stand up on its own, these supports need only be a couple of feet (60 cm) above ground. The idea is to hold the tree in place while it puts out roots, while allowing the stem to grow naturally.

To determine how high to put the ties, hold

the stem just below the lowest branch with one hand and pull the crown to one side with the other. When you let the top go, the crown will return to upright. Repeat this several times, moving your hand six inches (15 cm) down the stem each time. When you get to the place where the top no longer returns to upright, put the ties just above that.

Getting the stake ready before you start to dig the hole is one of the jobs Mr. Murphy alluded to in his law. If you forget, you can use a garden cane or piece of wood to mark the place where the stake is to go. This way you won't damage roots when you hammer it into place. For the strongest support, place the stakes so they are in undisturbed soil, rather than in the hole you dug.

Large evergreens, especially broad-leaved ones or tall coniferous plants purchased with a rootball, should be staked for the first year to prevent them blowing over in a gale. Use two stakes driven into the ground outside the rootball. You can either tie the plant to the stakes or nail a cross-brace to the stakes and tie the stem to this. Remember to leave room for growth.

Planting bare-root plants

Now comes the time when you will see why nature gave you three arms. Holding the plant in place and at the right depth, you may have to hammer in a stake while you can see where the roots are. When the plant and stake are properly positioned, shovel the soil back in, gently jiggling the plant up and down to work the soil in under the roots. I usually start with the plant slightly lower than the desired level, since I find it lifts a little while I jiggle.

When the hole is about half-full, the plant should be steady enough that it won't fall over. If so, firm the soil down carefully between the roots with your foot, using only a light pressure on heavy soils, or water well to wash the soil in between the roots. Then, holding the plant again

(so it doesn't develop a lean), continue to fill in the hole.

We will leave the hole partly filled at this point while I tell you about the slightly different techniques you will use with potted and B & B plants. The final filling is the same for all three types of root system.

Planting potted or B & B plants

If your plant is potted, it may be in a container made of several different materials. The most common are plastic, a sort of rubberized plastic, or heavy cardboard (fiber).

Plants in fiber pots can be planted pot and all, but you should cut several vertical slashes in the sides to allow the roots to escape. The pot will eventually rot but these cuts help the plant establish faster. Most importantly, break the rim off the pot to below soil level, all the way around. If you leave the rim in place, it acts as a wick, allowing moisture to evaporate from the soil and drying out the rootball faster than you would expect.

If the plant has not been in the pot for long, or if it is early in the season, remove fiber pots entirely. If the plant has been potted for some time, it will have rooted into the walls of the pot (ready to make a breakthrough as soon as you plant it), and taking it out of the pot will damage the fine root hairs through which the plant absorbs nutrients and water. How do I know if this plant has been potted for long or not, I hear you muttering. Look at the drainage holes at the base. If there are roots showing, it is probably rooted into the pot. Turn it upside down and tap the rim of the pot on the edge of the wheelbarrow. If, after a couple of taps, the pot doesn't slide off, leave it alone and plant as directed above.

Hard pots must always be removed before planting. To avoid lifting a plant in and out of the hole several times while you adjust for the correct depth, use a flower stake or piece of wood, marked to the soil depth inside the container, as a guide. With any luck, one test heave with the pot still on will ensure you only handle the plant the minimum amount once the pot is removed. With plants that have not been potted for long, the soil falls away very easily and plants react badly to having most of the soil around their roots removed when they are in full leaf. If the plants are still dormant, this is not a problem.

When you slide the roots out of the pot, give them a critical look before you shove the plant in its hole. If they are evenly distributed over the ball, with at least 30 percent soil showing, the plant is okay to plant as is. If there is little or no soil showing, the plant is probably potbound. Look at the base of the ball and see if there are roots curled round and round. If so, these should be teased out and either cut off (this is often the easiest way) or spread out in the planting hole. If possible, ask staff to remove the pot in the nursery before you buy, so you can check the condition of the roots. Plants that are potbound are best avoided. They can take longer to establish and may die at a comparatively early age because of girdled roots.

Balled and burlapped plants are often heavy and you will want to lug them around as little as possible. Also, every time you move a B & B plant, you tear a few more of the fibrous roots. Use your measuring stick to get the hole to the correct depth before you lower the ball into place. Make a rope sling that goes under the rootball; you can then pick it up with two pieces of lumber (and a little help from a friend) and lower it into place with comparative ease, and take it out again if the depth is not right (Figure 3.4).

Once the ball is at the right depth, start to fill in around it, making sure the soil gets worked under the curve. When the hole is half-full, untie the burlap from the neck of the plant or cut it with an old sharp knife (burlap is full of soil par-

Figure 3.4
A rope sling and two poles helps when moving B & B plants.

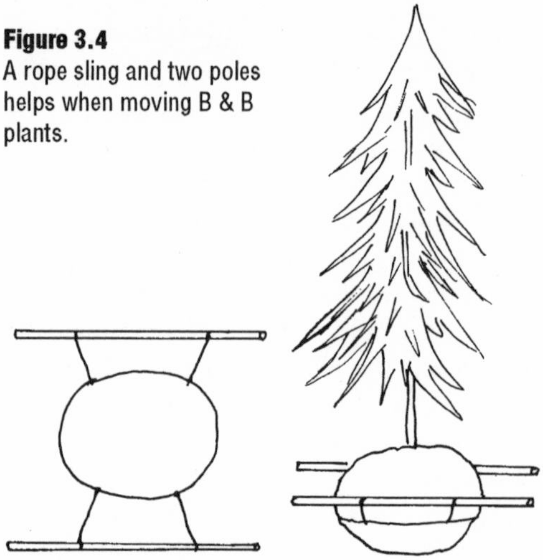

ticles and is not kind to good gardening knives).

Lay the burlap back across the soil you have filled in, so the top of the ball is exposed, then continue to fill and firm. If you leave the burlap in place, it will shed water off the rootball; by opening it across the hole, you are directing water towards the rootball.

Occasionally nurseries use a plastic burlap that is almost impossible to tell from the real thing. Like most plastics, it will not break down in the soil and will hinder the expansion of roots and the flow of water into the rootball. If left in place it may eventually girdle any roots that do manage to push through. To check which type of burlap your plant is wrapped in, pull a thread out of the weave and set fire to it. Real burlap will either smoulder or catch fire; plastic will melt first even if it catches fire eventually.

If this is the new plastic burlap, you will have to proceed slightly differently. Only put in enough soil to hold the rootball upright, then untie the burlap and cut off as much as possible. If you try to remove the burlap completely, you will probably ruin the soil ball, but at least cut off the surplus rather than laying it out in the hole. Again, put the stakes (if needed) in place alongside the rootball, start to fill in with the soil, and firm down as you go.

Filling the hole and afterwards

Continue to fill the hole almost to the soil mark on the stem of the tree or shrub. Leave a slight depression around the trunk and use the extra soil to make a small ridge around the outside edge of the hole (Figure 3.5). This will help retain water and stop it from flowing everywhere but onto the roots. Leave the moat in place for the first summer and level the planting site in fall.

Now is the time to water in your plant. You may decide to use a liquid plant-starter fertilizer, one with a high middle number, such as 10-52-10. The high level of phosphorus in these fertilizers stimulates the production of roots and gets the plants off to a good start. They work fine for annuals and perennials, which are fairly fast growing, but may not have much effect on slow-growing woody plants. There is not much research on this but I generally use them. They certainly do no harm and, since phosphorus is not washed out

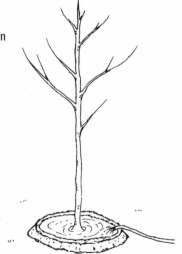

Figure 3.5
Build a moat to keep the water in the root zone.

of the soil, they probably help in root production. In any case, water thoroughly.

I wish there was some magic watering formula, but there isn't. Light sandy soils will take a lot of water in a short time, while heavy clays will need less but spread over a longer period to give time for it to soak through. All I can say is that your plants need a good soak at this stage to wash the soil particles into intimate contact with the roots.

Do not sow new grass or lay sod under newly planted trees or specimen shrubs. It competes for moisture and nutrients and the woody plants will grow at a slower rate. In the fall, when the moat is gone, you can lay a circle of landscape fabric round the trunk and cover it with a mulch of wood chips, shredded bark, cocoa hulls or, if you planted an evergreen, pine cones. Applying a mulch at this time allows the soil to thaw more evenly in spring, reducing the likelihood of frost-heave.

Landscape fabric is a finely woven artificial cloth that is used to suppress weed growth. When placed on the ground, it allows water and soluble plant foods to pass through, but is fine enough to stop weed seedlings (or pieces of perennial weeds) from growing through. It breaks down in sunlight, hence the need to cover it with some form of mulch. It is available in sheets, ideal to lay between shrubs, and in ready-formed circles with a hole in the center and slit to go round a tree.

In addition to reducing root competition for your young tree or shrub, leaving a space around your plant eliminates the need to mow close to the stem. This serves a double purpose; it reduces the area you have to mow, and it makes it almost impossible for careless drivers to knock pieces of bark off the trunk with the mower.

If you are planting in the fall, do not use landscape fabric or mulch until the following year. You want the soil to warm as fast as possible next spring to stimulate root growth.

Instant gardening

Some gardeners are not content to plant small and wait for nature to take its course; they prefer to spend megabucks and plant large specimens. If the plants are really large, the contractor will do everything for you, including digging the hole and staking the plant. Medium-sized specimens, which often come in wire baskets, may be manageable by an energetic gardener. The mechanics of digging the hole and planting are the same, there is just more of it.

The main difference is that larger plants need to be staked more firmly, since they have had more of their roots removed. They are most often held in place by three guy wires, fastened round the trunk and attached to pickets driven evenly into the soil around the tree. To allow the trunk to develop normally, keep the guys as low as possible, usually at the first side branch. Protect the trunk with a wide band of a soft material (such as old carpet) or a commercial tree-tie. Passing the wire through a piece of old hose pipe, the standard practice for many years, has now been shown to damage the bark. Finally, do not try and make the guy wires very tight. They are there to prevent the tree blowing over, not to hold it motionless.

Pruning at planting time

If you haven't already done so, trim back any damaged twigs and small branches to just above the scar where there was a leaf last summer. Try and trim to an outward-facing bud, even if it means cutting a bit more than necessary. This ensures the new growth will be away from the center of the plant, giving it a more open appearance.

When I was learning the craft of gardening, we were always told that you should cut back all the growing shoots on a newly planted tree or shrub by about one-third to compensate for the loss of roots. Recent research has shown that a chemical produced in the tips of shoots stimulates the growth of new roots. It is now suggested that you compensate for root loss by selectively removing a few shoots at the base and leaving the rest untouched (Figure 3.6).

Figure 3.6
Remove a few shoots completely after planting.

If the plant you buy is very full, with many branches, or is a shrub with a large number of shoots, then some pruning would be beneficial. The majority of plants in garden centers are not like this and pruning is probably unnecessary. Remember, the leaves are producing food that the plant needs to grow new roots. If you reduce the leaf surface too much, the roots will suffer.

One final word. Do not expect any woody plant to put on a lot of growth the first year. One of the most common comments I hear is that a plant hardly grew at all. It did. It grew below soil level where you can't see. Depending on the species, a tree or shrub may spend one to five years developing a good root system before it makes significant top growth.

Caring for New Plants

However you are using them in the garden—as specimen plants, foundation planting, mixed borders, screens and hedges, or climbing plants—the first few weeks are critical to the future growth and success of new plants. Proper care at the beginning will save many heartaches later on.

Getting them established

One way to minimize loss of newly planted shrubs and speed up their establishment is to protect them from drying winds for the first few weeks. The following method works particularly well with small bare-root plants (such as those prepackaged in plastic bags) and container-grown shrubs in one- and two-gallon (4- and 8-L) containers.

Before you even start to dig the planting hole, beg, borrow or, as a last resort, buy a large opaque plastic bag or paper sack. I use the 40- to 50-pound (20- to 25-kg) bird-seed bags made of several layers of paper. They stand up well to the weather and take a lot of rain and sun before they tear. Cut off the bottom so the bag forms a sleeve. Depending on the size of the plant, it may be possible to cut this in half and make two short sleeves. They are ideal for newly planted perennials even if you do make them too short for shrubs. Plastic

sleeves (from bags) work well, but both clear and dark-colored bags heat up too much in the sun and can scorch new foliage. Try to find white or a pale color. You will also need three or four bamboo canes or stakes, tough enough to withstand wind pressure, for each shrub.

After planting and watering, push two canes into the soil on one side of the plant and slip the tube over the canes and the plant. Stretch it out with the remaining cane(s) so that it forms a tight triangle or square around the plant and push these canes into the soil (Figure 4.1). With very small plants or those with an upright shape a triangle is sufficient; a shrub with a spreading shape will need a square to give it enough space.

Site the wind protectors with one corner of the shape facing into the prevailing wind so the wind can flow down either side, rather than hitting a side flat on. Make sure they are pulled down

Figure 4.1
Wind protection on
newly planted shrubs.

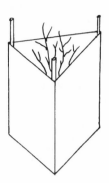

to soil level. In windy locations, it helps to actually bury the bottom of the sleeve in the soil to prevent the wind from getting underneath. Tall sleeves also shade the plant, preventing wilting in strong sun.

How long you leave them in place depends on the state of the plant you put in. A bare-root plant—particularly if it was already starting to leaf out—will need more protection than a potted plant that was moved with little root disturbance, but I would suggest a minimum of two weeks.

General care

While it is true that providing sufficient water is critical during the first few years of a woody plant's life, you must also keep in mind that, in the early stages, the plant has very few roots and cannot take up vast quantities of water. Overwatering can be a major cause of plant death in the first summer's growth. It's the old problem of knowing your soil. Gardens with a light sandy soil, or a well-drained loam, have little to worry about, but plants on heavy clay or water-retentive muck soils have to be watered with care.

The weather also has to be taken into consideration. It is obvious that you need to water very infrequently in rainy weather, and yet, I have heard people wonder why their tree died when they watered it twice a week during one of the wettest springs on record. Bright days dry the soil faster than cloudy ones, and strong winds suck moisture out of leaves and soil alike.

Coastal regions may get periods of misty, drizzly weather that we think of as wet, but from the plant's point of view the rainfall is negligible. Even though you think the weather has been terrible, your newly planted shrubs and trees may be dying for lack of water. If you have a rain gauge, you should give additional water to newly planted plants if there is less than one inch (2.5 cm) of rain in a week.

There is no magic formula that will tell you when to water. You have to be guided by instinct, by common sense, by experience, and above all by sticking your fingers into the soil to see how dry it is. Push deep into the soil, not just the surface, which may be wet from a recent shower. If the soil is hard, use a trowel to take out a sample.

Apart from the plant starter you may have used when you first watered in your tree or shrub, fertilizer is rarely required the first year on most garden soils. If you are gardening on a very sandy or gravelly soil, or in regions with high rainfall where leaching is excessive, feed with a high-nitrogen fertilizer in late June. Do not leave it too late or you may stimulate growth that will not have time to ripen properly before winter arrives. You cannot use the amount of new growth as an indicator that the plant needs fertilizing, as it will not put on much top-growth the first year. This is a good guide once the plant is established, but not until then.

Remember to check all ties that fasten the plant to a supporting stake in midsummer, and loosen them if they are tight. It is very easy to overlook this and you may suddenly find the stem is constricted, or the top snaps off the plant.

Preparing for winter

The first few winters are critical in the life of a young woody plant. This may be hard to realize. Surely, you say, when the plant is dormant, nothing can happen to it. The summers are critical too, but you are taking care of your new plants then, watering, inspecting, generally making them comfy in the garden. When the cold weather comes, we often retire to the fireside and read gardening books until spring, but there are several things that should be done to protect plants over the winter months.

Animals

Mice do not hibernate; they continue to run about all winter looking for tasty things to eat. If you fail to protect your plants, come January, when all the succulent seeds have been eaten, bark is the food of choice. Mouse populations go in cycles and when the population is at a peak, they do a tremendous amount of damage to young shrubs and trees.

The dissolved minerals the plant uses for growth are taken in by the roots and move up through the plant in the outer wood. The manufactured foods produced by the leaves in sunlight are transported down the stems in the layer immediately under the bark. They are used to build food reserves and grow new roots in combination with the minerals.

If an animal (such as a mouse) removes a ring of bark and the tissue immediately beneath it, food can no longer travel to the root zone. The plant will leaf out normally in spring, using the food reserves from storage which travel upwards in the wood, but the food manufactured by the leaves can no longer get down to the roots, which eventually starve, and the plant dies.

Discourage mice by placing a physical barrier around the stem if possible. This is fairly simple on trees. You can use one of the plastic tree spirals that are wound round the trunk in late fall and removed in spring. Mind you, if the mice are really desperate, they will chew through the plastic first. The only really sure way is to wrap the trunk in small-mesh chicken wire, several turns, to the average depth of snow in your area.

I have always had success with the plastic spirals, but have known the mice to go through them on the odd occasion. I always like to take them off for the summer for two reasons. First, they deteriorate in sunlight and you can lengthen their life considerably by storing them out of the sun. Second, they provide a wonderful hiding place for earwigs and ants. If these are a problem in your neighborhood, you will want to give them as few hiding places as possible. Also, leaving the spirals on the tree all summer slows the natural hardening of the bark, leaving it softer and more likely to be damaged by careless mowing. Finally, even on mature trees, bark contains chlorophyll. If you cover it up, you are cutting off a potential food factory that can help the plant grow.

It is very difficult to protect shrubs with tree guards; it is almost impossible to wrap them around several stems without leaving holes the mice can get into. In this case, you must resort to the use of chemicals—not the kind that kill but nasty-tasting medicine the mice won't want to eat, such as the commercially available spray-on repellents.

In theory, this is easier than trying to wrap shrubs in tree guards, but there is a snag. You don't want your sprayer freezing up as you apply the repellent and there is a fine line between the last rainfall and the onset of weather so cold that spraying is a problem. Being water-soluble, if it rains after you apply it, the repellent may wash off. If it is just a drizzle, you are probably okay, but after a downpour you will have to reapply.

One other method of keeping mice from your plants is worth a mention. If you live in an area where snow is reliable, go out after each snowfall and walk several times around all the plants you need to protect. This packs the snow down and makes it difficult for mice to tunnel underneath.

For areas where deer browsing is a problem, I have no real solution. This is becoming a great problem and many botanical gardens are spending a lot of money to erect deerproof fences each fall to protect their collections. For the home gardener, this may be impractical. There are several deterrents that work for a while, and if you haven't tried them, they may keep you deer-free for a winter or two.

Bags of human hair, collected from barbers and hung on the perimeter fence, may work for a while. The hair has to be replaced quite often since it loses its human smell in a few days. Bars of deodorant soap also work for some people, until the deer get used to the smell. Maybe changing brands every few days would work. It has to be deodorant-type soap; regular soap has no effect.

One correspondent in a national gardening magazine found that human urine applied round the boundaries of his country property kept groundhogs away. Maybe it would also work with deer. It might be worth a try if you have no neighbors close by!

Household pets, particularly male dogs, can also affect shrubs. By repeatedly cocking their legs in the same place while marking their territories, dogs can kill the lower branches on some shrubs or cause brown patches on the bottom of evergreen hedges, such as cedar. The bigger the dog, the higher the damage. Corgis rather than St. Bernards.

Cold

Providing you are growing plants that are hardy for your area, cold temperatures are no problem. Of course, there is always the particularly harsh winter that comes along once in a while, when the hardiness of plants is put on trial, but these are few and far between.

It is when you start experimenting and trying to push hardiness to its limit that problems occur. No matter where you live, there is always the challenge of growing something that may not be quite hardy. Probably the best example is bush roses. In much of northern North America, hybrid tea and floribunda roses are not quite hardy. Yet we continue to make the nurserymen rich by trying to grow them year after year.

There are certain precautions you can take if you are trying to grow plants at their limit. First, try to ensure the plant you get is from a northern strain, not from plants or seed from a much warmer climate. Second, give it protection.

It doesn't take much to keep the temperature a few degrees warmer, and often this is all it takes. A circle of wire or snow fence around a plant will make an enclosure. Fill this with leaves, making sure to work them down under the branches. Oak leaves are best, since they don't pack down, but any leaves can be used. Cover the top of the enclosure to keep the leaves from blowing away and the snow from packing them down. Depending on the size, you may get away with using a garbage can lid or you may have to make something to fit from scrap lumber (Figure 4.2).

Figure 4.2
A snow-fence enclosure filled with leaves should be covered to stop them packing down.

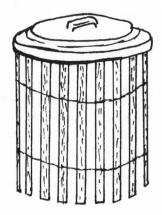

This sort of enclosure works well to protect slightly tender shrubs or rhododendron and magnolia buds, which can be killed in a hard winter even though the plants survive. The enclosures also make an ideal winter home for mice and voles, which can then feed at leisure. Put some poisoned bait on the ground inside the enclosure before you add the leaves. To keep the bait away from birds, and to make it easy to remove in spring, enlarge the opening on a regular pop can and put the bait inside.

Wind

Plants are not affected by wind-chill factors. It is only warm-blooded creatures who feel colder in a wind. Nevertheless, winter winds do play an important part in plant survival.

If the plant roots are still above the frost line, once the ground freezes they can no longer take up water from the soil, but the top of the plant is still losing some moisture to the air. More moisture is lost from evergreen plants than deciduous, and I sometimes wonder why it is that the main trees of the northern forest are evergreens. Moisture loss is increased when the wind blows, a point to consider when siting plants in spring. If you plant an evergreen in a place you know to be drafty, such as at the end of an opening between the house and garage, you are asking for trouble.

You can help reduce the drying effect of wind by wrapping the plant in burlap, or by erecting a temporary windbreak. If you do this, remember that a complete barrier does not necessarily give a dead-air region on the other side. The wind swirls over a solid object and can actually be stronger in places on the lee side than it would be without a windbreak. A porous barrier that lets some wind through is more effective than a solid one. Any windbreak must be firmly fixed before winter starts; if a gale blows it down, it is very difficult to hammer posts into ground that is frozen solid.

Anti-desiccant sprays can be used on conifers that have become too large to wrap. Like the mouse repellent, they should be applied as close to winter as possible. They put a waxy film over the needles, which helps to reduce water loss, but they also slow down subsequent growth. This may not matter with large plants, but can be important on smaller ones.

Sun

The combination of wind and sun is often deadly for evergreens, yews in particular. In some cases, the entire side that faces the sun turns brown over winter, while a similar yew that is shaded during the day comes through unscathed. Wrapping or an anti-desiccant will give protection.

The big problem caused by winter sun in cold regions is vertical splitting on tree trunks. Cracks appear on the main trunk, and occasionally on main branches, normally on the south to west sides. Although they are known as frost cracks, they are caused by the sun warming the trunk, followed by rapid cooling when the sun goes down or the tree is shaded by a nearby structure.

Frost cracks rarely occur in the wild, except along the edge of a woodland, since each tree shades its neighbor. They are more likely on specimen trees growing on their own in a lawn and may extend into the center of the tree. They close during the summer and if winter didn't happen with monotonous regularity would heal themselves. However, every winter the cycle begins again and the cracks open once more.

They are rare on conifers, possibly because of the shading effect of the needles, but even old evergreens with no lower branches rarely suffer. This condition is most likely to occur on trees that are growing vigorously. Newly planted trees seldom suffer, nor do old mature specimens.

It is the teenage trees that cause problems!

Once the trunk splits, it allows access to fungal diseases. Trees that are growing well will probably not be infected, but those under stress from poor conditions are more susceptible. Protecting the trunk each winter with a wrap of burlap or kraft paper will help prevent cracks from developing.

When pruning, try to leave the lower branches on the south and west sides of the tree to shade and help protect the trunk. Trees with dark bark can be given a coat of white interior latex paint in late fall. The pale color will stop them heating as much and interior paint will break down gradually over winter.

A trunk that is already split can be protected by tying a plank of wood to the trunk on the sunny side each winter. The superior insulation of wood will stop the trunk from heating and help prevent the existing split from opening, giving it a chance to heal, although it does not add to the beauty of the winter garden.

Sometimes, especially in regions with reliable snow cover, a circle of snow fence that traps snow is sufficient to protect slightly tender shrubs. I use this method to shield the leaves of Oregon grape from sun and wind burn. Without this little bit of protection, the top half of the plant is dead by spring.

Snow

By itself, snow is a great insulator. I always tell people who want to grow roses in a harsh climate to put them close to a laneway so they can easily shovel lots of snow over them. There are times, however, when snow is a nuisance. When it slides off the roof and smashes the foundation planting you put in last spring, it makes you say "Oh bother!" at least.

While the plants are small, wooden A-frames placed over them in early winter will deflect the

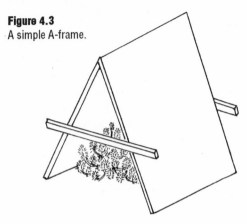

Figure 4.3
A simple A-frame.

snow (Figure 4.3). They are not a cold protection, they simply stop the snow from crushing your plants. If you clean your laneway with a snowblower, protect nearby plants with these frames, facing the solid side towards the drive.

As plants grow, it becomes increasingly difficult to protect them. Depending on the style of house, it may be possible to lay boards against the soffit above the plants, but this is difficult on two- and three-story homes. These problems really result from selecting the wrong plants initially.

On upright evergreens, snow can weigh down the individual branchlets, setting them in a curved position. Even when the snow has melted, they don't spring back into place. I once had a 'Skyrocket' juniper that was ruined by a snowfall. Instead of a skyrocket, it looked more like a skyporcupine.

The solution is to wrap the plant to hold the branchlets in place, which has the added benefit of helping to protect the conifer from windburn if you use burlap. You can also get a stretchy mesh, like an overgrown net stocking. Carefully work it over the plant to the ground, then stretch it up to the top and tie it shut. Even circling an upright conifer with a few spirals of twine can be effective.

Salt

If you live close to a main road in an area where winters are hard and roads are cleared with salt, you should take precautions to minimize salt damage. If plants are there already, you may have to protect them from drift. It is amazing how far salt-laden spray will travel in a winter wind. The ideal solution is to put up a length of snow fence, well supported with frequent stakes, and cover this with a piece of burlap to catch the spray.

Individual plants can be protected, but make sure the burlap is not in contact with the foliage or damage can still occur. Plants that retain their foliage all winter are most at risk, but even some deciduous plants can be affected by salt—either through residues in the soil or by direct contact. A row of mature crab apples on a busy highway in Ottawa flowers much better on the side away from the highway. Even flower buds many feet above the ground are affected by the spray.

See chapter 11 for a list of salt-tolerant and salt-susceptible plants.

CHAPTER 5

Care of Established Plants

If, like many people, you have moved into a second-hand home, in all probability there are already trees and shrubs growing in the garden. Even with newly built homes there could well be mature trees preserved by the builder. Suddenly you are faced with a host of questions about which you probably know very little, including the types of plants you have inherited.

It is difficult for a novice gardener to identify trees and shrubs, but it's quite important to know what you have, if only to know what and when to prune. You can try asking your neighbors, especially if they have a nice garden, but probably the best way is to join the local horticultural society or garden club. For good identification books, see the Suggested Reading list at the end of the book.

Watering

Established shrubs and trees that have been growing for at least five years will have an extensive root system. This, in a typical plant, will have several large anchor roots that penetrate deep into the soil, and a network of feeder roots that extend out all round the plant at least as far as the plant is tall. These feeder roots are mostly in the top 3 feet (1 m) of soil, although this depends to some extent on the fertility and texture of the soil and on the individual species.

Because of the widespread nature of the roots, it is difficult to give enough water to be of any use to large mature trees. In most home situations, unless there is a watering ban, the lawn is watered to keep it green during a summer drought. This water undoubtedly helps the shrubs and younger trees whose roots have not spread beyond the lawn's boundaries. However, once the plants are well established, it is seldom absolutely necessary to water them unless you have a very gravelly or sandy soil.

During a record-breaking drought in Ottawa, watering was banned and the lawns all turned brown, but I saw few signs of wilting on any of the woody plants. The plants did suffer, however, and the following spring there was an unusual amount of tip kill. There was also poor flowering on many species, caused no doubt by the water limitation at the time the plants were forming their buds for the following year. But these were temporary setbacks, and the plants themselves were basically unharmed.

Fertilizing

In nature, when the plants in the forest lose their leaves each fall, they form a carpet under the branches. This carpet gradually breaks down and releases nutrients back into the soil, which, in turn, help the plants grow. Once you move these forest plants into the city, human nature insists on immaculate surroundings. Even the most untidy person, whose house is cluttered with piles of books, three-week-old newspapers and something spread on every surface, has a compulsion to rake leaves.

If you fertilize your lawn each spring, enough fertilizer will probably wash down to the tree roots to keep the tree growing well. Shrubs growing in a bed will also get sufficient nutrients if you are fertilizing for other plants in that bed. Look at the plants and compare their vigor with the previous year. Are the leaves smaller than last year? Are they a paler green? Memory plays us tricks, but one sure way is to compare the length of growth from one year to the next.

Don't be in a rush to compare. It is not fair to go and look at a shoot a couple of weeks after the leaves unfurl. You must give the plant time to make a normal season's growth. If you look at a twig, you will see a ring of small scars on the bark, and usually a change in color where the current year's growth started. Look back down the twig about the same amount and you should find a similar ring of scars from the previous year's growth. These will not be as easy to see and you may have to look at several branchlets. As long as the distance between the scars is about the same, the plant is growing normally and doesn't need feeding.

When you feed a plant, the results will not be instantaneous: the elements you add often have to be converted into forms the plant can use by microbes and bacteria in the soil before you see any benefits. Patience is a part of feeding plants—and of gardening in general.

On mature trees, dieback in the crown may be a symptom of poor nutrition, although some dieback is normal and small twigs die for no apparent reason. It may be caused by wind damage, squirrels feeding, or birds injuring the branches while gathering nesting materials. If the dieback gets to the stage of being whole branches, it is more than casual wear and tear. Some diseases are also associated with crown dieback, but they usually attack plants that are already under stress. This stress may be caused by being planted in the wrong soil (for example, plants that prefer dryish soil may suffer dieback on a site that floods each spring) or poor nutrition.

Before starting on a major fertilization routine, look at some of the other factors mentioned. Compare leaf size and color with trees of the same species in gardens nearby. If possible, look at growth rates on your plant and see if they are decreasing.

If there is a reason to suspect the tree or shrub is lacking nutrients, apply fertilizer at between 1 and 2 pounds per inch (.5 to 1 kg per 2.5 cm) of trunk diameter measured at chest height. Double this rate for trees over 6 inches (15 cm) in diameter. Use a fertilizer with a slightly higher nitrogen ratio, such as 10-8-6. The commonly available lawn fertilizer 10-6-4 is quite acceptable, but be sure not to use one containing a weed killer. Spread the fertilizer on the ground in late winter or very early spring (once the frost is out of the ground if you live in a harsh climate) and water it in. The following day, irrigate again to move the nitrogen down to the plant's root zone and avoid overstimulating the grass.

In regions where the time between the ground thawing and the grass starting to grow is short—everywhere with a hard winter and almost no spring—it is better to put the fertilizer into the soil. Using a crowbar (hard work), an industrial electric drill with a large auger-type bit, or a small post-hole borer, make a ring of holes about 18 inches (45 cm) deep and 3 feet (1 m) apart under the drip-line of the tree—a circle under the tips of the branches. Make a second ring of holes about 3 feet (1 m) farther out. Count the number of holes and divide the fertilizer into equal parts. Pour the fertilizer into the holes (a large funnel helps) and fill them with a mix of sand and soil. Water the area well to dissolve the fertilizer.

You can also inject the fertilizer directly into the root zone with a root feeder. Push it into the soil in the same pattern as the holes described above and connect it to a hose. The block of solid fertilizer inside the feeder dissolves slowly as the water passes over it and the liquid fertilizer is injected directly into the soil.

Another choice is tree spike fertilizer. These solid, tapered blocks of slow-release fertilizer are hammered into the ground, still in the same pattern, and dissolve slowly during rain or irrigation. I find they tend to disintegrate while being hammered and it is best to make a hole with a crowbar first.

Whichever method you use, it is important that you apply the fertilizer early in the year, either as soon as you can walk on the lawn without leaving footmarks, or when the plants are in active growth. Fertilizing later than this may stimulate the plant to put on a flush of late growth that will not have time to ripen before winter comes. In cold climates this will result in a large amount of winter injury.

On normal soils, mature trees and shrubs should not need feeding more often than once every three or four years. On light, sandy or very poor soils, annual feeding may be necessary. Be guided by the growth pattern of your tree.

Old trees in new subdivisions

It often happens that, when clearing land for new subdivisions, a builder will work around some of the existing trees. While this does give shade and an air of permanency, it is often a mistake to expect those trees to survive.

The trees may hang on for several years, but most of them eventually die. They are victims of soil compaction, root disturbance (remember how far roots spread), changes in the water table, changes in the grade which could bury or expose roots (see chapter 7 for more on this), builder's waste, paving the area with blacktop or pollution from vehicles.

If you have recently bought a house in this type of situation, it might be a wise investment to plant another tree as a replacement for that old-timer. On a more positive note, builders are beginning to realize the needs of trees and take extra precautions to preserve existing specimens, and you may find this was the case on your lot.

On country properties this is less likely to be a problem. But changes in growth and signs of decline along the path into the site are generally attributable to compaction from delivery trucks and/or trenching to bring in services.

Pruning trees

Pruning is a topic that causes a great deal of anxiety in many home-owners. They don't know how to do it themselves and are reluctant to call in a professional because of the expense. Trees are mostly pruned for shape and to keep them healthy, while shrubs are pruned to ensure a good display of flowers or fruit. Pruning shrubs is covered in a later section, since the pruning requirements are different.

The following points may help you decide if pruning is needed, and whether you can attend to your own trees or if professional help will be needed.

Are there broken branches hanging in the tree? These may result from wind or ice storms and, if left, they can tear a long strip of bark off the tree when they fall, leaving it more suscepti-ble to disease. Broken branches should be re-moved as soon as possible. The jagged break is also a good spot for disease to gain a hold.

If small, or within reach, you can take them off yourself. Make your first cut upwards on the underside of the branch, a little way out from the trunk, cutting about one-third of the way through. Then cut downwards, slightly outside the first cut. This prevents the bark from tearing when the branch falls. Remove the stub in the same way, but try to make the two cuts meet. Don't cut flush to the trunk; a cut made an inch or so (2.5 cm) away will heal faster. Look for the branch collar (Figure 5.1) and cut just outside it. Do not use

Figure 5.1
The branch collar, and where to cut.

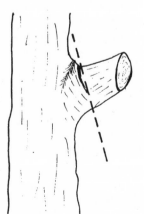

wound paint on the cuts; it has now been shown to actually slow down the healing process.

Most of the remaining conditions are more serious and you should probably get professional advice.

Are there large dead branches in the tree? Some dieback of small branches is quite common, as mentioned, but large dead branches are a dif-ferent matter and should be pruned out. You can do it yourself if they are within easy reach, but if you have to balance on top of a ladder and saw above shoulder height, call in a professional. And if there is any chance that the falling branch could cause damage to your own or a neighbor's prop-erty, let the expert do it. He has the equipment to deal with it and he carries insurance.

Does the tree have cavities or rotten wood on the trunk or along major branches? This is a sign of a major disease and needs prompt atten-tion from a qualified arborist. This is not the sort of thing you can tackle yourself unless the cavi-ties are very small.

Are there cracks or splits in the trunk, espe-cially where branches are attached? Splits on the south side of the trunk are common and are prob-ably not a problem (see chapter 4). Splits where branches arise are a cause for concern, since they can indicate a weakness in that branch. This can usually be cured by cabling the branch to others to give additional support.

Does the tree have a pronounced lean? Few trees grow perfectly upright; most develop a slight lean away from the prevailing wind. A tree that is leaning more than a few degrees is likely to fall over in a strong wind. Providing there is no dan-ger of it falling on something (a house or car, for example) it can be left, but if there is danger of it causing damage, it should have attention. De-pending on the degree of lean, it may need re-moving, but often thinning the branches will be enough, since this reduces the wind resistance.

There are a couple more areas that, while not strictly pruning, may also need the attention of a qualified arborist.

Do most of the major branches arise from the same point on the trunk? The crotches on a tree that grows and then divides into several branches are much weaker than those where the branches come from the side of the trunk. This shape of tree may need to be braced so all the branches are supported by each other.

Are there mushrooms present at the base of the tree? These may be a sign of heart rot if growing on the trunk. Mushrooms growing in the soil close to the tree may indicate damaged roots, or may be growing on the remains of an old tree left in the ground. They are different species of mushroom and a tree expert should be able to tell you if you have cause for alarm.

Pruning tools

Before you can start pruning, you need some specialized tools: pruning shears (known as secateurs), loppers and a pruning saw. You will need these for both tree and shrub pruning.

Secateurs come in two main types, anvil, where one blade cuts onto a flat plate, and bypass, where one blade moves past the other as in scissors. Which type you prefer will probably depend on which you first used. In either case, buy the best you can afford. Secateurs are always expected to cut thicker wood than they should. Instead of fetching the loppers (which are really just giant-sized pruners), we struggle to cut an oversized branch. Wood varies in hardness as well. I bought my loppers to prune a honeysuckle. Even branches no larger than my finger were too tough for the pruners, or else my grip is very weak.

Loppers also come in both anvil and bypass types, although the latter are more common. You can get them with telescopic handles, which increases the pressure you can put on a cut. Always try loppers in the store before you buy. Put lots of pressure on the handles (with them extended to full length if adjustable) to be sure they will take the strain. I have seen pairs that, even under moderate pressure, slowly bent where the handles were attached. You can possibly manage without loppers for a year or two.

Pruning saws are special. You cannot do the same job with a regular carpentry saw. There are several types available, but they all have one thing in common: the teeth point backwards. Pruning saws cut best on the pull stroke, not the push. If you are standing on a ladder cutting a branch you will appreciate that you pull yourself into the tree, not push yourself away.

Pruning saws based on a Japanese style are now available. The teeth do not have a kerf (the slight outward bend); instead the entire blade tapers from teeth to back. They are made of extremely hard steel and cut very fast. At the same time they give a smooth cut that feels as though you had sandpapered the surface. The cut leaves no ridges where disease spores could lodge and start an infection.

Knowing when to prune

Pruning is generally carried out while the tree is dormant. The timing varies depending on the species involved. Those species that have an early sap flow (maples and birch especially) are best pruned in late fall or early winter. This gives the cut surfaces time to dry and seal before the sap starts to run. Pruning them late in winter results in sap dripping from the cuts. Unless the pruning was very extensive it does not really hurt the tree, but it makes us feel bad since we tend to associate it with bleeding. If extensive pruning was done, the sooty mold which may grow on the residues from the sap can be unsightly.

With most species, pruning is best done in late winter, once the worst of the cold weather is past (for our comfort) but before the buds start to swell. The worst time to prune is when the leaves have just finished opening, since this is when reserves of food are at their lowest and the leaves are needed to work at replenishing these reserves.

The two instances when you don't wait for the proper season to prune are when your tree is damaged (broken branches should be cut off as soon as possible after the injury occurs) and when you find a bad attack of pest or disease that cannot be controlled by other means. This doesn't mean that every time you find a twig covered in aphids you should prune it off. Aphids are easy to control. A few pests and diseases are difficult or impossible to control and should be removed as soon as noticed. The more common of these are identified in chapter 6.

Knowing what to prune

When you stand and gaze perplexed at your tree, trying to decide if it needs pruning and if so, which bits you should cut off, remember that trees grow. If you make any errors, the tree will repair them if you wait long enough. Keep in mind that pruning stimulates new growth. Within reason, the more you cut off, the more the tree will grow the following season.

If you take pruning step by step, you can easily decide if pruning is needed at all and how to go about it. In younger trees, the main task is pruning for shape. Remove branches that will grow in the wrong direction or cause the tree to become one-sided. How you prune depends on the type of tree. The branches on an upright tree, with a central leader, should be evenly spaced around the trunk, while a spreading tree needs a more open center.

Remove branches that grow into the center. Look for branches that are crossing and rubbing on other branches, a potential site for disease. It

is usually obvious which is the best one to remove; if not, leave the one that has the widest angle with the main stem. The closer it is to a right angle, the stronger the branch will be.

Some species, crab apples in particular, have a tendency to send up water shoots. These are rapidly growing shoots that arise mostly on the upper side of branches and grow straight up. If left, they form a thicket in a few years and spoil the character of the tree. They can be removed in summer, once the season's growth is finished, or be left until winter pruning.

As trees mature, they need less and less pruning. In the first few years, while you are controlling the ultimate shape of the tree, it requires pruning every year. As the tree grows, try to remove the lower branches, one at a time over the course of several years, to give yourself room to walk under the tree without ducking. Of course, this must be done with an eye to the eventual shape. It will often not be possible on spreading species like crab apples, and it would spoil the character of a blue spruce. In colder regions you should also keep in mind the advantage of winter shade to prevent trunk splitting.

When you remove part of a shoot, the part remaining gets all the nutrients and grows accordingly. You can use this to your advantage. If you have a bare spot on a tree, removing the end of the shoot will cause all the side shoots to grow faster. If a branch breaks in a storm and leaves a hole in the crown, removing the side shoots on a suitable small branch will cause it to elongate faster and grow into the hole.

Occasionally, the main shoot on a tree with an upright growth habit may be damaged. When this happens on a deciduous tree, another shoot just below the break will become dominant and take over. If left alone, this will result in a kink in the stem. If possible (depending on the size of the tree) tie the shoot to a cane that is fastened to the stem lower down, so that the shoot is as up-right as possible. Remember to loosen any ties in early spring so the stem and shoot have room to grow during the spring flush of growth.

With evergreens, especially pine, a ring of new shoots will develop at the top tier of branches if the leader is damaged. If they are all allowed to grow, the tree will become top-heavy and may snap in a wind eventually. If you can reach them, remove all the shoots except one, which will become the new leader.

Choosing an arborist

Have you ever had a stranger knock on your door and tell you your trees needed trimming? Have you ever looked through the yellow pages trying to select a reliable arborist? Beware of door-knock-ers. Most reputable tree-trimming firms have plenty of work and do not need to go door-to-door looking for jobs. This is especially true after wind or ice storms, when home-owners are worried about repairing the damage. Unqualified tree workers can cause even more damage than the ice storm, so make sure to check the references of anyone you hire.

If your trees need pruning and it is a bigger task than you are willing or able to tackle, remem-ber that anyone can put a listing in the yellow pages as an arborist. Get more than one estimate, even if you have to pay for it. If the estimates and descriptions of work to be done differ greatly, get a third estimate.

To be sure you are being fair, especially when getting an estimate for thinning a crown, ask what size branch they prune to. A company that thins to branches of 1-inch (2.5-cm) diameter will take off a lot more than one that only goes to 2-inch (5-cm) diameter. This will take more time and cost accordingly.

Before you sign a contract, insist on seeing the company's certificates of insurance, includ-ing proof of liability for personal and property damage. You may be held responsible for damage done to a neighbor's property by uninsured operators. Ask for local references and follow them up.

The International Society of Arboriculture runs a certification program in both Canada and the U.S. that indicates the arborist has met pro-fessional standards and has a good level of tech-nical knowledge. While this program is too new to expect all local arborists to be certified, it cer-tainly would not hurt to ask if they have the I.S.A. Certificate or belong to an arboriculture associa-tion. Many of the larger firms that operate in sev-eral cities run their own education and training courses for their staff at slack times.

A good arborist will offer a range of services, including fertilizing and pest control. Any com-pany that only wants to rush in with the pruning saw may be suspect. Tree-topping (removing the growing top of the tree) is usually necessary only after major storm damage. It should be recom-mended only as a last resort and may eventually kill your tree anyway.

Beware of persons who immediately say the tree should be removed. It is usually easier (and more profitable) to take a tree down than save it. Removal takes minutes, but it takes years to grow a replacement. A good arborist will work with you to save a tree if at all possible. The chainsaw mechanic will prefer to remove the problem permanently.

Pruning shrubs

Unlike trees, most shrubs are not pruned while they are dormant. They are pruned immediately after flowering. This is not to say that you should dash out and chop back all your shrubs every time they flower; some shrubs need very little prun-ing. Fast-growing shrubs such as honeysuckle and mock orange will probably need some pruning every year once they are mature, while slow-growing ones like cinquefoil may need some work once every five years or so.

Assuming you are growing shrubs for flowers or fruit, the worst thing you can do is clip them all over—sort of a haircut pruning. All this does is remove the buds that would have given you flowers next season, especially if you do it late in the year.

The aim, when pruning shrubs, is to remove some of the older branches and encourage new growth from the base to replace them. In this way, you get a continual renewal of the flowering shoots and the shrub never becomes overgrown. This way of pruning is called the renewal method. The speed with which a species grows governs the frequency of branch removal. Lilacs, for example, which have a few main branches that divide to form the crown, can often go four or five years between each major pruning. Mock orange, on the other hand, which sends up a thicket of thin branches, will probably need some branches removed almost every year.

The majority of shrubs flower in spring or early summer and these are pruned, when required, immediately after flowering. If the branches are getting crowded, or the flowers less profuse, it is time to prune. If the shrub is growing and flowering well, leave it alone. When you think pruning is needed, remove about one-third of the oldest (thickest) branches close to ground level. This is a job for loppers or a pruning saw. Generally, if the branches are still thin enough to cut with pruners, they are not very old.

It is often difficult to remove branches with a saw without damaging the bark on adjoining branches. This is where the small pruning saws with very thin blades are handy. You may have to cut the branches into sections to remove them if the shrubs were very overgrown.

Following pruning, new shoots will grow from the base of the old branches. Later in the summer, once these shoots are large enough to handle, prune out the weakest, leaving about the same number as branches removed. These shoots may not flower next spring in some species, but should do so the following year.

Early-flowering shrubs bloom on the previous year's wood, while shrubs that flower late in the season produce their blooms on that year's growth. These are pruned early in the year and the previous year's wood is cut back to encourage lots of new growth. Cutting back almost to ground level will help keep these shrubs small. Hydrangea and butterfly bush are the best-known examples of late-flowering shrubs. Plants that have special pruning requirements are detailed in chapter 10.

CHAPTER 6

Stress and Pest Management

Plants that are grown in good soil, kept watered, fed and growing well are less likely to be attacked by pests and diseases and are better able to fight off these attacks when they occur. However, even the sturdiest plant will occasionally fall prey to a problem and that is when we must take action.

A certain amount of damage is acceptable, but you must decide at what point the health and appearance of the plant justifies the use of control measures. These controls need not be highly toxic chemicals; the majority of problems can be cured using substances of low toxicity. We now know that the indiscriminate use of chemical sprays, as practiced in the 1950s and '60s, is not good for us or our planet.

People pressure disease

It has been estimated that over 90 percent of the problems afflicting trees in the urban landscape are attributable to what has become known as people pressure disease. People are crowding trees and the trees have to stand and bear it—they cannot walk away.

Major or minor construction work is the cause of many tree woes. Putting in a swimming pool is obviously going to affect the root system of trees nearby, but a new walkway is not so obvious. Repairing sewer lines or septic systems, putting in underground hydro or telephone lines, installing automatic irrigation systems, leaks from natural gas, spills of all kinds, including gasoline from lawn mowers—all play a part in PPD.

Overdosing with fertilizer, using salt for deicing, spraying herbicides for weed control, and compaction caused by cars, foot traffic and riding mowers are all detrimental to tree health. All contribute to stress, and stress leaves a plant open to attack from pests and diseases. People pressure disease is not something that strikes suddenly. It takes time to find that a problem exists and by then it may be too late for effective action.

It is strange that we will go to great lengths to prepare the soil, plant and care for a dozen tulips, but we take a magnificent tree completely for granted and do little or nothing to ensure its continuing health.

Stress prevention

Curing a plant problem after it develops is more difficult, time-consuming and costly than preventing the problem in the first place. A regular tree inspection will do much to ensure that any problems that may arise do not get out of hand. This should be a continual process and should be done periodically throughout the growing season, but especially in spring and early summer.

Look at the leaf size and color and compare the rates of growth, as explained in chapter 5. Look for pest and disease build-up and spray, prune or treat accordingly. Inspect any ties to be sure they are not becoming tight; as a guide, there should be room for two fingers as well as the tree inside any tie. Look at support stakes to be sure they are needed (undo the tie and see what happens), and that they are not rubbing on the trunk, or haven't rotted at the ground.

Look for ants running up and down the trunk. A few are normal but a steady stream indicates either a nest inside the tree (hollow crown) or aphids. The presence of woodpeckers may also indicate a problem with bark beetles or other pests, although woodpeckers feed mainly on insects sheltering in bark crevices. Also remember, it matters little how carefully you take note of your tree's growth if you damage the plants by careless mowing or by using nylon line trimmers around the base of trees and shrubs to cut long grass. These can eat away even the bark on old mature trees, let alone the soft green bark of young plants. A circle of bare or mulch-covered soil around the base of every tree and shrub means the roots are not competing with grass for moisture. Also, the mower comes nowhere near the trunk and there is no need to use a weed-eater.

Integrated pest management

This is a fancy way of saying "getting Mother Nature to help you control bugs," but it is well worthwhile and cuts down on the amount of poisons we use in our gardens. You are using the natural predators that feed on plant pests to control these pests for you. Some, like birds, are present in our gardens anyway but others have to be introduced. Many garden centers now sell insect predators, or you can order them by mail. You have to realize that using IPM does not eliminate pests in most instances, it just keeps their numbers down to acceptable levels.

If you are relying on natural predators to keep pest populations down, keep in mind that the predators always follow the pest. By this I mean that the predators need the pest to feed on; when a pest population is low, so is the predator population. The pest must increase in order for the predators to have a food supply. Predators never wipe out their meal ticket, otherwise they, too, will perish.

IPM is most effective in the closed environment of a greenhouse, but can be used in the open garden. Ladybugs, which eat aphids, and praying mantises, which eat just about anything, are available by mail order (ask at your local garden center). As mentioned, it is no use ordering ladybugs if you don't have any aphids. They will just fly off to a neighbor's garden in search of a meal. Mantises do best in places with hot summers and may not be successful in coastal regions.

Aside from ordering insect predators for your garden, you can encourage a variety of animals, with zero, two, four or eight feet to help with pest control. Unfortunately, many people react negatively to some of them. Snakes will eat a large number of mice, beetles, slugs and snails, but many people are afraid of them, even though poisonous snakes are absent from most of the cold regions of this continent. In fact, you can have a considerable population of harmless garter snakes in your garden and never see one.

Most people, on the other hand, enjoy having birds in the garden. They eat an incredible number of insects, both good and bad, and by providing the kind of habitat birds need, you can encourage them to visit and stay. Providing food and shelter in winter, especially in the colder parts, will bring many benefits. Chickadees, for instance, will search out overwintering egg clusters laid by insects if they have a clump of evergreens in which to shelter and a feeder to balance their diet.

My garden is alive all winter with our resident sparrows who more than pay for their keep by attracting the returning spring birds that soon fill every available nesting spot.

By putting up nesting boxes and planting trees and shrubs to give suitable sites for birds that won't use boxes, you can encourage birds in summer, when insects are at their peak. Even hummingbirds eat insects if you lure them into the garden with a feeder.

Bats may not eat many plant pests, but they feed on flying insects, including mosquitos, thus making the garden more enjoyable for us. Often under stress in their natural environment, bats can be encouraged in the garden by putting up bat boxes—like bird boxes but with a slot in the base rather than a hole in the front.

The principal four-footed predator we encourage is not a favorite with many people; toads feed mainly on crawling pests, such as slugs, snails and earwigs. Unlike frogs, toads don't need water. They will live happily in any cool damp place. Our biggest one lives under the concrete back steps, but we find small ones in many places. They come out at dusk and spend the night hunting for tasty morsels. The upsurge in interest in garden pools will help increase frog and toad populations.

Many people who would happily eat a crab turn pale when faced with its cousin, the spider. Although the sexual habits of some spider species leave something to be desired, they do eat a lot of things other than their husbands and are very useful in the garden. As well as the familiar web-makers, which catch flying insects, the hunters, commonly known as jumping spiders, eat at ground level. While all spiders paralyze their prey by injecting poison when biting, few can puncture our tough skins. Those that can are not toxic enough to do permanent harm, although the itchy effect of their venom might last several days. Now, if you go farther south, that's another matter.

Garden hygiene

Some pests, such as leaf miners, and many diseases overwinter on dead foliage left from the previous summer. By being a bit more careful about cleaning up the garden in the fall, many of these problems can be avoided. If you have noticed problems such as mildew on your trees and shrubs, it could pay dividends to be extra thorough with raking the leaves. It seems ironic that it is the removal of leaves and the nutrients they release as they break down that can lead to plants being under stress in the first place and thus more susceptible to attack from diseases. But if a pest or disease is present, it is wise to remove old foliage.

When you must spray

Sometimes, pest or disease levels reach epidemic proportions and it may become a case of spray or lose the plant. While established plants can take being defoliated once in a season without too much harm, if the second crop of leaves is eaten off the plant starts to decline. If the same pest attacks for several years in succession (as with birch leaf miner) the plants can be killed.

If you have decided to spray, use the least toxic chemical that will do the job. The first essential is to identify the problem, be it pest or disease. If you don't know what you are spraying for, don't spray. In most cases, the problems you encounter will be the common ones. Often it is not necessary to identify a pest as a three-lined stink beetle; just knowing it is a beetle and not a caterpillar is enough. Pests and diseases that attack a wide range of plants are listed later in this chapter; those that are specific to particular plants are detailed in the plant listings in chapter 10.

Whatever type of chemical you use, treat it with respect. Read the directions on the packet and follow them exactly; doubling the dose may not kill more pests but it does put the user at twice the risk. Chemicals must always be used as specified; for example a wettable powder must only be used as a spray, never as a dust. Before applying a pesticide, make sure your equipment is working properly. If you haven't used a sprayer for some time, test spray with water first.

Even when using those with very low toxicity, wear unlined rubber gloves, especially while handling the concentrate, and preferably throughout the entire spraying operation. You should also wear a long-sleeved shirt and long pants, which should be washed after spraying. Use a dust mask if you are applying an insecticide or fungicide in powdered form, in addition to the protective clothing. Triple rinse sprayers after use and then have a shower yourself.

Pest control

In some cases, chemicals have got an unduly bad press because of careless use, while some organic pesticides, once considered very safe, are proving to have side effects. Be that as it may, both petro-chemical and organic insecticides and fungicides should be used with care. They can harm both the user and beneficial insects; even though some organic compounds are fairly target specific, they kill similar insects which are doing no harm.

The following list of the most common and readily available pest controls is arranged in increasing degree of toxicity. Use the least toxic spray that will control the targeted pest.

Bacillus thuringiensis. Commonly sold as BT, Dipel or Thuricide. This is a bacteria that attacks the caterpillars of many species of butterflies and moths. It is very specific and short-lived. Use it when the pests are visible, not as a preventative. It must be ingested to work. If it rains shortly after spraying, you will have to respray.

Insecticidal soap. This is made up of special selections of fatty acids (the basis of soap) that cause paralysis in many insects so they starve to death. The pest may not always fall off the plant after being sprayed, but a lack of movement shows the spray was effective. While ordinary soaps (but not detergents) work to a degree, they are not as good as these special formulations. They are short-lived, breaking down after a few days, and should be used when the pest is visible.

Oils. Dormant oil is a heavy distillation of oil used before leaves appear. It kills overwintering eggs and larvae, especially in crevices on the bark. When used in conjunction with lime sulphur, overwintering fungal spores will be killed as well. This combination is particularly useful on crab apples, which are prone to a number of pests and diseases. Read the directions carefully, as some plants are very sensitive to either the oil alone or the mixture. Dormant oil will kill plants once the leaves have opened.

Also on the market is summer, or superior, oil. This is a lighter oil that can be sprayed onto foliage (when mixed according to directions) at temperatures below 85°F (30°C). Summer oils will control aphids, mites, mealybugs and some caterpillars. Vegetable cooking oils will give the same control.

Diatomaceous earth. Although used mainly for controlling pests at soil level, diatomaceous earth can also be mixed with water (and a little soap) and sprayed onto shrubs and trees. It is composed of the spiny shells of tiny sea creatures called diatoms. It works by puncturing the skins of soft-bodied insects.

Methoxychlor. A long-lasting insecticidal spray used mainly for borers but that will also control most sucking insects.

Pyrethrins. Originally a plant derivative, pyrethrins are now produced synthetically. They are used in many "house and garden" and "flying insect" sprays. If using a spray can, be sure it is suitable for use on plants: some propellants can damage foliage. Pyrethrins are very toxic to fish and should never be used near garden ponds or streams. They break down very rapidly and have no residual effect.

Malathion. A commonly used organo-phosphate spray that controls a wide range of chewing and sucking pests. Its chief drawback is a repulsive smell when first diluted.

Carbaryl (Sevin). Controls many pests but is highly toxic to bees and should never be used on plants in flower. It is available as a spray or dust.

Dimethoate (Cygon). This systemic insecticide is absorbed into the sap-stream of the plant and makes it toxic to chewing insects. It may be sprayed onto the foliage, watered into the soil or, with some trees, painted on the bark. If applied as a soil drench it will kill any other living things it encounters in the soil. Systemics will control pests (such as leaf miners) that ordinary chemicals cannot reach. Read the label carefully; some plants are damaged by this chemical. Like Malathion, it stinks.

Rotenone. A plant derivative, available as a dust or spray, it remains effective for about a week.

Like pyrethrins, it is highly toxic to fish, but also affects birds, pigs and, it is now suspected, dogs.

Diazinon. A broad-spectrum insecticidal spray that can be used to control many of the more common pests. Being broad-spectrum, it also kills many neutral or beneficial insects as well.

Insects aren't the only problem

As if pests weren't enough to deal with, trees and shrubs are also attacked by other simple forms of plant life, especially fungi. They can sometimes be controlled with a fungicide, but in general they are more difficult to identify and control than pests. The following are some of the many controls available, again in increasing order of toxicity.

Baking soda. A mixture of 1 teaspoon (5 mL) of baking soda, a few drops of soap and 2 quarts (2 L) of water is reported to prevent fungal spores from becoming established. It has to be reapplied after rain, but could serve as a useful tool during a vulnerable period.

Sulphur. While sulphur deters many diseases, it is also harmful to the good fungi that live in the soil and to some plants. Lime sulphur, as mentioned earlier, will kill overwintering spores, but it can also be used after the leaves have developed providing the temperature is below 85°F (30°C).

Copper. While it can be used as a dust or liquid, copper is even more harmful to the soil than sulphur. When mixed with lime to form Bordeaux mixture, it becomes a much safer compound.

Folpet (Phaltan). A spray that controls powdery mildew, some leaf spots and certain other diseases.

Benomyl (Benlate). The first systemic fungicide, it controls a wide range of diseases. It is highly toxic to earthworms and should be used with care since excess spray dripping off a tree onto the lawn may have devastating effects on the beneficial worm population.

Maneb. A spray used chiefly for leaf spot diseases.

Triforine (Funginex). A good preventative spray for mildews and some leaf spots.

Ferbam. A spray for rust diseases, scab on crab apples, and some leaf spots.

Common pests

Aphids. Also known as greenfly or plant lice, aphids are tiny (1/4 in/6 mm) and can be green, yellow, pink, gray, black, two-toned or almost colorless. They feed on a wide range of plants, including many trees and shrubs. They tend to congregate on the new growth and excrete a sticky residue, known as honeydew, that can drip from trees and stain paving or cars. Ants farm aphid colonies for honeydew and will move the aphids to new shoots when colonies become overcrowded. Aphids may also be responsible for spreading some virus diseases, although since they are mostly wingless, this is not a big consideration.

The honeydew often supports a black secondary fungus called sooty mold. It lives on the honeydew, not the plants, but it forms a coating on the leaves, cutting off light. This can be as damaging to the plant as the original aphid attack.

Different races of aphids are fairly specific on their host plants. For example, the black aphids that feed on cherry and plum would not be found on linden, which is host to a yellow aphid. The woolly aphid, commonly found on crab apples, protects itself with a white, wool-like covering that repels water, making it difficult to control.

Control: Aphids are the preferred food of ladybugs and each species of ladybug has its favorite aphid. The orange one with two spots, for example, feeds almost exclusively on the aphid that attacks roses. The ladybug larva has a voracious appetite and will devour several times its own weight in aphids each day. These larvae are a dark purple with yellow spots and don't look at all like the adults, but like little dragons. If chemical control is necessary for aphids, the insecticidal soaps work well, as do garden sprays containing pyrethrins.

Leaf Miners. These are the larvae of several different types of insects, from moths to midges, but they all have the same effect on the plant. Eggs are laid either on the surface of the leaf or in a slit made in the leaf cover. On hatching, the larvae start to eat their way along inside the leaf, between the upper and lower surfaces. There are two main types of miner, those that mine galleries and leave a long winding passage behind them, and those that eat out an irregular chamber inside the leaf, leaving a large pale area.

Because they reduce the amount of leaf surface available for the manufacture of food (photosynthesis), a bad attack can weaken a plant and severe attacks for several years can kill it. They may cause premature defoliation, which can make the plant use energy in putting out a second batch of leaves, only to have them attacked in turn. Leaf miners are most common on birch, but also attack lilac, oak, dogwood, elm, and other species.

Control: The larvae may emerge from the leaf and fall to the ground to pupate, or they may remain inside the leaf until it falls. If you have a tree or shrub with leaf miner tunnels visible in the leaves, good hygiene is a must. Rake up the leaves frequently and dispose of them in the garbage. You may be able to prevent the larvae overwintering in the soil under the plant and thus break the cycle of infection.

Chemical control is rather difficult. Since the larvae are protected by the leaves themselves, most chemicals have no effect. You have to make the whole plant poisonous and for this you need a systemic insecticide. Dimethoate is the one most commonly used and it can either be sprayed onto the leaves (which absorb it), watered into the ground to be taken up by the root system, or, in a few cases, painted onto the bark to be absorbed into the sap-stream.

Caterpillars. A great number of caterpillars feed on trees and shrubs. With most caterpillars, it is not generally necessary to know what the actual pest is, as long as you recognize it as a caterpillar. In general they are the young stage of butterflies and moths, but some of the caterpillar look-alikes such as inchworms (a.k.a. loopers) are the larvae of sawflies.

Mostly caterpillars do not do a great deal of harm since the numbers are few and the damage they do is minimal. A few, however, are major pests and a careful watch must be kept for them. Most are quite specific as to their host plants and they are dealt with in those plant listings in chapter 10. The gypsy moth, which is causing concern in eastern provinces and states, is an exception. It is an eclectic feeder, although it does have favorite foods. Oaks, lindens, hawthorns and apples are its choice, but it will feed on just about any tree or shrub, and in the absence of anything else will eat grass.

The adults are small brown moths and the female lays eggs in late fall in crevices or under loose bark. Chickadees feed on them during the winter, and a dormant oil spray will kill any it touches. Even so, if you live where gypsy moths occur, you would be well advised to keep a careful watch for small, hairy, brown caterpillars, with blue spots at the front end and chestnut ones at the rear, that strip branches of all foliage in a short time. The newly hatched caterpillars are covered with small bristles that catch the wind. They can be carried for miles by a stiff breeze, so you might find the odd one without having a major outbreak.

Two other caterpillars that attack a wide range of plants are the tent caterpillar and the fall webworm. The first is a problem in spring and favors apple and cherry trees, although it will also feed on other species. The caterpillars form a nest in the fork of a branch to which they retreat each evening, fanning out during the day to strip all the leaves off nearby branches. Fall webworms are similar, but they form their nest on the ends of branches.

Control: The true caterpillars can be controlled with *Bacillus thuringiensis*, and insecticidal soap is fatal to both caterpillars and inchworms. The aerosol sprays containing pyrethrins also work well on these pests and are especially useful on tent caterpillars and webworms. These are usually in small colonies so it is wasteful to mix up a special spray in quantity. Break open the nests with a stick before spraying so the spray can reach the pests. The aerosols sold to control wasps and hornets put out a jet, rather than a spray, and are good for caterpillar infestations higher up the tree.

Borers and Bark Beetles. While it is true that a few perennial plants have stem borers, it is only in woody plants that they become a major pest. Borers pose serious problems for a few species (for example, black locust), and a constant watch must be kept for piles of sawdust beneath the tree—these indicate a borer at work. It is very considerate of borers to advertise their presence in this way, but finding the hole is not always so easy. If you can catch them in the early stages, a fine piece of wire pushed into the hole will spear the occupant.

Bark beetles lay their eggs in crevices on the bark. When the eggs hatch, the young tunnel into the bark and eat their way along until they mature. If several eggs were laid at the same spot, the tunnels form a much-branched gallery which is invisible until the bark is peeled off. With most trees, it is often the presence of woodpeckers digging into the bark for grubs that lets us know all is not well up there. It was the elm bark beetle that was responsible for the spread of Dutch elm disease, which decimated the American elm in much of North America.

Borers have a similar method of egg-laying,

but the larvae tend to tunnel into the stem or trunk, rather than just below the bark. Unless the attack is heavy, borers and bark beetles don't do a lot of harm, although willows can suffer badly from their presence.

Borers can be found on many species, including both deciduous and evergreen trees and shrubs. True bark beetles are more discriminating and attack only hickories, junipers, pines and elms.

Control: Since the pests are enclosed in the plant, only a systemic insecticide can control them. Even a systemic poison may not affect borers since the wood in the center of a branch is dead and has no sap flow. Larvae that are feeding on the central core are almost impossible to kill.

Mealybugs. These are closely related to scale and aphids; some of the mealybugs look like aphids in a wedding dress, all white and frothy. Their white waxy coating makes them easy to see but, as with woolly aphid, it helps to repel many sprays so they are somewhat difficult to kill. They differ from aphids in not having six distinct legs in the adult form.

They are chiefly pests of warm climates (or indoor plants) but hardy species can overwinter on yew, cedar, crab apple, maple and basswood in some regions.

Control: Insecticidal soap will cut through the wax and generally gives good control.

Mites. Probably better known as pests of house plants and greenhouses, mites also attack a range of woody plants. They are minute members of the spider family, with eight legs, but unless you have the eyesight of Superman, you will not know this without the aid of a strong hand lens. As they are so tiny, they are often overlooked until their damage is noticed, by which time the population is huge.

They feed on the foliage, generally on the underside, and cause tiny yellowish spots which can run together in a severe attack. Their feeding often results in the leaves taking on a slightly purplish or coppery tinge, often the first indication of a problem.

Mites occur chiefly on birch, hawthorns, hollies, crab apples, rhododendrons, roses and basswood without causing too much harm. They are more harmful on evergreens where the needles do not regenerate easily. Fir, spruce and hemlock are the principal hosts and I have seen a dwarf Alberta spruce almost killed down one side by mites in an exceptionally hot summer. Evergreens may also be defoliated by winter desiccation, but this generally shows up early in the year, whereas mite damage is a summer problem.

Control: Since they are not insects, many insecticides do not kill them. In fact, some insecticides kill off their natural predators and allow the mite populations to explode. In enclosed situations, you can introduce natural predators, but outdoors these have little effect. Spraying the plant with water, directing a strong jet upwards, will wash many of the pests off the underside of the leaves. Repeat every few days. You can also use malathion or dimethoate if the plant is not too large. These chemicals are too poisonous to spray without care and may drift onto food plants if large trees are sprayed.

Mites are generally only a problem in very hot summers and by the time populations have built up enough to show symptoms, the plant has stored enough food to survive. If you do get a bad attack of mites, be sure to use a dormant oil spray in late winter to kill off any that are overwintering in crevices on the bark.

Scale. Female scale insects must be the couch potatoes of all time. After a brief bout of exercise shortly after hatching, when they move away from Mum and branch out on their own, they settle down in one spot, put down a feeding tube and that's it. Male scale insects have a more active, but very brief, life—often only a few days. Perhaps they wear themselves out.

Scales are classified as soft or hard, depending on the type of covering they produce. Many soft scales are difficult to tell from mealybugs, except they hardly move. They produce a cottony mass containing eggs but the front part of the scale can usually be seen poking out of this. With many of these soft scales, the young stage (called crawlers) feed on the leaves for the summer and only migrate to their permanent home in fall. The commonest soft scale is the cottony maple scale, which attacks many plants other than maple.

Hard scales cover themselves with a hard wax coating—black, brown, yellow or green, depending on the species—once they reach their chosen location. They often blend in with the twig they are feeding on, making them hard to see. Because they insert a feeding tube into the sap flow of the host, they tend to feed on young branches where the bark is not developed, rather than on the more mature shoots.

Where infestations have escaped detection for some time, scale can build up a dense colony. The crawlers only move far enough to find a piece of exposed twig before settling down for a summer-long feed. Often, as they grow, their shells overlap those of their neighbors, producing a multi-level parking-lot effect.

In a typical scale, the female lays eggs under her canopy in late fall and then dies. These eggs hatch in spring, break out of the cover and crawl away to set up housekeeping on their own— presumably being visited by the short-lived male in the process.

A great number of woody plants are afflicted with scale. Maple, elm, oak, lilac, camellia, euonymus, holly, spruce, pine and hemlock are probably the most prone. As with all these pests, a tree already under stress is more at risk.

Control: The best time to control scale is when the crawlers are house-hunting. Use superior oil, methoxychlor, carbaryl or diazinon. In winter, a dormant oil spray will kill many, but where infestations are heavy, complete control is unlikely.

Common diseases

Like the pests, many fungi and bacteria find an easy living on the woody plants we grow. Many of them produce similar effects and are listed by symptom without being specific as to the agent involved. Most diseases are more difficult to control than pests. Often only the fruiting bodies are produced above the surface of the plant; the bulk of the problem is hidden inside the leaf or twig where sprays cannot penetrate.

Anthracnose. This is one of the many diseases that are known collectively as leaf blights or blotches and is characterized by the suddenness of the attack. Brown spots appear on the leaves, seemingly overnight. These may run together to form large blotches and are usually between the veins. The leaves may wilt and fall early, or may turn brown and not drop all winter.

Mature trees can take early defoliation for a year or two, but it weakens them and makes them more liable to further attack. Help the tree recover by watering during prolonged drought and by feeding.

Anthracnose has become a major problem on chestnuts, flowering dogwood, maples, oaks, sycamores and lindens growing in stressful city situations. It can also attack spindle trees, Boston ivy and Virginia creeper, currants, roses and snowberry, but is not common on these.

Control: Good sanitation is essential. Remove and dispose of all the affected foliage. This may mean raking leaves in July, but at least you will beat the rush for pick-up. If the tree is small enough, spray with lime sulphur in late winter and with Bordeaux mixture as the leaves start to unfurl.

Blight. This is a general term used to describe similar symptoms caused by several different fungi and bacteria. It is often linked with the name of the part affected, as in leaf blight, flower blight, or the appearance of the affected part, as in brown blight, fire blight. Young growth is most commonly attacked; wilting and death of that part is rapid.

Probably the most important, certainly the most notorious, of all the blights is fire blight. This bacterial disease attacks members of the rose family such as crab apple, serviceberry, hawthorn, plum and cherry and most frequently, mountain ash. The disease starts on one branch; the leaves turn brown and hang down but are not shed. It looks as if someone had gone along the branch with a blow torch.

Control: As soon as you see symptoms that could be fire blight, remove that branch, cutting well outside the affected area. Sterilize the pruning saw with rubbing alcohol after making each cut, just in case. If you are very lucky, and act quickly enough, the tree will be saved. Infected wood left on the tree will produce spores which are spread by splashing rain and wind. Prunings should be put in the garbage or burned.

Other blights may cause symptoms similar to anthracnose if fungal in origin, or water-soaked blotches if bacterial. The treatment is the same as for anthracnose.

Canker. Canker may attack roots, stems or twigs and is best described as dead areas of tissue, often sunken or cracked. Canker is often the result of mechanical injury, such as hitting the trunk with a lawn mower, or it may follow an exceptionally hard winter. It is caused by both fungi and bacteria and may spread slowly to girdle a branch, killing all the growth beyond.

Control: If possible, prune out the affected part as soon as noticed. Cut well inside the damaged area to remove all discolored wood. Burn the wood

or dispose of it in the garbage and be sure to disinfect the pruning saw. Root cankers usually go unnoticed until the plant dies and are only discovered on digging up the remains. Luckily they are rare.

Galls. A gall is a swelling on a shoot, branch or root and may be caused by insects or fungi. The swollen leaves on honey locust and the lumpy leaf stalks on poplar are insect-caused, but the black swellings on plum branches (black knot) are fungal in origin.

Insect-caused galls are often numerous and appear suddenly. They are generally cyclic in nature, building up to a high level when almost every leaf is attacked. Then when the appropriate natural predator has also multiplied, the pest level drops dramatically and the problem seems solved—for a year or two. They are unsightly but seldom life-threatening for your plant.

Fungus-caused galls are normally few in number and may escape early detection for this reason. Frequent tree inspection will help in spotting them.

Control: Insect-caused galls can generally be controlled by good sanitation or, if really bad, by treating the ground under the affected plant with a soil drench to kill any larvae in the soil. Remedial pruning will remove fungus-caused galls but it may reappear if the fungus has spread into the plant. Sterilization of pruning tools is a must after each cut.

Leaf spots and blotches. There are a multitude of things that can cause leaves to develop dead areas, ranging from air pollution, insect feeding and mechanical damage, to fungus, bacteria and viral attacks. Leaf spots are one of the hardest things to pin down and can cause home-owners considerable worry. Unless spots are widespread and the plant starts losing leaves, there is no need to panic. As noted earlier, once the disease is inside the leaf it is very difficult to control it.

Viruses are minute organisms that live inside the cells of plants and animals. They cause many strange symptoms in plants (and some of humanity's worst diseases) and are easy to confuse with other fungal and bacterial problems. They are almost impossible for the home gardener to control and may be the cause of witches' brooms (a tangled mass of branching stems) in conifers.

Fungal leaf spots can normally be distinguished from insect damage by a ring of paler tissue surrounding the spot. In some cases (black spot on roses, tar spot on maples) the spots are black. Sometimes the center falls out of the spot, giving a shot-hole effect, and making it difficult to tell from insect damage.

Almost all plants are likely to be attacked by one or more of the many, many diseases that cause leaf spots, but they are seldom fatal. They are likely to be more in evidence during wet summers or in regions with high rainfall.

Control: This is the same as for anthracnose: good sanitation and a dormant spray.

Rusts. Two distinct host plants are needed for the majority of rusts to reproduce successfully. These are often widely different, as in the case of wheat and barberry. Growing many types of barberry is now banned in Canada since they are the alternate host of a serious rust disease of wheat. In the U.S., the rust that attacks currants and pines has resulted in a ban on currant-growing in many states. This may be a futile effort, as an alternate host to currant is goldenrod.

In the home garden, the most important rust is probably the one that alternates between junipers and many members of the rose family. It is found on crab apple, ornamental pear, chokecherry, serviceberry, mountain ash, hawthorn and flowering quince. In late summer, small spots on the underside of the leaf or on the fruit give rise to tiny fruiting bodies that release spores into the air. On juniper, rusts produce reddish galls that put out bright orange tendrils in spring to release their spores.

Control: The galls on juniper are quite easy to spot, especially in spring, and can be pruned off; dispose of them in the garbage. This is the best method of control.

Mildew. The two mildews that attack trees and shrubs are quite different and easy to tell apart. Downy mildew is not common but does occur sometimes. It shows up as a pale patch on the upper leaf surface and a downy, gray growth on the lower. In time the leaf wilts, withers and dies.

Powdery mildew, as its name suggests, is a white to light gray powder on the leaves, buds and shoots. If the attack is severe, the leaves will become distorted and turn yellow. The mildew may cover the entire leaf, causing premature leaf drop. Both of these diseases gain a foothold during periods of high humidity, warm days and cool nights, but powdery mildew is encouraged by stagnant air. Lilacs in need of rejuvenation, with a thicket of suckers, are prime targets for powdery mildew, but it can occur on a wide range of plants.

Control: Good sanitation will remove much of the source of infection. Thinning thickets of suckers on shrubs such as lilacs will allow better air circulation and reduce the chances of infection. On plants that are particularly prone to attack (possibly because of location) spraying with baking soda, folpet or triforine on a regular basis will help.

Wilt and Dieback. Anything that interferes with the normal uptake of water to a shoot will cause wilting. Causes can range from insufficient water in the soil, to an excess of water that cuts off oxygen to the roots and kills them, to root damage, to fungal or bacterial infections. If the entire plant is affected, suspect the first three. If it is only one or two shoots, suspect the last two.

Sometimes the wilting goes unnoticed, especially if it is high in a large tree, and the branch is killed. The disease moves down towards the trunk, killing as it goes. This is described as dieback. A large number of diseases can cause dieback, but it is also a symptom of people pressure disease.

If your tree or shrub is infected, there is often a discoloration of the wood. A long diagonal cut through the wilting shoot will reveal discoloration if it is there (a cut made at right angles across a branch may expose too small an area to be certain).

Control: Prune well below the wilting part of the shoot and hope you removed it all. If the dieback was stress-related, there may be no disease involved.

Wood rot. Older trees can be attacked by various wood-rotting fungi. These are slow-acting and may be present for years before the production of fruiting bodies reveals the attack. The fungi gain entrance through wounds, such as pruning cuts, insect, bird or squirrel damage, mower knocks and frost cracks. They can also attack through weak crotches that collect rain and provide the perfect incubation ground.

Fungi most often attack the heartwood in the center of the tree but can also infect living wood. The presence of bracket fungi on the trunk or clusters of small fungi at the base of the tree indicates a wood rot fungus attack.

There is very little you can do if the heartwood is infected. It is virtually impossible to remove all the infected wood, and many a hollow tree will carry on growing for years in seemingly good health.

* * *

Let me finish this chapter of gloom and doom on a bright note. While all these things (and a great many more I haven't described) can attack woody plants, it is most unlikely they all will. As long as your shrubs and trees are growing well and are not under stress, you will probably see only a few of these pests and no more serious a disease than mildew.

CHAPTER 7

Changing the Landscape

One of the good things about gardening is that mistakes can usually be rectified. If you make a mistake building furniture you have to live with it, but an error in planting a garden is generally easy to put right.

These errors can happen in many ways. You may have chosen the wrong-sized plant for a specific place; subsequent reading may indicate an inappropriate location—a sun-loving plant in a shady spot, for example; you may have overplanted initially so that mature plants are now crowded; or you may have decided to change the entire landscape design of your garden.

While most plants can be moved, some are easier to relocate than others. Perennial plants can be moved even after many years in the same place; in fact, most benefit from being divided and replanted in fresh soil. Woody plants are a different matter. The length of time they have been planted is the major factor governing their movability, but the species involved, the type of plant, how it was purchased, and even the kind of soil in which it is growing contribute to the success or failure of transplanting.

Moving trees and shrubs

Before you start to dig the plant up, think back and remember how it was packaged when you bought it. If it was a large tree planted by a tree-moving company, you will have to call them in again to move it for you. If it was a container-grown tree or shrub and has been planted less than three years, it should move without much problem. If planted longer than this, its chances of survival depend on several factors. Some species make many fibrous roots, others a few anchor roots with feeding roots coming off these. You will retain more feeding roots on the first type. In general, shrubs have a shallower root system than trees and will survive transplanting more easily.

The type of soil also affects survival. Plants in light soil are easier to dig than those in clay so you will be more inclined to dig a large rootball. Plants in sandy soils tend to develop more roots because the soil is not rich. Finally, survival depends on the amount of work you are willing to do. A plant with a large rootball will survive better than a small one, but it is harder to keep a rootball together in sandy soil; it tends to fall apart.

Bare-root trees and prepackaged shrubs, because they don't have as many roots as those in containers, are slower to grow away when first planted. You can probably move these successfully for about five years, but the factors mentioned above still apply. Once you start to dig, you will discover what sort of roots your plant has. If it seems impossible to move, you may want to give up and fill the trench back in. The plant will probably survive; you just did a bit of root pruning.

The time of year you try to move established plants is just as critical as when you first planted them. See "The best time to plant" in chapter 3.

Problems with roots

Many home-owners are concerned that foundation plants could damage the basement walls. The probability of this happening depends on the type of plant, the kind of soil it is growing in, and its distance away from the house. Many large shrubs or small trees are used as foundation planting without ever causing problems. Cedars

(arborvitae), and junipers are probably the most common and seldom cause any problems because they all have fibrous root systems with few large roots.

Roots on their own are not strong enough to penetrate brick or concrete foundations—unless a crack already exists—but a root alongside a wall exerts tremendous pressure as it increases in size year by year. The worst offenders are trees with shallow root systems, such as poplar, willow and silver maple, none of which are good candidates for a small city lot anyway.

The majority of trees will seldom cause damage, providing they are planted a reasonable distance away from the dwelling. A reasonable distance is at least half of the eventual height of the fully grown tree. While the root spread will be greater than the tree height, the roots are unlikely to be thick enough at this distance to cause problems. People who plant trees right next to their foundations, or allow seedling trees to grow close to their house, garage or swimming pool are asking for trouble. These plants should be removed before they have time to cause problems.

Trees that are normally safe may cause problems during prolonged droughts on clay soil. Locally, two consecutive summers with severe droughts produced several instances where basements had cracked due to settlement caused by soil shrinkage. In each case, there was at least one large tree with roots under the house, taking the water from a clay soil.

Changing grades

After a time, you may find you are dissatisfied with the way your garden looks and decide to relandscape. Hopefully, many of the existing trees and shrubs can be incorporated into the new design. Providing your new plans do not include any changes in grade, you have nothing to worry about except the work. If, however, you intend to excavate or truck in extra soil, you need to take care to preserve your existing plants.

The roots of all plants breathe; they take in oxygen from the air spaces between the soil particles and give off carbon dioxide. This does not happen at the same rate at which we breathe, but then roots aren't as active as even the worst couch potato. If you add a layer of soil you reduce the amount of oxygen that can percolate down through the soil to the root zone. Deprived of oxygen, the roots die, and then the tree dies. This is what happens when beavers flood a section of woodland. Water replaces the air between the soil particles and the trees die from lack of oxygen at the roots.

The feeding roots for most plants extend out beyond the ends of the branches. While most instructions for feeding woody plants recommend putting the fertilizer at the drip-line, it is now known that the feeding roots actually go well beyond this. If you excavate close to a tree or large shrub, you will be removing a proportion of these roots and the plant will suffer, and possibly die. Consider the "specimen" trees that are left on some of the more affluent building estates. By the time the roads have been excavated, basements dug and services buried, the poor trees have little root system left. No wonder they slowly die over the next few years.

If you must increase the grade around existing trees and the increase is only 4 to 6 inches (10 to 15 cm), use a sandy soil and, if possible, add it over two growing seasons. Different species vary widely in their ability to tolerate having their roots buried. Maples (especially sugar and silver maples), beech, dogwood, most oaks, pines and spruce are very sensitive. Birch, cedars and hemlock are less sensitive, while elm, poplar, willow, pin oaks and locusts can survive large grade changes.

To change the grade by up to a foot (30 cm), cover the area with a layer of coarse crushed stone (up to 2-inch/5-cm diameter) and put a layer of gravel over this. About 6 inches (15 cm) of soil is recommended to grow a good lawn. Slope the soil up from the tree so the trunk is not buried below its original depth (Figure 7.1).

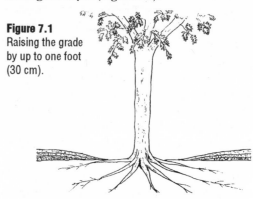

Figure 7.1
Raising the grade by up to one foot (30 cm).

To raise the grade by more than a foot (30 cm), first lay agricultural drainage tiles or plastic drainage pipe radiating away from the trunk and extending at least to the drip-line (Figure 7.2). Then build a dry-stone wall round

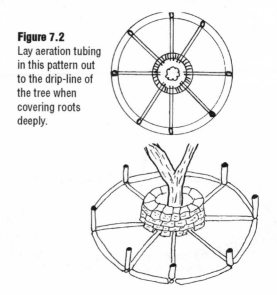

Figure 7.2
Lay aeration tubing in this pattern out to the drip-line of the tree when covering roots deeply.

the trunk of the tree, leaving room for the tree to grow, with the ends of the tiles poking through. If using tiles, cover the joints with heavy plastic to prevent soil from being washed in. Set upright tiles filled with large crushed stone at the ends of the spokes to allow air in. Place a layer of broken rock between the spokes and cover this with large-grade crushed stone. Top this in turn with gravel and then finish with a sandy soil. The wall should lean away from the tree to take the pressure of the soil.

When excavating around existing trees, leave as much of the old grade in place as possible, certainly out to the drip-line of the tree. It may be possible to slope the soil up to meet the old grade, or you may have to construct a retaining wall (Figure 7.3). If a retaining wall is needed, the drip-line should be the absolute minimum in mild climates. Where winters are cold, the old grade should extend well beyond the drip-line. Cold penetrates an exposed wall and can damage roots on species that are generally considered hardy.

Figure 7.3
When lowering the grade, leave as much room as possible.

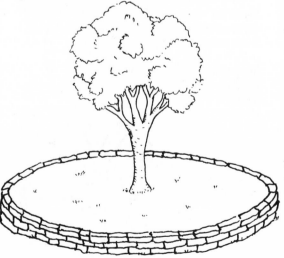

Tree and shrub removal

Sometimes plants die. It may be from old age; even trees don't live forever. It may be from damage, such as mice girdling the trunks in winter or overenthusiastic use of a weed-eater. It may be from winter injury in a year that is colder than normal. It may be from pest or disease attack that has been allowed to continue for several years (such as birch leaf miner) or for which there is no cure (like Dutch elm disease). If the plant has not been a resident in your garden for long, you can probably dig it out without difficulty. If it is an old-timer, other measures are needed.

Very large trees should always be left to the professional. Even on large properties, where the tree can do no damage as it falls, it might fall on you. Reasonable-sized trees can be taken down by the home-owner providing there is no chance of them causing damage to your own or a neighbor's property.

First remove the major branches; cut them up and remove them from the site before tackling the trunk. If you intend to remove the stump, do not cut the trunk down too low, as it gives leverage to break the roots. Depending on the location you might decide to keep the stump; there are several vines that could clothe it and make it a garden feature.

Large shrubs should be removed in the same way. Cut off the top branches and clear the site before starting to dig. Leave several feet (at least a metre) of the main branches as an aid when digging out the stump.

Many trees and shrubs will sprout from the base if they are not completely dead. This is particularly true for winter-killed or girdled plants where only the top is killed; the roots are still active and may stimulate new growth in time. However, many named forms of trees are grafted onto a seedling rootstock and basal growth will probably be the rootstock, rather than the form you bought. Species trees and most of the common shrubs propagated by cuttings will come true from the roots. Depending on the cause of death, you may want to delay stump removal until you know if the roots are still alive. With an active root system to support it, new growth is fast and a good-sized shrub or tree can grow quickly.

How to kill roots and decay stumps

Poplars and willows are very hard to kill and cutting them down only causes the roots to produce a multitude of suckers. Providing you realize this ahead of time, you can take steps to kill the stumps and their offspring. When cutting these species down, leave at least a foot (30 cm) of stump above ground. Using a drill and the largest bit you can borrow, drill a series of deep holes into the top surface of the stump. You will need the equivalent of a one-inch (2.5-cm) hole, at least four inches (10 cm) deep, for each three inches (8 cm) of diameter.

Mix up some 2,4-D lawn weed killer, diluting it with an equal amount of water and fill the holes with this. Cap them with modeling clay or staple plastic over them. This will reduce evaporation, prevent rain from diluting the solution, and prevent the accidental poisoning of birds. Check the levels every day or so and refill as needed. The 2,4-D is absorbed by the stump, goes into the roots

and kills the suckers from inside. This is more environmentally friendly than spraying the entire garden with weedkiller, and it gets the suckers growing where you can't spray.

Be cautious if you have two similar trees growing in the same part of the garden and are only removing one. Roots can graft themselves together underground and the weedkiller you applied to one stump can move into an adjacent plant you want to keep.

This method leaves the roots in the soil and in a year or two you will get a crop of fungi growing on the decaying roots, which may develop into fairy-rings. These will eventually disappear once the roots have decomposed.

When the roots are dead, cut the old stump down to ground level. If the stump is accessible from the street, you can call in one of the stump-grinding companies to chip it away to below ground level. With soft woods, like poplar and willow, simply mounding soil over the stump will rot it away in three or four years. For hardwood stumps, commercial stump destroyers do a reasonably fast job.

Beware of stump removers that you soak into the wood and, after a period of time, set alight. If the tree is anywhere near a dwelling, you have no way of knowing where the roots go and they may carry the fire under your house!

Making New Plants

While it is easy to go out and buy plants, there is great satisfaction in being able to say you knew a plant when it was just a young green slip of a thing. This chapter is about the various ways in which you can propagate your own woody plants.

Seed

The most obvious method of propagation is seed, and for some plants this works great, but it is a fairly slow process: if you are drawing your old age pension, don't expect to be able to swing your hammock from the two acorns you just planted.

One point to keep in mind is the provenance (original source) of the seed you plant. This is quite important in northern climates where a plant may be close to the limit of its hardiness. Seed coming from a southern source will be less likely to survive than seed from a local tree or equally cold place.

Another point to consider is what other trees of related species were growing close by. Most botanical gardens have stopped collecting seed from the woody plants they grow; once you have a collection of different but closely related plants, cross-pollination will occur and your seedling may not be what you expected. Picking up a few acorns

in the local park may not be such a good idea unless all the oaks are the same species. Reputable commercial sources generally get their seed from pure stands in the wild or isolated trees in cultivation.

As a general rule, seed from woody plants that grow where winters are harsh need a cold treatment to germinate. This is a self-protection mechanism for the plant: if the seed germinated soon after it was shed in late summer or fall, the seedlings might not be strong enough to survive the winter. By having a built-in inhibitor that is broken down by cold temperatures, seeds cannot germinate until spring and the seedlings have all summer to grow and store food for winter. There are exceptions to this rule; some early-flowering species shed their seed quickly and germination takes place immediately.

Those seeds that require a period of cold to break dormancy must be kept below 41°F (5°C).

The length of time varies greatly and can be anywhere from 30 to 120 days, depending on the species. See the books in Suggested Reading at the back of the book for the time required for individual species. For the home gardener who wishes to start plants indoors, this is rather important. While you can find a spot in the fridge where the temperature is below 41°F (5°C), you need to know when to start the chilling to have seeds ready to germinate in early spring.

This process is known as stratification, and you will find many of the plants listed in chapter 10 can be propagated by stratified seed.

Some plants have seed with a very hard coat. In nature this may take a couple of years to break down, but we can speed up the process by scarifying the seed, that is, rubbing the seed coat with a nail file, emery paper or sand to scratch through the hard layer and allow water to penetrate. In extreme cases, commercial growers use concentrated sulphuric acid to eat through the coating, but I wouldn't recommend that for the home gardener. You could, however, experiment with vinegar, a dilute acid, or Javel water, a concentrated alkaline; both will dissolve the seed coat in time.

When asked how to grow any woody plant from seed, my reply is "Make like a squirrel, bury it in the garden in the fall and see what happens." Except in the mildest climates, fall planting outside meets all the requirements for successful germination. The temperature is below the critical level and stays there for longer than needed. When the soil warms up, the seed will sprout. After all, that's the way nature has been doing it for longer than humans have been gardening. If scarification is needed, either do it before you plant the seed, or be patient; in time the seed coat will break down.

There are a few things to consider when planting outside. First, depth of planting: it should be two to three times the smallest diameter of the seed. If you have a large, flat seed, plant it flat, just under the surface. Second, label the spot where you put the seed—both ends of the row so you won't plant something else on top. Third, if squirrels are a problem in your area, place chicken wire over the seed bed to stop them from digging. Be sure to lift it daily to prevent it freezing to the soil, and remove it entirely when the ground is frozen, just in case the seeds sprout in early spring.

There are a few species that take two years to show, so don't be too disappointed if nothing happens at first. They may make a root the first spring and not put up a shoot until the second, or they may have a very hard seed coat. Be patient, it takes several years to make a good-sized plant anyway, so a few months will make little difference.

Be warned: don't sow a great quantity of any plant. We gardeners have a built-in reluctance to throw out any living plant (except maybe weeds) and having grown it oneself from seed makes this reluctance ten times worse. If you sow a hundred seeds when you want one plant, you may end up living in a forest. Don't sow seeds from hybrids (named forms) and expect them to look like the parent. If you collect seed from 'Charles Joly' lilac (a good dark form) and sow it, you will end up with a whole range of shades, most of which will be inferior. You may get the odd seedling that is a similar color, but you will have to wait several years before you know.

Cuttings

A great many plants can be raised from cuttings if you go about it in the right way. The advantages of cuttings over seed are that you can often start named forms this way, the plant is several inches tall immediately, and it grows much faster.

The critical factor is timing: getting the new growth at just the right stage of ripeness. This will vary from season to season, from region to region, and from plant to plant. Those that leaf out in early spring will be ready sooner than those that are slower to leaf out. The best stage for getting roots to form is something you learn with practice, so don't be afraid to experiment.

When a plant puts out new growth in the spring, it is known as "soft." The bright green shoots are flexible, and have thin, easily torn leaves. As the season progresses, the stems become more rigid, turn a darker green and the leaves toughen up. This stage is known as semi-ripe and is the best for easy rooting on most species.

If you have something you really want to grow, take a few cuttings every week or ten days, from the time the wood starts to ripen until it is mature. They only take up a little space and this way you will learn the best time to root that species.

Before you rush out into the garden to try out this great way of getting new plants for nothing, there are certain things you will need. Get a sharp knife or one-sided razor blade (try a paint store—they sell them in holders to scrape paint off glass) and some rooting hormone—use the number 2 grade for semi-hardwoods. Gather up several small sheets of clear plastic, some old coathangers and a pair of wire cutters. You'll need some horticultural-grade or washed river sand; don't use builder's sand as there are too many fine particles in it that cake the soil. You will also need a shady spot in the garden, with good drainage, that is free of plants. If you have a heavy clay soil, don't try to root cuttings outside; use the indoor method described later.

Taking, making and sticking cuttings

To prepare the site where you intend to put the cuttings, mix some of the coarse sand into the soil to improve the drainage and water the area if it is dry. Cut the coathangers into pieces a little longer than the width of your plastic sheets and bend them into hoops. These will be pushed into the soil and covered with the plastic to form a mini-greenhouse (Figure 8.1). Make it large enough to hold several cuttings without them touching the sides, but also without crowding them.

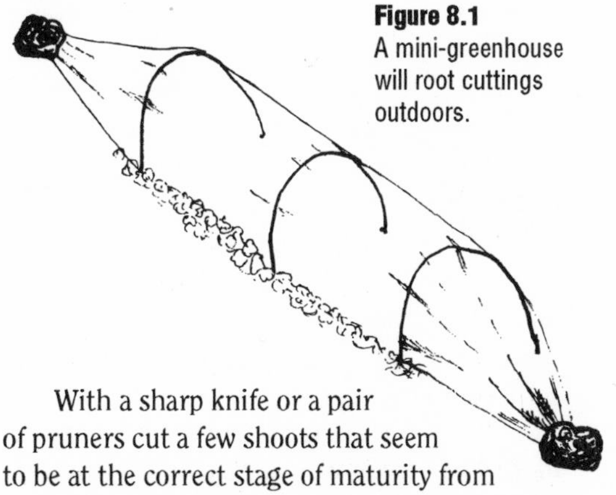

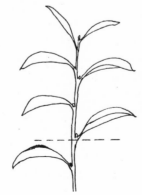

Figure 8.1
A mini-greenhouse will root cuttings outdoors.

With a sharp knife or a pair of pruners cut a few shoots that seem to be at the correct stage of maturity from the parent plant. Because the rates of growth vary so much between species, it is not practical to say cuttings should be a particular length; instead cut shoots that have about six pairs of leaves, or about eight leaves if they are not in pairs. Put the shoots in a plastic bag containing a piece of moist paper toweling to keep them fresh.

Figure 8.2
Making a cutting—showing the node.

You are now ready to make the cuttings. Using the knife or one-sided razor blade, cut just below the place where a leaf, or pair of leaves, joins the stem (Figure 8.2). This is called a node and most plants root better here.

Trim off the lowest leaves to bare about

Figure 8.3
A cutting ready for planting with trimmed leaves.

half the stem. If the remaining leaves are very large, they can be cut in half (Figure 8.3). Keep both the unmade and freshly made cuttings in the plastic bag while you work. You may be slow at first but will improve with practice. Form the prepared cuttings into a bunch with the bases all level, and dip the ends of the cuttings into water. Shake off the excess so they are just damp, and then dip them about half an inch (1 cm) into the rooting powder. Tap the cuttings on the edge of the tin to remove loose powder and you are ready to take them to your rooting bed. If you are using a liquid rooting hormone, simply dip the bottom half inch (1 cm) of the cuttings into this without wetting them first. Pop them back in the bag to keep them fresh.

If you cannot find any of the rooting hormones, you can make your own using willow twigs. Known as willow-water, many gardeners find it gives as good or better results than commercial compounds.

Use shoots from any available willow, but the common weeping willow works well. Select shoots ranging from the thickness of your little finger to pencil-sized, at the time the willows are just showing the first signs of new foliage, when the tree starts to look yellowish from a distance. Cut these shoots into 1-inch (2.5-cm) lengths, giving a slanting cut to expose more of the ends.

Place one measure of cut shoots and two measures of water in a container and keep this in a warm place (on top of the refrigerator works well) for about 72 hours, then strain out the shoots and keep the liquid in the refrigerator. If you leave the shoots to soak for a longer period, the liquid will not keep well.

When you are ready to make cuttings, take a small container of the willow-water into the garden with you and put the shoots you cut off into it. As you make the cuttings, put them back into the liquid and, after you have put the cuttings into the prepared bed, water them with the willow-water you were soaking them in.

With a pencil, piece of bamboo cane or sharp stick, make a hole about as deep as the bare part of the cuttings in the soil of your prepared bed. Put a cutting into the hole and firm the soil round the base with your fingers. Don't try to use the cutting to make the hole; you will probably break it. When all the cuttings are in place, mist them gently with water. Stretch the plastic over the frame and bury the edges. Gather the ends into a bunch and hold them in place with a stone.

Inspect the cuttings every few days without taking the cover off the wires. If the cover is completely free of condensation on the inside, gently water the soil round it. This will provide enough moisture to stop the cuttings from wilting.

After about three weeks, on a cloudy day or in the evening, remove the cover and give one of the cuttings a gentle tug. If it comes up easily, replace it, put the cover back on and wait another three weeks. If there is slight resistance, rooting has started, so replace the cover and wait about ten days. If there is good resistance, the cuttings have rooted and you can proceed to the next stage.

By now the cuttings are used to a humid environment, and if you suddenly remove the cover they will probably die. Instead, make a few small holes in the top of the cover to let some of the humidity escape and begin hardening off the cuttings. A few days later make more holes, and a few days after this, remove the cover completely.

Leave the cuttings in place until they lose their leaves. Once they are dormant, it is safe to dig them up, carefully separating their roots, which are probably growing into one another, and replant them farther apart. In regions with harsh winters, separating the cuttings is probably best left until spring.

If you find that cuttings root, but do not make good root systems, try this technique the following year. When you are preparing the cuttings, slice the skin off one side for about an inch (2.5 cm) above the base to create a wound, or slit the base of the cutting for about an inch (2.5 cm). Use the rooting hormone as usual. Try doing some cuttings each way and keep notes on which is more effective.

Rooting indoors

If you have a fluorescent light set-up in your basement or a bright window in a spare room, try the following method. To root a single kind of cutting, bend two pieces of wire to form a dome over a 5-inch (13 cm) flower pot. Fill this pot with a mix of 50 percent damp peat moss or vermiculite and 50 percent washed sand. Make the cuttings as described above, dip them in the rooting hormone and insert them into the pot. Water lightly, stand the pot on a saucer, push the wire frame in place and put the plastic bag on. It may be easier to place everything in the bag, pull it up over the frame and close it at the top (Figure 8.4).

If this works well, and you want to experiment with more varieties, try making your own mini-misting unit instead of having the place cluttered with pots in bags. Build a small frame to make a mini-room and cover the sides and top with clear plastic sheeting. The size and shape depends on the number of cuttings you expect to make, and the space you have available.

Put the cuttings in the pots and place them in the rooting room with a cool vaporizer. This gives a very fine mist and is as good as a commercial mist unit for rooting (Figure 8.5). This ar-

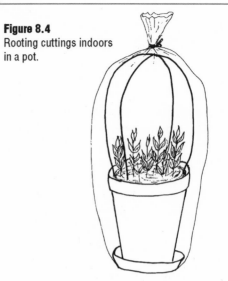

Figure 8.4
Rooting cuttings indoors in a pot.

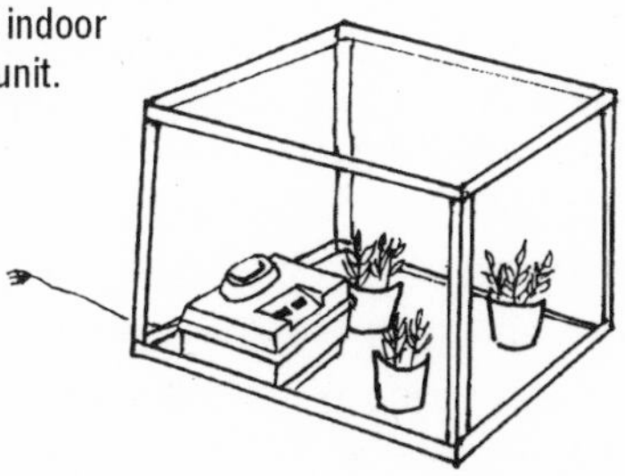

Figure 8.5
A cool vaporizer can make a good indoor propagating unit.

rangement will enable you to root many species that would not root easily in the open ground, such as magnolia.

To harden off the cuttings in the misting chamber, use a multi-cycle timer which shuts the mister off for progressively longer periods. Start with two hours mist and one hour off. After a few days, go to one on and one off, then to one on and two off. Before cold weather sets in, you should have the plants weaned to non-humid conditions so you can plant them out in the garden. In cold regions, don't separate the cuttings in the fall; just remove them from the pot and plant the entire clump, leaving division until spring.

Hardwood cuttings

Some plants can be propagated most easily from hardwood cuttings. This is particularly true in milder climates, but well worth trying even where winters are harsh. Make the cuttings after leaf-fall, choosing stems that have fully matured. Several cuttings can often be made from a single long shoot and they are generally made about 8 inches (20 cm) long. Dip the ends in a hardwood-strength rooting hormone. You can then either set them out in fall in a trench about 4 inches (10 cm) apart, leaving only two or three buds above soil level, or tie the cuttings in a bundle, bury them in the garden over winter and line them out in spring.

Many conifers can be propagated from winter cuttings, but they must be kept indoors in a cool location. If you are the adventurous sort and have a spare room where you can regulate the temperature to keep it just above freezing, it is worth a try.

Layering

One of the simplest and most foolproof methods of increasing plants is by layering, but it has limited uses. Trees are impossible to layer, upright shrubs are very hard, and some species will not make roots no matter how hard you try. But for suitable shrubs it is a successful, if slow, method of propagation.

A few nurseries use this method for plants that are almost impossible to root any other way, but the main drawback commercially is the limited number of plants that can be made from each parent plant, and the considerable space needed to bend down branches all around the stock plant. But for the home gardener who only wants to grow an extra plant or two, these are not important considerations.

Layering is best carried out in spring, and you should have a new plant ready to move by fall in most cases. Because the plant has been produced in your local climate, you don't have to worry about it not being hardened off enough for fall transplanting.

In early spring, as soon as the soil has dried out enough to be able to walk on it, decide which shrubs you want to propagate. Select outside branches that can be brought down to soil level a little way back from the tip. Mark the place where the branch meets the soil and also the point on the branch that will be in contact.

Lightly fork the soil, working in some coarse sand if it is not well drained. At the point where the branch will meet the soil, make a long slanting cut halfway through towards the tip. Dust the cut surface with a little rooting powder and slide in a piece of toothpick to hold the cut open (Figure 8.6). If you allow it to close, it may heal without making roots. Alternatively, you can take a sliver off the bark—enough to expose the wood beneath.

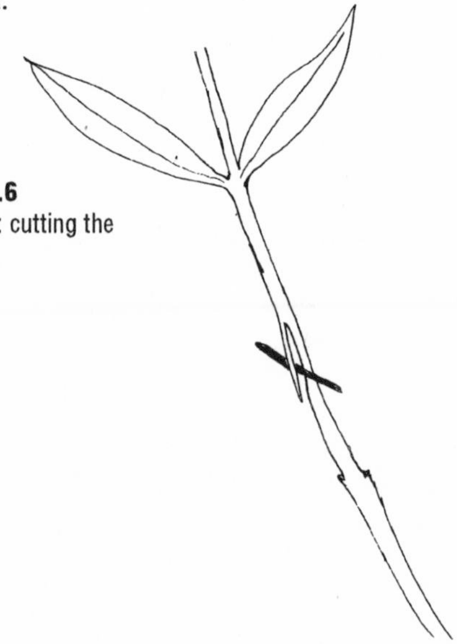

Figure 8.6
Layering: cutting the branch.

Bring the wounded part into contact with the soil and peg it down into position. You can use a piece of coathanger wire to make a small hook that will hold the branch in place. Very springy branches may have to be held down with a piece of string fastened further down the branch and tied to a tent peg. Mound soil over the wounded part. Depending on the shape of the shrub, it may be helpful to tie the end of the branch to a small cane to give an upright habit to your new plant (Figure 8.7).

Figure 8.7
Layering: burying the shoot.

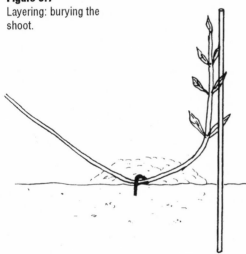

Water the entire area and make sure you keep it reasonably moist all summer. Rooting should take place during the summer. In early fall, remove the mound of soil carefully and pull out the peg used to hold the branch in place. A gentle tug on the shoot will soon tell you if it has rooted or if you will have to wait another year—a few species are very slow rooting. If rooting was successful, cut through the shoot, dig up the new plant and move it to its new home.

Air layering

While layering works well for shrubs with an arching habit, where it is possible to bend branches down to the ground, it is not easy to do on shrubs with an upright shape. Here you can try air layering. This is more usually done on indoor plants, but it can be used on many woody plants as well. It is too slow for commercial use, but for the home gardener this may not matter.

You will need a double handful of sphagnum moss (not peat moss—try your local florist), a sheet of plastic about 12 inches (30 cm) square and some plastic twist ties or waterproof tape.

Make the cut 12 to 15 inches (30 to 38 cm) from the tip of the shoot, dust with hormone powder and insert a piece of toothpick just as with regular layering. Then cover the wound with just-damp sphagnum moss. Holding it in place with both hands, wrap the whole thing with the plastic sheet and secure it top and bottom with twist ties or tape (Figure 8.8). It helps if you have an assistant for this job!

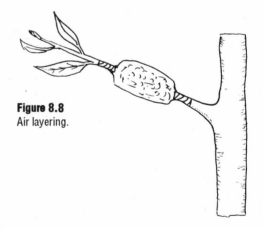

Figure 8.8
Air layering.

Check occasionally to make sure the moss hasn't dried out. Undo the top tie and push your finger into the moss. If it feels dry, add a little water and refasten the tie. The next day, loosen the bottom tie for a while to allow any excess water to drain out.

Roots will grow out from the wound into the moss, although it can take a couple of years in extreme cases. When you can see the roots inside the plastic, it is time to cut the branch off, remove the plastic carefully and plant the new plant. This should be done at normal planting time, spring or early fall.

Grafting

This is a rather complicated method of plant propagation that is used chiefly by commercial nurseries that need to produce large numbers of identical plants. Grafting, including budding, is mostly used for roses, fruit trees, named forms of many ornamental trees, and the special blue spruces. It is a highly skilled operation that can require very specific conditions in order to be successful.

I am not trying to put you off by saying that, and many amateur gardeners produce good plants by grafting. If you think you would like to try your hand at it, I suggest you join your local horticultural society or garden club. There may well be a member who is a tree enthusiast or amateur fruit grower, who can teach you the various grafting techniques. This is one case where hands-on experience is far better than book learning.

CHAPTER 9

Wallpapers and Carpets

While the primary use of woody plants in the garden is to provide major focal points, they also fill other roles.

Hedges can enclose a space, provide a windbreak, or screen a view; climbers can cover walls or fences; and ground covers can replace lawn in areas where grass will not survive or may be difficult to mow.

Hedges

Hedges have been used in the garden almost since there were gardens to put them in. Very early Greek and Islamic gardens built around a courtyard do not seem to have had hedges, but by the fifteenth century, low hedges were commonly used to delineate plots.

The popularity of hedges waxes and wanes with changing tastes in gardens. The great change in English gardens sparked by Capability Brown, where everything was open and naturalized, was probably the lowest point on the hedge popularity scale.

In today's North American gardens, hedges are used for a multitude of purposes. The most common use is to give privacy. A hedge is nicer to look at than a chain-link fence and less expensive than a wooden one. It doesn't do as good a job of sound-proofing your yard as a solid fence, but it helps. A bonus is that the wind turbulence associated with solid fences is absent with a hedge. You may find you can grow plants that would not previously survive in the microclimate it provides.

Hedges are often used to screen unsightly views, either in the garden or outside it. While it is true it would need a very tall hedge to hide a 20-story apartment building, a hedge draws the eye and provides a focus other than the building. In my garden a 10-foot (3-m) length of hedge does a great job of screening a utility area from the patio.

Remember, if you are planting a boundary hedge, do not plant it on the lot line. You must plant it on your own property with a reasonable clearance to allow room for growth. If you and your neighbor decide to plant a joint hedge, then it can be planted on the property line, but keep a written copy of the agreement in case of future disputes with a new owner.

What constitutes reasonable clearance depends on the plant chosen for the hedge, how tall you let it grow, and how often you trim. Hedges can last for many years (some in England are over 200 years old), and I would suggest a minimum of 2 feet (60 cm) clearance between the trunk and the lot line for a formal hedge.

Hedges that are allowed to grow almost unclipped are known as informal ones. As a rough guide, informal hedge plants often have an arching habit and an extended flowering period or attractive fruit that would be removed by trimming. There are only one or two species that can be used for both informal and the more common formal hedges.

Because of their habit of growth, informal hedges will be a lot wider and should be planted farther inside the boundary line. While they make a great show and can be very attractive, they are not really suited to small city lots because of space limitations. On a larger lot, especially where labour-saving gardening is the idea, they are a plus. Instead of regular clipping, they only need to have straggly branches removed at the end of the growing season.

Do deciduous or evergreen plants make the best hedges? Deciduous plants give you a greater range of leaf textures and colors, they may flower well and/or have showy fruit, and in winter they may have attractive colored bark. Evergreen hedges form a denser barrier, if you are looking for privacy, and they remain green all winter, forming a backdrop for other shrubs with attractive bark. Because they are denser, evergreens are a more effective wind barrier, but in winter the snow may build up against the hedge and spoil its shape.

A wide range of plants can be used for hedges.

If possible, visit the nearest botanical garden or arboretum, most of which have demonstration hedge collections. There is no need to grow exactly the same hedge as the rest of the neighborhood. Be different and help diversify the plantings so our plants are not so open to pests and diseases. The lists in chapter 11 give plants suitable for use as formal and informal hedges.

Planting. Your hedge will be in place for many years and it makes sense to prepare the site properly. Dig the area over thoroughly, removing rocks, rubble and perennial weeds. Unless the soil is poor and sandy, do not enrich it by the addition of manure; you want the plant roots to grow out into the surrounding soil in search of nutrients. Heavy clay soils will benefit from the addition of coarse sand at planting time.

Measure the length of the proposed hedge and work out the number of plants needed. For hedges that will be kept low (under 4 feet/1.2 m), use one plant for each third of the eventual height. For taller hedges, use one plant for every half of the final height. Thus a six-foot (1.8-m) hedge needs a plant every three feet (.9 m).

These distances are for formal hedges using expensive plants. If you are planting bare-root plants sold specifically for hedging in bulk, you can double the quantities. For instance, cedar hedging plants dug from the wild (the most commonly planted hedging in most of the east), could be planted much more thickly than nursery-grown plants of the cedar variety 'Nigra', although the latter makes a superior hedge.

With informal hedges, plant a little closer than the eventual spread of the plants. Thus if the plants will grow to four feet (1.2 m) across, plant them about three feet (.9 m) apart.

The easiest way to plant is to excavate a trench, piling all the soil on one side. Stretch a garden line down the center of the trench at soil level and pull it tight. When you plant, put the trunk of each shrub against the line and fill in round the roots. This will give you a straight row of plants. You either need three hands or an assistant to be able to plant a hedge efficiently.

As you fill in the trench, leave a slight depression along the line of plants as an aid to getting water down to their roots. After several waterings you can fill it in. Once the soil is leveled, it is helpful to lay a strip of landscape fabric down either side of the row and cover it with mulch, to stop weeds from competing with the newly planted hedge.

The next important step is one that is frequently overlooked: trimming the new plants to the same height. Find the shortest plant in the row and cut it back by about 10 percent (about one inch for each foot/2.5 cm per 30 cm). Then cut all the other plants to the same height. You may want to stretch a line along the hedge to be sure they are even.

Having paid good money to get a certain size of plant, you may not be happy to cut them back, but it quickly results in a better hedge. All the plants will grow at about the same rate, so if you don't even them up at the beginning, they will always be uneven. Removing the tops stimulates the side branches to put out new growth, so your hedge thickens up faster and soon looks established.

Trimming. A formal hedge should be trimmed on a regular basis. How often this is done depends on the plants used and how long they have been planted. New hedges should be trimmed frequently to encourage them to thicken up and form a dense screen. You can expect to clip a new hedge twice as often as a mature hedge for the first two or three years.

In my time, I have had a variety of hedges in various gardens. The worst by far was an established Chinese elm hedge which grew at a fantastic rate and needed clipping every two weeks throughout the summer. I dug it out after the first year.

I now have about 500 feet (150 m) of mature cedar hedge which, luckily, only needs cutting once a year. Depending on the species you use, the frequency of clipping will fall somewhere between these two extremes. Most deciduous hedges seem to need cutting two or three times a summer, and most evergreen ones only once.

When trimming any hedge, try to make the base slightly wider than the top. This allows light to reach the sides and there is less tendency for them to die off. The top should never be wider than the base, and in areas with heavy snowfalls, the tops of evergreen hedges should be pointed or rounded. A flat-topped hedge may allow the snow to build up and force the branches out, spoiling the shape. On deciduous hedges the snow can sift down through the bare branches and the shape of the top is not as critical.

Windbreaks/Shelterbelts

All hedges are windbreaks, but not all windbreaks are hedges. Windbreaks and shelterbelts can help considerably in reducing the cost of home heating. By siting them on the windward side of the house and planting them dense enough to slow the wind, you can cut a good slice off your fuel bill.

The height of the windbreak is important. Use plants that will grow about as high as the top of the ground-floor windows (or the eaves on a bungalow). Locate them twice this height away from the house; they will then lift the wind over the house. If planted farther away, there will be some turbulence between the hedge and the house but most of the wind will be lifted. The greater the distance, the less effective the windbreak will be.

If space allows, the planting should extend several feet (2 or 3 m) on either side of the house to allow for variations in the prevailing wind direction. Curve the ends of the hedge inwards slightly; there will be less swirl effect round the ends of the hedge, and less snow will collect there.

Climbers

Climbers play an important part in garden design and can often be, if not the leading lady, then certainly the chief supporting actress.

Climbers can be used to clothe a wall, cover a pergola or arbor, or hide a fence. Use them anywhere you want a vertical accent without devoting the space needed by a tree. Just remember that climbers climb in different ways and you need to provide the right type of support.

Many, like honeysuckles, climb by twining. The growing tip moves in a circle as it grows (either clockwise or counterclockwise) and wraps itself around any still object it encounters. These species need slightly rough supports; they will slide down smooth bamboo or plastic-covered metal canes. They do not grow well on the standard trellises sold in garden centers because the slats are often larger than the circles the plant tip makes.

Some climbers have special tendrils, which are often a modified leaf. They may be one side of a pair of leaves, or the end leaflet on a compound leaf (a leaf divided into smaller leaflets). In other plants, it is the leaf stalk itself that twines. If you have ever tried to untangle the new shoots on a clematis, you will know all about this method of climbing. This type of climber needs a mesh, but it should not be too fine or the tendrils may not get through the openings.

Some climbers do not actually climb, they sprawl. They push their way through another shrub and then lean on it for support. They also may have backward-pointing thorns to hook onto their unwilling host and stop them from sliding down. Climbing roses are a good example of this type. Strictly speaking, they are not really climbers, as you have to tie them to a trellis.

The climbers that grow well on brickwork have small rootlets that grow from the stems and push their way into the crevices between the bricks—for example English ivy. Some, like Virginia creeper, have special tendrils, called holdfasts, that, in addition to twining, have a sticky pad on the end that will attach itself to anything, including aluminum siding. Be careful where you plant this type: I grew it on a stucco-covered house and it pulled most of the stones off when I had to take it down.

Ground covers

Many people tell me they don't have a garden, they just have grass. To my mind, this is an unrewarding form of intensive gardening. What other area of the garden do you groom weekly, fertilize regularly, weed rigorously and rake every leaf almost as soon as it falls from the tree? If you would like to break this cycle of being a lawn slave, consider ground covers other than grass!

Ground covers do not have to be low, ground-hugging plants, although they often are. Any plant that will make a solid mat and keep out other, unwanted plants can be considered a ground cover. A good example of this is daylilies. They could never be considered low carpeting plants, but they make an ideal ground cover.

If you have a tiny garden with only a scrap of lawn, however, don't be tempted to replace it with a ground cover. You need somewhere to sit and enjoy life and nothing takes hard wear like grass. Few other plants, and certainly no woody ones, will stand up to constant foot traffic.

Woody ground covers will not provide an instant, low-maintenance garden. They are usually slow growing and will need hand-weeding several times each summer for the first year or two. Once they form a thick mat, however, they become virtually maintenance-free. Using landscape fabric and mulch between the plants can greatly reduce the work, but the mulch will be visible for a year or two.

Woody ground covers are best used in difficult situations, such as a steep bank, or a small area inside low retaining walls where mowing would be difficult. They can also be used under a canopy of tall trees. In a situation where grass will not thrive, shade-tolerant ground covers come into their own.

This is the ideal site to combine spring-flowering bulbs (which flower before the trees leaf out) and a low, shade-loving plant like dwarf periwinkle. If you intend planting bulbs between the shrubs, you cannot use landscape fabric to keep weeds down, but weeds are seldom a serious problem in woodland situations anyway.

If you are planting on a slope, make pockets to retain the water. Excavate the planting holes at the back, bringing the soil forward to make a lip that prevents the water from running down the slope (Figure 9.1). If you are using plants in large containers, or are planting on a steep slope, simply making a lip of soil may not be sufficient. You may need to make a small terrace with a piece of board to keep the soil in place and ensure correct watering (Figure 9.2).

With plants that have an arching habit or grow flat to the ground, layering the shoots each spring for the first couple of years will help create a thick stand. You don't need to sever the shoots once the tips have rooted, as the rooted layers will grow much quicker with the extra nutrition.

Figure 9.1
Planting on a shallow slope.

Figure 9.2
Water-retaining terraces on a steep slope.

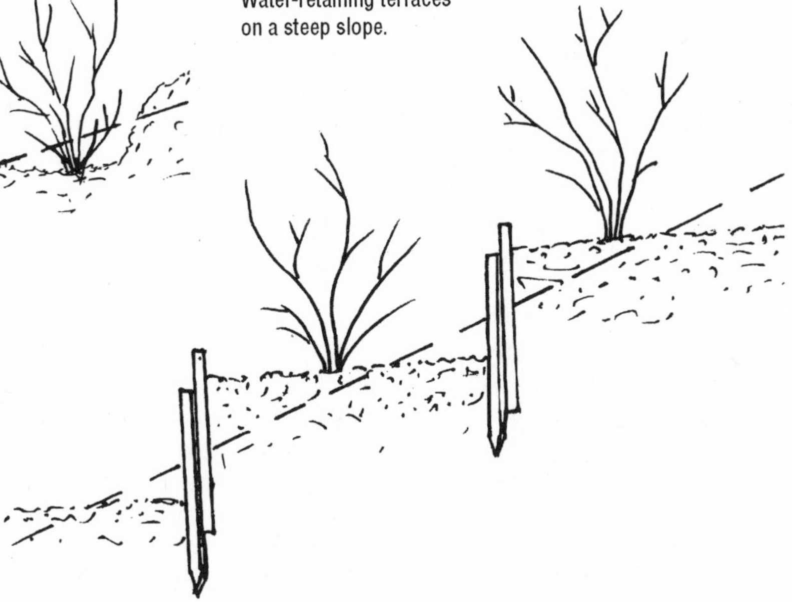

CHAPTER 10

Plant Listings

This chapter covers some of the many trees and shrubs that may be suitable for your garden, listing their size, hardiness, good points, bad points, growing information and the best of the named forms available. The plants are arranged alphabetically by botanical name and divided into five sections: deciduous trees, shrubs, conifers, ground covers and climbers.

The plants are listed by their botanical name because common names tend to be regional—one person's burning bush is another's fishwood and the same common name may apply to more than one plant. For instance, burning bush can refer to a shrub, a perennial or an annual, depending on the plant in question. To help you find your way around the listings, a cross-index of common and botanical names is given at the end of the book.

The hardiness zones are a guideline, rather than a carved-in-stone certainty, and there is some disagreement between the U.S. and Canadian zones in some cases. Even the best reference books give differing zone ratings for some trees. To add to the confusion, there are three different hardiness maps in use in the United States which, although they are similar, are not identical. In time, the latest (1990) U.S.D.A. map will prob-

ably become the standard, but at the moment confusion reigns.

Occasionally, particularly with the more unusual plants that haven't been widely grown, there is some doubt about the hardiness listing. Where I suspect that the plant is actually hardier than listed, there is a question mark after the zone number. If you live in a slightly colder zone, you may want to experiment.

Availability changes as plants become better known, but this is fairly gradual for woody plants. A general idea of the availability is indicated as follows:

M – Most nurseries carry it;

A – quite readily Available;

F – may take a bit of Finding;

S – Scarce;

H – you will probably really have to Hunt for it.

Nurseries in zone 3 will not carry zone 5 plants, even if availability is rated *most nurseries,* but most of the nurseries in zone 5 should have them. Conversely a plant may be common in your area but scarce in general, and thus rated "**S.**"

There are a couple of books that will help you find something you have really set your heart on but cannot find locally. In the U.S., the Andersen Horticultural Library has a *Source List of Plants and Seeds.* This is updated periodically and is available from the Andersen Horticultural Library, Minnesota Landscape Arboretum, 3675 Arboretum Drive, Box 39, Chanhassen, MN 55317-0039. Canadians can get information from *The Canadian Plant Sourcebook,* available from 93 Fentiman Ave., Ottawa, Ontario, K1S 0T7.

Sometimes the sources given are wholesale only, but your local nurseries might be willing to order for you. While they are unlikely to order a single plant, they will often add a plant to an existing order to please a customer. It is worth searching out nurseries that specialize in this type of customer service.

The height and spread given are for the mature species; with trees this could take 50 or 60 years. If the size of the cultivar is widely different (as with many evergreens) this is noted in the cultivar description. Flowering period and size of bloom are also similar to the species if not stated otherwise. The majority of woody plants are deciduous, so only those that keep their leaves all winter are specifically noted as being evergreen.

Just a reminder: the word cultivar stands for CULTIvated VARiety, generally a form that originated in a garden or nursery, not in the wild. It is abbreviated to cv. and cultivar names are shown in single quotes, while botanical varieties (var.) are in italics. A multiplication sign in front of a species name indicates a hybrid. See "Plant names" in chapter 1 for a fuller explanation of these terms.

DECIDUOUS TREES

Acer spp.   Maple

The symbol of Canada—although no one seems sure just which maple—this genus has many large trees suitable only for country properties, but also some good small trees for city use. Most maples have excellent fall color. A few are quite weedy, seeding readily. Prune in late fall to early winter—many species will bleed badly if pruned later than this.

Acer griseum   Paperbark maple

Comments: A small tree with bark that is more attractive than that of white birch, it transplants best in spring as a container-grown tree.

Hardiness: Canadian zone 6; U.S. zone 5.

Availability: **A.**

Height: 25' (7.5 m). *Spread:* 20' (6 m).

Propagation: Seed, but this is difficult and slow.

Soil preferences: Most.

Location: Sun.

Good points: The bark starts to lift on two-year-old wood to show a cinnamon to reddish inner bark. It has good fall color most years, but the bark is the main attraction.

Bad points: Not hardy for many of us.

Uses: Specimen tree.

Acer negundo   Manitoba maple, box elder

Comments: This rather weedy tree has leaves that look like those of the elder, rather than being maple-like. It is a very tough, pollution-resistant tree that will survive even in the harsh environment of a city core.

Hardiness: Canadian zone 1b; U.S. zone 2.

Availability: **M.**

Height: 40' (12 m). *Spread:* 50' (15 m).

Propagation: Seed.

Soil preferences: Any.

Location: Sun.

Good points: It gives a good dappled shade and the seeds attract birds in winter.

Bad points: It is brittle and sheds branches in ice storms. Each seed the birds miss germinates three times I'm sure. Manitoba maples resist air pollution but not salt and get badly infested with aphids some years, so honeydew drips on pavement, sidewalks and cars.

Uses: Shade tree.

Acer pensylvanicum   Striped maple

Comments: An understory tree in eastern woods, its green bark is marked with long, vertical, whitish stripes.

Hardiness: Canadian zone 2b; U.S. zone 3.

Availability: **F**.

Height: 20' (6 m). *Spread:* 15' (4.5 m).

Propagation: Stratified seed.

Soil preferences: Moist, slightly acidic.

Location: Shade.

Good points: This makes a useful small tree for shady locations and has bark that is attractive year-round.

Bad points: It dies in 3 to 4 years if the location is too sunny.

Uses: Shady border; naturalizing.

Acer platanoides   Norway maple

Comments: This maple is much used as a street tree because it tolerates pollution. There are a great many forms with a wide range of sizes but only the most readily available are listed below.

Hardiness: Canadian zone 5; U.S. zone 4.

Availability: **M**.

Height: 50' (15 m). *Spread:* 40' (12 m).

Propagation: Seed and grafting.

Soil preferences: Most.

Location: Sun.

Good points: The many cultivars give a wide range of shapes, sizes and colors. Pollution- and salt-tolerance make this a good choice for city homes—but be sure to pick one whose final size is right for your property.

Bad points: It is susceptible to 2,4-D so don't use lawn weedkiller over the root spread. Most cultivars cast a dense shade so growing grass is difficult; trunk splitting is common in winter; tar-spot disease causes black blotches on the leaves (unsightly but not serious) and wilt can be a problem if the trees are under stress. Fall color is not consistent and often poor.

Uses: Specimen; shade tree.

Cultivars: See table opposite.

Acer rubrum   Red maple

Comments: Red maples are one of the fall glories of northern hardwood forests. Plant in spring, and, for more reliable fall color, plant the named forms, rather than the species. Look for the very early flowers, which are small but attractive.

Hardiness: Canadian zone 3; U.S. zone 3.

Availability: **M**.

Height: 60' (18 m). *Spread:* 50' (15 m).

Propagation: Seed for the species; grafting for the cultivars.

Soil preferences: Slightly acidic, but adaptable.

Location: Sun.

Good points: Smooth gray bark and red leaf stalks make this tree easy to identify. It has excellent red fall color.

Bad points: It gives dense shade so growing grass beneath it is difficult. Frost cracks can cause problems if the trunks are not shaded when young, and leaves may be disfigured by tar-spot disease.

Uses: Specimen; shade tree.

Cultivars: 'Armstrong' is a cross between red and silver maples *(Acer x freemanii)* with a narrow upright form growing to 50 feet (15 m)

Norway maple variety	Height	Spread	Comments
'Cleveland'	40 ft (12 m)	30 ft (9 m)	Somewhat upright, dark green.
'Columnare'	50 ft (15 m)	15 ft (4.5 m)	Very upright; use on small lots.
'Crimson King'	45 ft (13.5 m)	45 ft (13.5 m)	Dark purple foliage all summer.
'Crimson Sentry'	25 ft (7.5 m)	15 ft (4.5 m)	A columnar form of 'Crimson King'.
'Deborah'	45 ft (13.5 m)	40 ft (12 m)	Red new foliage turns green.
'Drummondii' (harlequin maple)	25 ft (7.5 m)	20 ft (6 m)	Green and white foliage. Remove branches reverting to green quickly.
'Emerald Queen'	50 ft (15 m)	40 ft (12 m)	Dark green, oval-shaped.
'Globosum'	25 ft (7.5 m)	20 ft (6 m)	A garden lollipop.
'Royal Red'	45 ft (13.5 m)	40 ft (12 m)	Very similar to 'Crimson King'.
'Schwedleri'	40 ft (12 m)	45 ft (13.5 m)	Dark red foliage turns green.
'Summershade'	45 ft (13.5 m)	35 ft (10.5 m)	Dark green, leathery leaves.
'Superform'	50 ft (15 m)	45 ft (13.5 m)	Fast-growing and fairly upright.

by 15 feet (4.5 m); it has poor fall color some years. 'Autumn Flame' has reliable early color on a rounded tree growing to about 60 feet (18 m). 'Morgan' is a fast-growing selection reaching 65 feet (19.5 m) with good fall color, one of the brightest. 'Northwood' has good orange-red fall color, grows 60 feet (18 m) high, and was chosen for its oval shape and hardiness. 'October Glory' is late to color and may be caught by early frosts in the north; it grows to about 40 feet (12 m) with an oval outline. 'Red Sunset' is more pyramidal in shape, growing 45 feet (13.5 m) tall by 35 feet (10.5 m) wide with reliable, brilliant red fall color.

Acer saccharinum — Silver maple, soft maple

Comments: A large tree, this was once extensively used as a street tree, but has now been replaced with more pollution-tolerant species. The common name comes from the silvery undersides of the leaves.

Hardiness: Canadian zone 2b; U.S. zone 3.
Availability: **M**.
Height: 70' (21 m). *Spread:* 60' (18 m).
Propagation: Seed sown as soon as it ripens.
Soil preferences: Most.
Location: Sun.
Good points: It is fast growing, so it quickly gives shade in new gardens.
Bad points: Fast growth (hence soft maple) means the wood is brittle and branches are shed in storms. It seeds freely and germinates readily, too much so at times. The heavy canopy and surface roots make it hard to grow anything under this tree. Wilt causes dieback under stress; tar-spot disease causes black spots on leaves; leaf-gall mites cause unsightly blotches or pimples on leaves; and there are several other minor problems.
Uses: Shade tree.
Cultivars: 'Silver Queen' is an almost fruitless form; maybe it should have been called Silver King. 'Weiri' has finely cut leaves and drooping branches.

Acer saccharum Sugar maple, hard maple

Comments: Extensively planted in cities in the past, these trees are now suffering from people pressure disease. It is still a magnificent tree for larger country lots, if you are young. Plant B & B trees in spring and prune in late fall/early winter to avoid excessive bleeding.

Hardiness: Canadian zone 4; U.S. zone 4.

Availability: **M**.

Height: 60' (18 m). *Spread:* 45' (13.5 m).

Propagation: Stratified seed.

Soil preferences: Moist and slightly acidic.

Location: Sun to light shade.

Good points: Slow growth produces a hard wood. Good yellow to gold fall color makes this a beautiful specimen tree where space permits.

Bad points: The dense canopy and surface roots make it almost impossible to grow other plants under a mature sugar maple. It is not a good city tree: it is intolerant of pollution and salt and suffers from crown dieback (maple decline) when under stress. Leaves may be attacked by tar-spot and by leaf-gall mites which cause raised red pimples or red blotches, but neither of these are serious problems.

Uses: Specimen; shade tree.

Cultivars: 'Green Mountain' has an upright, oval shape with dark green leaves that turn yellow. 'Legacy' has thicker leaves that don't tear in summer storms and a good orange-yellow fall color. 'Newton Sentry' and 'Temple's Upright' are more columnar forms that are good for smaller gardens, but they are hard to find.

Aesculus spp. Buckeye and chestnut

These trees and large shrubs have attractive flowers and large fruit. Many are native to North America; Ohio calls itself the buckeye state.

Aesculus × *carnea* Red horse chestnut

Comments: A hybrid with the common horse chestnut as one parent; unlike most hybrids, this comes true from seed. The cultivar is the most commonly grown form.

Hardiness: Canadian zone 6; U.S. zone 5.

Availability: **M**.

Height: 50' (15 m). *Spread:* 50' (15 m).

Propagation: Seed for the hybrid, grafting for the cultivar.

Soil preferences: Deep and well drained.

Location: Sun.

Good points: Red flowers are carried in spikes up to 8" (20 cm) tall in spring. This species has some resistance to the leaf blotch.

Bad points: Few.

Uses: A specimen tree for large properties, parks, etc.

Cultivars: 'Briottii' has brighter, larger flowers.

Aesculus *glabra* Ohio buckeye

Comments: This is a good smaller tree that grows reasonably fast. Transplant container-grown or B & B plants only.

Hardiness: Canadian zone 3a; U.S. zone 3.

Availability: **M**.

Height: 35' (10.5 m). *Spread:* 25' (7.5 m).

Propagation: Stratified seed.

Soil preferences: Deep, well drained and slightly acidic.

Location: Sun.

Good points: Creamy yellow flowers grow in upright candles, not as dense as on the horse chestnut; fruit is not as large or as messy.

Bad points: This species is subject to the same problems as the horse chestnut; it also suffers damage from pollution in city locations and from people pressure disease.

Uses: A specimen tree for medium-sized gardens on city outskirts and larger properties.

Aesculus hippocastanum **Horse chestnut**

Comments: This is the spreading chestnut beneath which the village blacksmith stood. It makes a large tree and lives for a considerable time. The spiny fruit contains the conkers used in the traditional British schoolboys' game.

Hardiness: Canadian zone 5; U.S. zone 4a.

Availability: **M**.

Height: 50' (15 m). *Spread:* 40' (12 m).

Propagation: Scarified seed.

Soil preferences: Moist, but well drained.

Location: Sun.

Good points: Very showy spikes of white flowers appear in spring, and it has attractive finger-like leaves, especially when young.

Bad points: It is very susceptible to a leaf blotch, which can defoliate trees by mid-August. Japanese beetles can quickly eat large areas of the canopy in late summer. The fruit is messy and needs frequent raking as it is too large to go through the mower.

Uses: Specimen tree for estates, parks and country lots.

Cultivars: 'Baumannii' (Baumann's horse chestnut) has double flowers like small powder-puffs. They are sterile so there is no fruit to clean up (but no conkers either).

Ailanthus altissima **Tree of heaven**

Comments: This is a very weedy tree, seeding freely when growing well, but also very pollution-tolerant and able to survive in inhospitable city conditions. This was the tree in *A Tree Grows in Brooklyn*. Male and female flowers are on separate trees; the male flowers have a bad odor, while the female trees shed copious seed.

Hardiness: Canadian zone 6; U.S. zone 5.

Availability: **F**.

Height: 60' (18 m). *Spread:* 60' (18 m).

Propagation: Seed.

Soil preferences: Any, including seashore.

Location: Sun.

Good points: The compound leaves are almost palm-like; growth is fast, up to 5 feet (1.5 m) per year, and the bright red fruits on female trees can be attractive.

Bad points: There are bad litter problems after a high wind, as the wood is very soft and brittle. This is often advertised as "The perfect tree for new gardens—grows 5 feet (1.5 m) a year giving almost instant shade." Don't believe it. There is no perfect tree, and this is a long way from it; remember all those seedlings.

Uses: Shade tree in difficult conditions.

Alnus glutinosa **Common or black alder**

Comments: This is the most common of this group of shrubs and trees. They are useful for waterside planting and grow well in wet soils, but they're not as widely used as they might be.

Hardiness: Canadian zone 4; U.S. zone 3.

Availability: **S**.

Height: 40' (12 m). *Spread:* 30' (9 m), but may be much smaller in poor soils.

Propagation: Seed sown as soon as it is ripe. Old seed needs cold treatment.

Soil preferences: Most soil types except for very sandy.

Location: Sun to light shade.

Good points: The early spring catkins are attractive, as is the shiny dark green foliage. It grows well in difficult, wet locations where few other trees survive.

Bad points: Alders are subject to woolly aphid attack, but this seldom seems to harm the trees.

Uses: Specimen tree; shelterbelt on wet sites.

Amelanchier spp.   **Serviceberry**

This native North American species has a multitude of common names, including serviceberry, shadblow and shadbush (because it blooms when the shad are spawning), Juneberry, saskatoon and snowy mespilus.

These are excellent small trees or shrubs (see "Shrubs" in this chapter) and are becoming increasingly popular. The botanical names are undergoing revision so the species names for all the new cultivars that have recently appeared may vary from source to source. They are often wrongly named in nurseries but they are all equally nice, so the names may not be that important.

Serviceberries are pollution-tolerant and rarely need pruning, except for shape.

Amelanchier x   **Apple**
grandiflora   **serviceberry**

Comments: A cross between the Allegheny and downy serviceberries, this is the parent of many named forms. The young foliage is pinkish and but is covered in fine hairs. You need a hand lens to tell the serviceberries apart.

Hardiness: Canadian zone 4; U.S. zone 4.

Availability: **M.**

Height: 30' (9 m). *Spread:* 25' (7.5 m).

Propagation: Cuttings.

Soil preferences: Well drained.

Location: Sun.

Good points: It has larger flowers than other serviceberries and good red fall color most years.

Bad points: Fire blight and cedar-apple rust may attack this plant.

Uses: Specimen tree; shrub.

Cultivars: 'Autumn Brilliance' was selected for the fall color. 'Ballerina' is a more upright form.

'Cole' was also selected for its fall color. 'Princess Diana', generally grown as a shrub, is chosen for its fruit and fall color. (Yes, there is a Prince Charles as well.) 'Robin Hill' has flower buds that are pink and open to white. 'Strata' has horizontal branches; in flower they look like layers of cloud. 'Ballerina' and 'Princess Diana' grow about 20 feet (6 m) tall; the rest are the same size as the species.

Amelanchier laevis   **Allegheny serviceberry**

Comments: Generally grown as a small tree, the new foliage is bronzy and hairless.

Hardiness: Canadian zone 3b; U.S. zone 3.

Availability: **A.**

Height: 30' (9 m). *Spread:* 20' (6 m).

Propagation: Stratified seed.

Soil preferences: Well drained.

Location: Sun.

Good points: Frothy white flowers cover the branches in spring, while the very edible black fruit and good orange to red fall color make this well worth growing.

Bad points: There is a slight chance of fireblight, but this is not a high-risk plant most years. Cedar-apple rust can also attack it, especially the fruit, which is then inedible.

Uses: Specimen tree.

Cultivars: 'Cumulus', a form with a more oval shape, grows about 25 feet (7.5 m) tall and is better for small gardens.

Betula spp.   **Birch**

These stately trees, much used in the past for home gardens, are now going slightly out of favor since they do not take kindly to modern city conditions. They are not too bad in the suburbs, but are liable to dieback downtown. Prune all birches in late fall to early winter.

Betula alleghaniensis — Yellow birch
Betula lenta — Sweet birch

Comments: These two similar native birches have interesting yellow-brown to brown peeling bark.

Hardiness: Canadian zone 3b; U.S. zone 3.

Availability: **S**.

Height: 40' (12 m). *Spread:* 40' (12 m).

Propagation: Seed.

Soil preferences: Moist.

Location: Sun.

Good points: They have a better shape than the more commonly grown paper birch, and are not as prone to pest problems.

Bad points: Both are large for city homes and need spring moisture to grow well.

Uses: Shade tree, especially for parks and golf courses.

Betula nigra — River birch

Comments: This species needs a soil that is wet in spring, but it will tolerate dryness later in summer.

Hardiness: Canadian zone 3; U.S. zone 4?

Availability: **A**.

Height: 50' (15 m). *Spread:* 40' (12 m).

Propagation: Seed.

Soil preferences: Wet.

Location: Sun.

Good points: The very attractive brown bark flakes off to reveal a pale inner bark. It is quite pest- and disease-resistant and is fast growing.

Bad points: The need for wet spring soil limits where it can be grown.

Uses: Shade tree; accent tree for winter interest.

Cultivars: 'Heritage' is a fairly recent introduction; it is now becoming available but is still hard to find in Canada. It is less demanding of wet spring conditions, faster growing and slightly hardier than the species.

Betula papyrifera — Paper, canoe or white birch

Comments: This native tree is the most commonly grown of all birches. It is sold with a single trunk or with multiple stems, which form a wider plant at maturity. The peeling bark is the main attraction, but resist the temptation to pull off large strips—it detracts from the appearance.

Hardiness: Canadian and U.S. zone 2.

Availability: **M**.

Height: 60' (18 m). *Spread:* 40' (12 m).

Propagation: Seed.

Soil preferences: Slightly acidic and well drained.

Location: Sun.

Good points: The attractive bark adds winter interest to the garden. It is reasonably fast growing and grass grows well in light shade under the canopy.

Bad points: It is susceptible to leaf miners and birch borer. Miners can be controlled with dimethoate (Cygon) applied as a soil drench or as a band painted on the bark in spring. This must be applied at a different height each year or it causes the bark to peel. Borers are more difficult to control and trees under stress are often attacked. Cygon helps control them but is more effective with leaf miner.

Uses: Shade tree; accent tree in large properties.

Betula pendula — European white birch, weeping birch

Comments: The species itself is not widely planted but several of the named forms are.

Hardiness: Canadian zone 2; U.S. zone 2.

Availability: **M**.

Height: 50' (15 m). *Spread:* 40' (12 m).

Propagation: Seed.

Soil preferences: Well drained to moist.

Location: Sun.

Good points: The named forms are very striking in the right setting.

Bad points: They are too large for most city gardens and are susceptible to several pests (see *B. papyrifera*).

Uses: Specimen tree.

Cultivars: 'Laciniata', the most commonly planted form, has much-divided leaves and branches that weep down to the ground. 'Youngii' is a very weeping form that makes a smaller tree. In nature it would creep along the ground, so it is trained upright or grafted on the top of an upright seedling. The eventual height of the tree depends to a large extent on the height of the graft. In time, it forms a dome shape with the branches reaching the ground. 'Fastigiata' is an upright form that is not as readily available.

Betula utilis var. jacquemontii — Whitebark Himalayan birch

Comments: This introduction has recently become popular. It may be listed as Jacquemont's birch or *B. jacquemontii*.

Hardiness: Canadian zone 4; U.S. zone 5?

Availability: **M**.

Height: 30' (9 m)? *Spread:* 20' (6 m)? The height and spread are tentative as there are no mature specimens here yet.

Propagation: Grafting (seed gives variable bark colors).

Soil preferences: Well drained.

Location: Sun.

Good points: Has the whitest bark of all birches if propagated by grafting. From seed the bark may be creamy. Look these over in a nursery and select a good bark color, rather than buying by mail and taking a chance. They are not as prone to problems as some birches.

Bad points: None so far.

Uses: Shade tree; winter accent.

Carpinus spp. — Hornbeam

These medium-sized trees should do well in city locations, but they are not well known. The few I have seen planted have had no problems, even close to well-used roads. Prune (if needed) in early winter to avoid the sap bleeding.

Carpinus betulus — European hornbeam

Comments: This tree adapts well to varying soil types and moisture content. It is best planted in spring using smaller container-grown or B & B plants. Large plants dug with a tree spade do not transplant well.

Hardiness: Canadian zone 4; U.S. zone 4.

Availability: **A**.

Height: 35' (10.5 m). *Spread:* 35' (10.5 m).

Propagation: Seed or cuttings.

Soil preferences: Most.

Location: Sun.

Good points: In shade tree trials this tree rates highly; it will even survive in parking lots. It has a good pyramidal shape, and dark green foliage that turns a bronzy-red in fall.

Bad points: None.

Uses: Specimen; shade tree; screen; tall hedge.

Cultivars: 'Fastigiata' is a more upright selection, making a pear-shaped tree with age. It grows only half as wide as the species.

Carpinus carolinianus — American hornbeam, ironwood, musclewood, blue beech

Comments: The wood is very hard (hence ironwood), the trunk has curious swellings (musclewood), and the bark is smooth (blue beech). Plant B & B or container-grown trees in spring. It often grows in woods with hophornbeam *(Ostrya)*, also known as ironwood.

Hardiness: Canadian zone 3b; U.S. zone 3.

Availability: **F**.

Height: 30' (9 m). *Spread:* 30' (9 m).
Propagation: Stratified seed.
Soil preferences: Deep and moist.
Location: Sun to medium shade.
Good points: This is another understory tree that grows equally well in sun or shade. The light green foliage turns orange in fall and colors better in sun. The smooth bark is interesting in winter.
Bad points: None.
Uses: Specimen; shade tree; naturalizing; hedge.

Carya ovata   **Shagbark hickory**

Comments: This is a large tree with interesting bark that lifts in long strips. The edible fruit is the easiest of all the hickories to crack—comparatively.
Hardiness: Canadian zone 5; U.S. zone 4b.
Availability: **A**.
Height: 60' (18 m). *Spread:* 30' (9 m).
Propagation: Seed.
Soil preferences: Deep and well drained.
Location: Sun.
Good points: The bark is most distinctive and the dark green leaves turn gold in the fall. There are selections for superior fruit production, but these are harder to find.
Bad points: It is difficult to transplant due to the long tap root.
Uses: Specimen tree; shade tree.

Catalpa spp.   **Catalpa**

Catalpas are ornamental trees grown mainly for their flowers or shape. Their large leaves can smother grass and are difficult to rake.

Catalpa bignonioides   **Globe**
'Nana'   **catalpa**

Comments: This mop-headed tree makes an accent in the garden, but rarely flowers. It is a good choice if you like this shape of tree.

Hardiness: Canadian zone 5b; U.S. zone 5.
Availability: **M**.
Height: 12' (3.5 m). *Spread:* 10' (3 m).
Propagation: Grafting.
Soil preferences: Most.
Location: Sun.
Good points: It is useful in restricted sites, such as under utility wires, gives good shade, and is fairly pollution-tolerant.
Bad points: The large leaves of this cultivar smother grass as they fall and must be raked up frequently.
Uses: City gardens.

Catalpa speciosa   **Northern catalpa**

Comments: I am of two minds about this tree. It is late to leaf out and one of the first to shed its leaves. The fruit persists over winter and cleaning it up is an added chore in spring. The blooming time always seems to coincide with a summer storm, which beats the flowers to shreds. But in flower it is one of the showiest trees going. Transplant B & B only or container grown, never bare-root.
Hardiness: Canadian zone 5; U.S. zone 4.
Availability: **M**.
Height: 50' (15 m). *Spread:* 30' (9 m).
Propagation: Seed.
Soil preferences: Most.
Location: Sun to shade.
Good points: Flowers are creamy white with a yellow throat and up to 2 inches (5 cm) long. They are carried in 8-inch (20-cm) spikes and are most attractive. Long seed pods persist over winter and give added interest.
Bad points: The large leaves cast a dense shade, making it difficult to grow grass. The tree is rather coarse.
Uses: Specimen tree.

Celtis occidentalis   **Hackberry**

Comments: This large tree, native over much of eastern and central North America, has been recommended as a replacement for elms, although it doesn't have quite as good a vase shape. The fruit, small and cherry-like, is edible and quite tasty, but there is not much flesh surrounding the very hard stone.

Hardiness: Canadian zone 2b; U.S. zone 2.

Availability: **M**.

Height: 60' (18 m). *Spread:* 40' (12 m).

Propagation: Stratified seed.

Soil preferences: Any.

Location: Sun.

Good points: A versatile tree, it grows well in both wet and dry soils and in windy locations. It makes a good shade tree for large properties.

Bad points: Diseases such as leaf spot and powdery mildew are disfiguring, but rarely fatal.

Uses: Specimen; shade tree.

Cercidiphyllum japonicum   **Katsura tree**

Comments: Here is an excellent tree that is becoming increasingly popular. I hope it does not become overplanted so that problems develop, as happened with the little-leaf linden.

Hardiness: Canadian zone 4; U.S. zone 4.

Availability: **M**.

Height: 60' (18 m). *Spread:* 30' (9 m).

Propagation: Seed.

Soil preferences: Well drained but moist.

Location: Sun.

Good points: The pink to purple new foliage turns a blue-green, then colors well in the fall, becoming orange, dull red, or even pink depending on soil type and acidity; it also has a caramel scent as it changes color. Flowers are in small catkins and although they don't make a big show, they are nice when seen close up.

Bad points: The spread is quite variable and some plants may grow as wide as they are tall, a nuisance in a small garden.

Uses: Specimen; shade tree.

Cultivars: 'Pendula' is a weeping form that is much shorter, maybe 20' (6 m) maximum, but as much or more across.

Cercis canadensis   **Redbud**

Comments: An interesting native tree, if only because the flowers are often borne directly on the trunk and main branches, as well as on the twigs.

Hardiness: Canadian zone 5b; U.S. zone 4.

Availability: **M**.

Height: 25' (7.5 m). *Spread:* 20-30' (6-9 m).

Propagation: Stratified seed.

Soil preferences: Moist, but not wet.

Location: Sun.

Good points: Bright pink flowers bloom in early spring before the leaves, which open pale green, darken through the summer and turn yellow in fall. It's very showy when in flower, nice when not, and also has a good winter silhouette.

Bad points: It may get canker, but it's not a serious problem. Low branching makes mowing a little difficult, but the flowers are worth it.

Uses: Specimen; shade tree.

Cultivars: 'Alba' is the white-flowered version. 'Forest Pansy' has leaves that open a bright red, then fade to a red-purple. It is not as hardy as the species but is very striking.

Chionanthus virginicus   **Fringetree**

Comments: Here is another of the small trees or large shrubs that should be better known. Plants have survived -39° with only a little dieback; it may be hardier than thought.

Hardiness: Canadian zone 5 (4?); U.S. zone 3.

Availability: **S** in Canada; **A** in U.S.
Height: 15' (4.5 m). *Spread:* 15' (4.5 m).
Propagation: Seed (difficult).
Soil preferences: Deep and moist.
Location: Sun.
Good points: A multitude of white flowers with narrow, strap-like petals are borne in late spring and give a misty appearance, while the good golden-yellow fall color starts early and lasts quite a long time.
Bad points: None.
Uses: Specimen; border; screen.

Cladrastis lutea   Yellowwood

Comments: This good, medium-sized tree is quite slow growing and seems to be pollution- and salt-tolerant. The wood is a bright yellow. Plant B & B specimens in spring. It is surprisingly hardy for a Texas native.
Hardiness: Canadian zone 4b; U.S. zone 4.
Availability: **F**.
Height: 40' (12 m). *Spread:* 40' (12 m).
Propagation: Stratified seed.
Soil preferences: Well drained, acid or alkaline.
Location: Sun.
Good points: Think of this as a white-flowered goldenchain tree. The hanging trusses of fragrant flowers appear in early summer.
Bad points: Prune, if needed, in late summer. Excessive bleeding follows winter or spring pruning.
Uses: Specimen tree.

Cornus spp.   Dogwood

Ranging from low ground covers to medium-sized trees, the dogwoods are a very versatile group of plants. Mostly spring-flowering, they also have attractive fruits which are edible in some species. See also "Shrubs" and "Ground Covers" later in this chapter.

Cornus alternifolia   Pagoda dogwood

Comments: Horizontal branches turn up at the ends—like a pagoda. The leaves are also horizontal so the plant has a layered look. It grows wild on the edge of woods and does well in light shade, requiring it in southern regions.
Hardiness: Canadian zone 3b; U.S. zone 3.
Availability: **M**.
Height: 20' (6 m). *Spread:* 25' (7.5 m).
Propagation: Stratified seed.
Soil preferences: Acid and well drained.
Location: Light shade.
Good points: In late spring this is a most attractive tree with clusters of white flowers on the tops of the branches. Clusters of berries on red stalks are green, then red and finally blue-black when ripe. These trees seem quite adaptable; mine grows happily in an alkaline soil and full sun.
Bad points: A twig blight can cause dieback, especially if the plant is stressed.
Uses: Specimen; mixed border.

Cornus kousa   Kousa dogwood

Comments: The flowering and Pacific dogwoods are among the showiest of flowering trees but they are quite tender and are outside the scope of this book. The Japanese kousa dogwood is almost as showy, hardier, and drought-tolerant.
Hardiness: Canadian zone 6; U.S. zone 5.
Availability: **A**.
Height: 20' (6 m). *Spread:* 20' (6 m).
Propagation: Cuttings.
Soil preferences: Well drained.
Location: Sun.
Good points: Pointed white flowers on short stems above the leaves give this small tree a distinct appearance. It has good fall color most years and the globe-shaped showy fruit is red, raspberry-like and edible.

Bad points: Leaf spot diseases can cause early defoliation.

Uses: Specimen; border.

Cultivars: C. kousa var. *chinensis*, the Chinese form, has larger flowers and is slightly hardier than the species. 'Milky Way' is a free-flowering selection of *C. k. chinensis*. 'Summer Stars' has bracts that remain good for several weeks, giving a longer flowering period.

Corylus colurna   **Turkish hazel**

Comments: This forms a smallish tree that seems to stand up to city conditions and drought. It should be used more on medium-sized lots.

Hardiness: Canadian zone 5; U.S. zone 4.

Availability: **A.**

Height: 40' (12 m). *Spread:* 25' (7.5 m).

Propagation: Seed.

Soil preferences: Well drained.

Location: Sun.

Good points: Its pyramidal outline, dark green leaves, and few problems make this a good choice for city planting.

Bad points: None.

Uses: Specimen; shade tree.

Crataegus spp.   **Hawthorn**

This group of smaller trees, many of which are native to North America, includes some with edible (although not very palatable) fruit and others with vicious thorns. The thorniness limits their use in public places and many species that are otherwise excellent are not grown for this reason.

Crataegus crus-galli   **Cockspur hawthorn**

Comments: A wide-spreading tree, it has almost horizontal branches and conspicuous thorns.

Hardiness: Canadian zone 2b; U.S. zone 3.

Availability: **A.**

Height: 20' (6 m). *Spread:* 25' (7.5 m).

Propagation: Stratified seed.

Soil preferences: Well drained.

Location: Sun.

Good points: White flowers in clusters produce bright red fruit that persists well into winter. Dark green leaves turn dull red in the fall, and the branch structure provides winter interest.

Bad points: All hawthorns are subject to many of the same diseases that attack crab apples. Rusts can be a particular problem, attacking the fruit and causing it to drop prematurely.

Uses: Specimen; screen; crashproof hedge.

Cultivars: C. crus-galli var. *inermis* is similar to the species, but without the thorns.

Crataegus laevigata   **English hawthorn**

Comments: This is the most commonly grown haw in Europe, but it is very susceptible to diseases. It makes a round-topped tree. Usually only the cultivars are available.

Hardiness: Canadian zone 6; U.S. zone 5.

Availability: **M** to **A.**

Height: 20' (6 m). *Spread:* 15' (4.5 m).

Propagation: Grafting.

Soil preferences: Well drained.

Location: Sun.

Good points: Very showy flowers and fruit (except on the double form) make this spectacular when in bloom.

Bad points: 'Paul's Scarlet' is highly prone to leaf blight.

Uses: Specimen; screen.

Cultivars: 'Crimson Cloud' has bright red flowers and fruit and is resistant to blight. 'Paul's Scarlet', the most popular form, has double flowers.

**Crataegus x   Morden
mordenensis   hawthorn**

Comments: The English hawthorn 'Paul's Scar-
  let' is one parent of this hybrid, developed at
  Morden, Manitoba, so it is much hardier.
Hardiness: Canadian zone 3; U.S. zone 3b.
Availability: **M** in Canada; **A** in U.S.
Height: 20' (6 m). *Spread:* 20' (6 m).
Propagation: Grafting.
Soil preferences: Well drained.
Location: Sun.
Good points: The double flowers are like little
  powder-puffs in spring and are followed by
  red fruit and bronzy foliage in fall. The thorns
  are not as numerous as on many hawthorns.
Bad points: Disease problems. (See *C. crus-galli*.)
Uses: Specimen tree.
Cultivars: 'Snowbird' has white flowers. 'Toba' has
  light pink flowers that darken with age and
  is the most readily available.

**Crataegus   Washington
phaenopyrum   hawthorn**

Comments: This can be grown as a small tree or
  large shrub. It is not as troubled by diseases
  as some hawthorns and is widely grown.
Hardiness: Canadian zone 5; U.S. zone 4.
Availability: **M**.
Height: 25' (7.5 m). *Spread:* 20' (6 m).
Propagation: Seed.
Soil preferences: Well drained.
Location: Sun.
Good points: It extends the flowering season by
  opening its white flowers after all the other
  haws have bloomed. Dark green leaves turn
  orange-red to scarlet and fruit is small, red,
  plentiful and persistent.
Bad points: It may be difficult to transplant if it is
  not stored correctly; make sure you get a
  guarantee. Long thorns can be a hazard.
Uses: Specimen tree; screen.

Crataegus viridis   Green hawthorn

Comments: The cultivar listed below is a supe-
  rior selection and the form most usually avail-
  able. It makes a rounded tree.
Hardiness: Canadian zone 5; U.S. zone 4.
Availability: **S** in Canada; **A** in U.S.
Height: 20' (6 m). *Spread:* 15' (4.5 m).
Propagation: Grafting.
Soil preferences: Well drained.
Location: Sun.
Good points: The white flowers in spring give red
  fruit that lasts well; the flaking bark adds
  winter interest.
Bad points: This species still has some disease
  problems, but not as seriously as most other
  hawthorns.
Uses: Specimen tree.
Cultivars: 'Winter King' has larger fruit that per-
  sists longer, and better disease resistance.

Euonymus europaeus   Spindle tree

Comments: The wood is hard and was used to
  make spindles.
Hardiness: Canadian zone 4; U.S. zone 3.
Availability: **M**.
Height: 20' (6 m). *Spread:* 15' (4.5 m).
Propagation: Seed.
Soil preferences: Well drained.
Location: Sun.
Good points: This small tree has excellent fall
  color, more purple than the dwarf euonymus
  shrub. The pink and orange seed capsule re-
  mains attractive long after leaf-fall.
Bad points: Flowers are small, green and insig-
  nificant and the seeds are poisonous. Aphids
  and scale can be a problem.
Uses: Specimen tree.
Cultivars: 'Red Cascade' has fruit capsules that
  are red, not pink; they are freely produced
  and last well into winter.

Fagus spp.   Beech

These are large trees with smooth, attractive bark. People insist on carving names, initials and hearts on the trunks of these trees, which is fine until M.S. and J.B. split up.

Fagus grandifolia   American beech

Comments: This large tree is slightly more fussy about soil than the European beech, but it is hardier and well worth growing.

Hardiness: Canadian zone 4; U.S. zone 4a.

Availability: **F**.

Height: 70' (21 m). *Spread:* 60' (18 m).

Propagation: Seed.

Soil preferences: Well drained but moist.

Location: Sun.

Good points: It moves easily when young, grows away quickly, and has good fall color. The smooth, gray bark is very attractive, especially in winter, while the foliage turns brown in fall but only partly drops, giving added winter attraction. The fruit (beech nuts) is edible.

Bad points: It will not grow on wet soils. Surface roots make mowing grass difficult round mature trees and it is intolerant of city pollution.

Uses: A specimen or shade tree for large gardens, golf courses and parks. It makes a good hedge and can be kept under 10 feet (3 m).

Fagus sylvatica   European beech

Comments: This is a wonderful tree where it is hardy, with a multitude of named forms in a variety of shapes and colors. This is the tree of choice for stately homes, college campuses and the like.

Hardiness: Canadian zone 6; U.S. zone 5.

Availability: Species **A**; cultivars **A** to **H**.

Height: 60' (18 m). *Spread:* 40' (12 m).

Propagation: Seed for the species; cultivars by grafting.

Soil preferences: Well drained, slightly acidic.

Location: Sun.

Good points: This is an excellent shade tree that keeps its branches well down the trunk. It withstands heavy clipping and many of the famous hedges in English country homes are beech. Like its American counterpart, the smooth, gray bark is wonderful in winter, and its leaves turn brown in fall but do not drop until spring, giving winter interest.

Bad points: It is difficult to grow anything under it, and it is slow growing; plant for the next generation.

Uses: Shade or specimen tree for large properties. It makes a dense hedge that clips well.

Cultivars: 'Asplenifolia', the fern-leaved beech, is the hardiest of the selections and will just survive in the northern part of Canadian zone 5. It has finely cut leaves. 'Pendula' is a weeping form that may be spreading or like a half-closed umbrella. 'Purpurea-Pendula' is similar to 'Pendula' but with purple leaves and a smaller habit. 'Riversii' is a very dark purple; the newly opened foliage is almost black. 'Tricolor' has foliage that is a blend of purple, pink and cream: a very striking tree but a bit hard to fit into a color scheme. It is slower-growing and needs a partly shaded site in more southern regions.

Fraxinus spp.   Ash

These are mostly large trees that are much used as street and boulevard trees because of their pollution-tolerance. Some have brittle wood and suffer badly in ice storms. They all have smallish leaves, so grass grows well in their shade. The named forms must be propagated by grafting.

Fraxinus americana — White ash

Comments: This large native tree is best suited to country properties. It is quite pollution-tolerant, so is also used for shade in parking lots.
Hardiness: Canadian zone 3b; U.S. zone 4.
Availability: **M**.
Height: 70' (21 m). *Spread:* 40' (12 m).
Propagation: Seed (species only).
Soil preferences: Most soils except for very dry.
Location: Sun.
Good points: It is pollution-tolerant and has good fall color.
Bad points: It sets copious seed and seedlings can be a nuisance. The wood is fairly brittle and trees are subject to storm damage. There are many insect problems, especially when the trees are grown in urban settings and are under stress. Ash decline, now affecting many city trees, seems to be stress-related.
Uses: Shade tree.
Cultivars: 'Autumn Purple' is a seedless selection with extra good fall color. 'Manitou' is a Canadian introduction with a more upright habit.

Fraxinus excelsior — European ash

Comments: Not as widely grown as the native ashes, especially in the central U.S.
Hardiness: Canadian zone 5a; U.S. zone 4.
Availability: **F**.
Height: 60' (18 m). *Spread:* 40' (12 m).
Propagation: Seed.
Soil preferences: Moist; does well on alkaline soils.
Location: Sun.
Good points: It forms a more open tree than the white ash and has dark green foliage.
Bad points: There is no fall color worth speaking of, it is subject to borers, and the plentiful seeds are a clean-up problem.
Uses: Shade tree.

Cultivars: 'Rancho' has a more rounded form. 'Westhof's Glorie' is a seedless selection that produces no litter.

Fraxinus nigra — Black ash

Comments: This smaller tree does well on wettish soils. The twigs are used by some native peoples for basket-making.
Hardiness: Canadian zone 2b; U.S. zone 3a.
Availability: **M**.
Height: 35' (10.5 m). *Spread:* 30' (9 m).
Propagation: Seed.
Soil preferences: Wet.
Location: Sun.
Good points: It has good fall color, especially the cultivar, and is very hardy.
Bad points: It tends to have an open, straggly shape.
Uses: A good tree for wet locations.
Cultivars: 'Fallgold' has long-lasting fall color and a more upright shape.

Fraxinus pennsylvanica — Green ash, red ash

Comments: At one time the green ash was considered to be a variety of the red, but botanists now consider them the same. If a nursery is selling both, ask them to point out the difference!
Hardiness: Canadian zone 2b; U.S. zone 3.
Availability: **M**.
Height: 60' (18 m). *Spread:* 40' (12 m).
Propagation: Seed.
Soil preferences: Most.
Location: Sun.
Good points: This is very tolerant of poor soils and pollution, so it is used in parking lots and as a street tree.
Bad points: The species seeds freely, so plant a seedless form.
Uses: Shade tree for large gardens.

Cultivars: There are many named forms, but the following are the most readily available. 'Marshall's Seedless' is a seedless, male form. 'Patmore' is very hardy, seedless and slightly smaller. 'Summit' is an upright form with good fall color. It is not seedless but does not set a large amount of fruit.

Gleditsia triacanthos var. *inermis*   Thornless honeylocust

Comments: The species has multibranched thorns on the trunk and branches and is not grown, but the thornless variety has given us several named forms that are widely grown. Prune in late summer or fall if needed.
Hardiness: Canadian zone 4; U.S. zone 3.
Availability: **M**.
Height: 70' (21 m). *Spread:* 40' (12 m).
Propagation: Grafting.
Soil preferences: Deep, well drained.
Location: Sun.
Good points: It is salt-tolerant, with a range of eventual heights, shapes and foliage colors in the cultivars. The small foliage allows grass to grow well under the tree.
Bad points: It has been overplanted, with the result that pests and diseases are causing problems. Dieback of branches indicates stress, while pod gall midge causes disfiguring and inflation of leaflets. Webworm can also be bad some years.
Uses: Specimen; shade tree.
Cultivars: 'Imperial' is a round-headed form growing about 30 feet (9 m) tall. 'Shademaster' is more upright, taller and has some webworm resistance. 'Skyline' has good fall color and is even more upright, almost pyramidal, reaching 40 feet (12 m). 'Sunburst' has new foliage that is yellow, becoming bright green later. Widely used in gardens, it will grow to 35 feet (10.5 m) tall and wide.

Gymnocladus dioicus   Kentucky coffeetree

Comments: Male and female flowers are carried on separate trees. The female produces long pods that last into winter, but mostly male trees are propagated and sold. Plant B & B specimens. The mildly toxic beans were used as a coffee substitute by early settlers.
Hardiness: Canadian zone 5; U.S. zone 4.
Availability: **M**.
Height: 60' (18 m). *Spread:* 40' (12 m).
Propagation: Scarified seed or cuttings.
Soil preferences: Deep and well drained, but it is adaptable.
Location: Sun.
Good points: Large (24-inch/60-cm) feathery leaves give good shade that is not too dense for grass to survive. The trusses of white flowers are longest on the female tree.
Bad points: There is no fall color. The large leaves are difficult to clean up in fall, while the fruit makes a spring clean-up task.
Uses: Specimen; shade tree for large properties.

Halesia caroliniana   Silverbells

Comments: This interesting, spreading, native tree that grows from Virginia to Florida is a real attention-grabber when in bloom and attractive at other times. Plant B & B or container-grown plants only.
Hardiness: Canadian zone 5; U.S. zone 4.
Availability: **A**.
Height: 30' (9 m). *Spread:* 35' (10.5 m).
Propagation: Stratified seed.
Soil preferences: Moist, acidic.
Location: Sun to light shade.
Good points: White, bell-shaped flowers hang in clusters just below the branches as the leaves unfurl. The fruit is also attractive and there is good yellow fall color most years.
Bad points: None.
Uses: Specimen tree; border.

Heptacodium miconioides   **Chinese heptacodium, seven son flower**

Comments: A new plant that may be grown as a small tree or a shrub, its hardiness is unknown at present. At the time of writing, it has survived -15°F (-25°C) with very slight tip kill.
Hardiness: Canadian zone 5?; U.S. zone 4?
Availability: **H**.
Height: 20' (6 m)? *Spread:* 15' (4.5 m)?
Propagation: Seed.
Soil preferences: Well drained.
Location: Sun.
Good points: White flowers appear on the ends of the shoots in early fall when little else is in bloom. It is said to be fragrant, but this is only very slight in my experience. The shredding bark gives winter interest.
Bad points: None so far.
Uses: Specimen.

Juglans spp.   **Walnut**

These large trees are suitable only for country properties, parks or golf courses. They are slow growing, so plant them for the next generation. The fruit is edible but hard to husk without special equipment. All are difficult to transplant because of the long tap root. Plant young container-grown plants.

Juglans cinerea   **Butternut**

Comments: In native stands, trees may be almost double the height given here, but this is about average in cultivation. This species has the hardest nut to crack without smashing the meat.
Hardiness: Canadian zone 3; U.S. zone 3.
Availability: **A**.
Height: 45' (13.5 m). *Spread:* 40' (12 m).
Propagation: Stratified seed.
Soil preferences: Deep, rich and moist.

Location: Sun.
Good points: The butternut tree gives excellent wood for cabinet-making and forms a shapely specimen.
Bad points: The roots give off a toxic substance, juglone, that inhibits the growth of many plants. This makes it hard to grow other plants close to walnut trees. Luckily, the common lawn grasses are not affected.
Uses: Specimen; shade tree.

Juglans nigra   **Black walnut**

Comments: The w___ of this stately tree is highly prized for ver___ o the extent that tree rustling has bee___ to happen.
Hardiness: Canad___ U.S. zone 3.
Availability: **A**.
Height: 50' (15 m). ___ (15 m).
Propagation: Strati___
Soil preferences: De___
Location: Sun.
Good points: This make___ ee and gives a good shade, if you h___ t is the fastest growing of the walnu___
Bad points: The roots of this ___ nhibit other plants (see *J. cinerea*).
Uses: Specimen; shade tree.

Juglans regia   **English walnut, Persian walnut**

Comments: This is the source of the walnuts you buy in the grocery stores.
Hardiness: Canadian zone 6; U.S. zone 5.
Availability: **A**.
Height: 40' (12 m). *Spread:* 40' (12 m).
Propagation: Stratified seed for the species, grafting for the cultivars.
Soil preferences: Deep and dryish; not wet.
Location: Sun.
Good points: This species is the least demanding to grow and has the easiest nuts to crack.

Bad points: It is difficult to grow with some other plants (see *J. cinerea*).

Uses: Specimen; shade tree.

Cultivars: 'Carpathian' is much hardier (zone 4 in Canada; zone 3 in U.S.). There are many other cultivars of English walnut selected for nut production or flavor but they are only available from a few specialist nurseries.

Koelreuteria
paniculata
    Varnish tree,
    goldenrain tree

Comments: I first saw this tree in fruit and the inflated pods sent me scurrying across to look for a label. Two years later I saw it in flower and was equally impressed. Transplant small, either B & B or container-grown plants.

Hardiness: Canadian zone 5b?; U.S. zone 5.

Availability: **F** in Canada; **A** in U.S.

Height: 30' (9 m). *Spread:* 30' (9 m).

Propagation: Stratified seed.

Soil preferences: Most.

Location: Sun.

Good points: Copious spikes of conspicuous bright yellow flowers in midsummer are followed by inflated seed pods that are green, then yellow and finally a pinkish-brown. The bright green, fern-like foliage turns golden most autumns.

Bad points: None. Some references say it is liable to wind damage but others dispute this.

Uses: Specimen tree.

Laburnum x watereri   **Goldenchain tree**

Comments: Although there are other laburnums occasionally available, this hybrid, and particularly the cultivar below, are the most widely available and grown.

Hardiness: Canadian zone 6; U.S. zone 5.

Availability: **M**.

Height: 15' (4.5 m). *Spread:* 12' (3.5 m).

Propagation: Seed or cuttings.

Soil preferences: Well drained.

Location: Sun to light shade.

Good points: Long chains (up to 18 inches/45 cm in the cultivar) of golden yellow flowers in spring make this a popular small tree which also has attractive winter bark. It can be trained over a pergola to form a golden arch.

Bad points: Laburnum does not like excessive heat, so the range where it will grow well is limited; seed is poisonous.

Uses: Specimen tree; border.

Cultivars: 'Vossii' has longer flower trusses and is the form normally offered.

Liquidambar styraciflua   **Sweetgum**

Comments: In my student days we traveled to a garden in southern England in autumn especially to see the fall color on sweetgum and tupelo. Years later, we camped in southern Delaware, where it is a weed tree. How circumstances change our view. This species has fleshy roots, so planting B & B in spring is recommended. Check the provenance of the plant: trees from southern seed may not survive at the northern end of the range.

Hardiness: Canadian zone 6; U.S. zone 5.

Availability: **F** in Canada; **A** in U.S.

Height: 60' (18 m). *Spread:* 40' (12 m).

Propagation: Seed.

Soil preferences: Moist and slightly acidic.

Location: Sun.

Good points: This makes a good small tree (for many years at least) with a narrow, pyramidal outline. The main reason for planting this species is the fall color: yellow, red and bronze, often all together on a good tree.

Bad points: Chlorosis can be disfiguring on alkaline soils, and some plants do not have a good fall display every year.

Uses: Specimen tree.

Cultivars: Several, but none are readily available.

Liriodendron tulipifera — Tulip tree, yellow poplar

Comments: This tree is one of the easiest to identify in leaf because of the reverse point at the tip of the leaf; it ends in a shallow vee. Plant B & B specimens in spring and prune in winter.

Hardiness: Canadian zone 5b; U.S. zone 4.

Availability: **M**.

Height: 90' (27 m). *Spread:* 30' (9 m).

Propagation: Stratified seed.

Soil preferences: Deep, moist.

Location: Sun.

Good points: The unusual, bright green leaves turn gold in the fall. Flowers, a greenish-yellow with orange inside, are produced at the ends of the branches in late spring. They are very showy and look like 2-inch-long (5-cm) tulips.

Bad points: Attacks of aphids can be bad some years and a leaf spot can cause early leaf fall.

Uses: Specimen tree.

Maackia amurensis — Amur maackia

Comments: An unusual tree that has many good points, it should be used more.

Hardiness: Canadian zone 3b; U.S. zone 3.

Availability: **S**.

Height: 25' (7.5 m). *Spread:* 30' (9 m).

Propagation: Stratified seed.

Soil preferences: Well drained.

Location: Sun to light shade.

Good points: Long leaves with many small leaflets give light shade. Attractive yellowish bark adds winter interest. Erect spikes of pea-like flowers in summer, slightly fragrant.

Bad points: Tends to form a multistemmed tree.

Uses: Shade tree.

Malus spp. — Crab apple

There are a few species (with their related cultivars) that I will cover first, but the majority of crab apples available are complex hybrids. Normally grown as small specimen trees, they are occasionally available as shrubs.

Crab apples are subject to a few major, serious diseases, and the susceptibility of the individual hybrid varies greatly. Following are the chief diseases.

Cedar-apple rust causes yellowish spots on the leaves. These spots grow and may eventually cause leaf-drop. Rust diseases need two different host plants for stages in their life cycle; here the alternate host is juniper. That stage forms bright orange galls. They are highly visible and should be pruned out immediately when noticed.

Apple scab causes dark spots on the leaves and corky spots on the young fruit. It overwinters on twigs and in bark crevices and can be kept in check by spraying with lime sulphur in late winter.

Fire blight makes whole branches look as though someone had run a blow torch up and down them. The leaves turn black and shrivel but generally do not drop. Prune out the infected branches as soon as you notice them, well back from the affected area. Sterilize the pruning tools between cuts with Javel water or rubbing alcohol. Don't forget to oil the tools afterwards or they will rust in hours. Fire blight is difficult to control, and if the tree dies, it should be removed as soon as possible and the wood trashed to avoid spreading the spores.

Mildew. Several closely related fungi attack different groups of plants. See chapter 6 for more information on mildew and its control.

Malus baccata — Siberian crab apple

Comments: A small-fruited species with white flowers and yellow (or sometimes red) fruit. The fruit hangs on the tree over winter and is small enough for the birds to eat. If they don't eat them all in fall, they soon polish them off in spring. There are never any to rake up. It is susceptible to scab.

Hardiness: Canadian zone 2b; U.S. zone 2.
Availability: **A**.
Height: 30' (9 m). *Spread:* 25' (7.5 m).
Propagation: Seed.
Soil preferences: Heavy but well drained.
Location: Sun for at least half the day.
Cultivars: 'Columnaris' is a very narrow, upright form with almost vertical branches. Final size is about 30 feet by 5 feet (9 by 1.5 m). *M. baccata* var. *gracilis* is the reverse of 'Columnaris'; branches weep almost to the ground and the plant becomes wider than it is tall.

Malus	Japanese flowering
floribunda	**crab apple**

Comments: Dark pink buds open paler and then fade gradually almost to white. The fruit is yellow and red but drops early. This is one of the better crabs that is moderately resistant to diseases.

Hardiness: Canadian zone 5b; U.S. zone 4.
Availability: **S**.
Height: 20' (6 m). *Spread:* 15' (4.5 m).
Propagation: Seed or grafting.
Soil preferences: Well drained.
Location: Sun.

Malus ioensis   Prairie crab apple

Comments: Single, pink, fragrant flowers fade to white in time and the fruit is round and green, like a tiny 'Granny Smith' apple. This species is very susceptible to rust.

Hardiness: Canadian zone 4b; U.S. zone 4.
Availability: **F**.
Height: 25' (7.5 m). *Spread:* 30' (9 m).
Propagation: Seed or grafting.

Soil preferences: Most.
Location: Sun.
Cultivars: 'Plena' (Bechtel's crab) has fully double flowers that are fragrant and sets very few fruit. It is very disease-prone. 'Klems' is a selection of Bechtel's crab that is much more disease-resistant.

Malus sargentii   Sargent's crab apple

Comments: This is a comparatively dwarf species, although in time it becomes quite wide. Its buds are red, the flowers white and the fruit is small and bright red. It has good disease resistance.

Hardiness: Canadian zone 5; U.S. zone 4.
Availability: **A**.
Height: 6' (1.8 m). *Spread:* 10' (3 m).
Propagation: Seed.
Soil preferences: Well drained.
Location: Sun.
Cultivars: 'Rosea' is supposed to have darker buds, but I have never been able to see any difference. 'Tina' is reported to be even smaller than the species.

All the other named hybrid crab apples

There are around 500 named crab apples that cannot be grouped with any one species as they have a complex parentage. This group includes the majority of crab apples sold by nurseries.

Unfortunately, some of the more commonly available varieties are very susceptible to most (or all) of the diseases listed above and are best avoided. There are many good crab apples and it makes no sense to plant those that are known to have problems.

The following are not good choices as they are susceptible to most diseases: 'Almey', 'Hopa', 'Makamik', 'Oekonomierat Echtermeyer', 'Radiant', 'Royalty' and 'Snowcloud'.

Because of these diseases, and the resulting

quarantine regulations, the introduction into Canada of new varieties developed in the U.S. is a long process. They are slowly finding their way across the border, so by the time you are reading this, most of those mentioned may also be available in Canada (with a bit of a search).

Lake County Nursery in Ohio has recently introduced a new type of disease-resistant crab apple, called the Round Table series. The trees are much smaller and more suited to townhouse and condominium gardens; they are about 10 feet (3 m) tall at maturity, large enough to give shade, but not overpowering on a small lot. They have names like 'Excalibur', 'King Arthur', and 'Lancelot' and should be available from local nurseries soon.

Good, disease-resistant crab apples, readily available

Variety	Flowers	Fruit	Fruit size	Tree size	Comments
'Adams'	pink	red	5/8 in/16 mm	25 ft/7.5 m	
'Candied Apple'	pink	red	5/8 in/16 mm	15 ft/4.5 m	Weeping.
'Centurion'	red	red	5/8 in/16 mm	25 ft/7.5 m	
'Dolgo'	white	purple	1 1/4 in/30 mm	30 ft/9 m	Good for jelly.
'Donald Wyman'	white	red	3/8 in/9 mm	20 ft/6 m	
'Harvest Gold'	pink	yellow	3/4 in/19 mm	30 ft/9 m	Columnar.
'Indian Summer'	rose	red	5/8 in/16 mm	20 ft/6 m	
'Madonna'	white	yellow	1/2 in/13 mm	20 ft/6 m	Double flowers.
'Prairiefire'	dark pink	dark red	5/8 in/16 mm	20 ft/6 m	New leaves are reddish.
'Robinson'	pink	dark red	3/4 in/19 mm	25 ft/7.5 m	
'Sugar Tyme'	white	red	1/2 in/13 mm	15 ft/4.5 m	
'Thunderchild'	pink	dark red	1/2 in/13 mm	20 ft/6 m	

Good, disease-resistant crab apples less easy to find

Variety	Flowers	Fruit	Fruit size	Tree size	Comments
'Ames White'	white	yellow	5/8 in/16 mm	25 ft/7.5 m	
'Baskatong'	purple	dark red	1 in/25 mm	30 ft/9 m	
'Beauty'	white	red	1 1/2 in/37 mm	25 ft/7.5 m	Upright.
'Centennial'	white	striped	1 3/4 in/44 mm	30 ft/9 m	
'Color Parade'	white	pinkish	1/2 in/13 mm	12 ft/3.5 m	Weeping.
'Evelyn'	dark pink	greenish	11/4 in/30 mm	20 ft/6 m	
'Molten Lava'	white	red	3/8 in/9 mm	15 ft/4.5 m	Weeping.
'Professor Sprenger'	white	orange	5/8 in/16 mm	20 ft/6 m	
'Sea Foam'	white	red	3/8 in/9 mm	5 ft/1.5 m	Weeping.
'Strawberry Parfait'	pink, edged red	yellow	1/2 in/13 mm	20 ft/6 m	

Semi-resistant crab apples

Variety	Flowers	Fruit	Fruit size	Tree size	May get
'Beverley'	white	red	3/4 in/19 mm	25 ft/7.5 m	fire blight.
'Indian Magic'	dark pink	red	1/2 in/13 mm	20 ft/6 m	scab.
'Liset'	red	dark red	1/2 in/13 mm	20 ft/6 m	mildew.
'Mary Potter'	white	red	1/2 in/13 mm	15 ft/4.5 m	scab, mildew.
'Pink Spires' (upright)	mauve	dark red	3/4 in/19 mm	25 ft/7.5 m	scab.
'Red Jade' (weeping)	white	red	1/2 in/13 mm	15 ft/4.5 m	scab, mildew.
'Red Jewel'	white	red	1/2 in/13 mm	15 ft/4.5 m	fire blight, scab.
'Red Splendor'	pink	red	3/4 in/19 mm	25 ft/7.5 m	fire blight.
'Selkirk'	red	red	1 in/25 mm	25 ft/7.5 m	scab, fire blight.
'Snowdrift'	white	red	3/8 in/9 mm	20 ft/6 m	fire blight.

Morus alba — White mulberry

Comments: Introduced to Europe from China to feed silkworms, this plant soon naturalized itself there and has done the same here. The fruit is enjoyed by birds but to my taste it hasn't much flavor. The cultivar is the form most often grown. The native red mulberry (*Morus rubra*) is larger and tastes better, but is not as hardy or easy to find.

Hardiness: Canadian zone 3; U.S. zone 3.

Availability: **M**.

Height: 30' (9 m). *Spread:* 30' (9 m).

Propagation: Stratified seed or cuttings.

Soil preferences: Most.

Location: Sun to light shade.

Good points: It is pollution- and possibly salt-tolerant: it grows well close to the sea but suffered damage close to a major highway in Ontario. The leaves are interesting as they vary greatly in outline; some are simple, others have one to several lobes, making this plant easy to identify.

Bad points: Fruits stain sidewalks and are messy. Birds drop seeds which come up as weeds. There are male (non-fruiting) forms but these are difficult to find. Look for 'Chaparral' if you want to grow this species without the fruit.

Uses: Shade tree; screen.

Cultivars: 'Pendula' is a form with vertically weeping branches that are grafted on the top of a short stem. It is widely planted.

Nyssa sylvatica — Tupelo, black gum, sour gum

Comments: Although it also grows on dryish soils, this tree does best on wet ones. I first saw it growing beside a lake, ablaze in its outstanding fall color. Plant small plants, B & B, in spring.

Hardiness: Canadian zone 5b; U.S. zone 4.

Availability: **F** in Canada; **A** in U.S.

Height: 60' (18 m). *Spread:* 25' (7.5 m).

Propagation: Stratified seed.

Soil preferences: Moist, acidic.

Location: Sun but sheltered from wind.

Good points: The deep green summer foliage turns yellow-orange, then scarlet, then flame in fall.

Bad points: It is difficult to transplant due to its long taproot.

Uses: Specimen tree, especially where it can reflect in water.

Ostrya   **Hophornbeam,**
virginiana   **ironwood**

Comments: An underused native tree with flaking bark similar to shagbark hickory, it is mostly found as an understory tree in woodlands. Use container-grown plants only; it does not transplant well bare-root.

Hardiness: Canadian zone 3; U.S. zone 3.

Availability: **M**.

Height: 30' (9 m). *Spread:* 20' (6 m).

Propagation: Stratified seed.

Soil preferences: Well drained.

Location: Sun to medium shade.

Good points: The wood is very hard, so it is seldom damaged in wind or ice storms. Clusters of hop-like fruit form in fall when the leaves turn a pale yellow color.

Bad points: It is slow growing and very susceptible to salt damage. Do not plant close to roads where salt is used in winter.

Uses: Specimen tree; shade tree.

Parrotia persica   **Persian parrotia**

Comments: A very good small tree that should be planted more. It will survive in zone 5 as a low, spreading shrub if winter snow is reliable.

Hardiness: Canadian zone 6; U.S. zone 5.

Availability: **S** in Canada, **A** in U.S.

Height: 25' (7.5 m). *Spread:* 15' (4.5 m).

Propagation: Stratified seed.

Soil preferences: Well drained.

Location: Sun to light shade.

Good points: This species has very good orange to scarlet fall color; the bark on mature branches flakes off to reveal gray, green and brown inner bark.

Bad points: None.

Uses: Specimen tree (or shrub).

Paulownia tomentosa   **Empress tree**

Comments: When in flower, this tree, with leaves the size of dinner plates, is very striking.

Hardiness: Canadian zone 6; U.S. zone 5.

Availability: **S**.

Height: 60' (18 m). *Spread:* 30' (9 m).

Propagation: Seed.

Soil preferences: Well drained.

Location: Sun.

Good points: When young, this tree grows very rapidly, up to 10 feet (3 m) or more per year. The vanilla-scented, pale mauve, tubular flowers are up to 2 inches (5 cm) long.

Bad points: Flower buds are often killed by a late frost or an extra-cold winter. Because of the very dense shade it casts it is difficult to grow a lawn under this species and it tends to be weedy from seed in warm climates.

Uses: Specimen tree for large properties.

Phellodendron amurensis   **Amur corktree**

Comments: This is not the commercial source of cork (which comes from a species of oak), but the bark is spongy and attractive.

Hardiness: Canadian zone 3; U.S. zone 3.

Availability: **A**.

Height: 40' (12 m). *Spread:* 40' (12 m).

Propagation: Seed.

Soil preferences: Tolerates most soils.

Location: Sun.

Good points: Older trees have interesting ridged bark. Long strings of black berries smelling strongly of resin persist well into winter on female trees (providing there is a male tree nearby). It is pollution-tolerant, so does well in cities, and has no pest problems.

Bad points: On mature trees, some roots tend to grow to the surface and get scalped by mowers.

Uses: Specimen tree.

Cultivars: 'Macho' is a male clone that is seed-free.

Platanus spp.   Plane tree

These large trees are suitable for parks, golf courses and large properties. I have seen wonderful specimens on some university campuses in Pennsylvania and Ohio.

Platanus x *acerifolia*   London plane

Comments: A hybrid between the American and oriental plane trees, this is the main street tree in London, England, where it is often pollarded. (In winter all the branches are cut back to the main crown, and the tree puts out extensive new growth each year.)

Hardiness: Canadian zone 5b; U.S. zone 4.

Availability: **S** in Canada; **A** in U.S.

Height: 70' (21 m). *Spread:* 70' (21 m).

Propagation: Stratified seed.

Soil preferences: Deep and moist.

Location: Sun.

Good points: It withstands city conditions well.

Bad points: A disease called canker stain can kill trees in a few years and is prevalent in the southeastern U.S. This species is not as susceptible to anthracnose as the American plane tree, but it can happen.

Uses: Specimen; street tree; shade tree.

Cultivars: 'Bloodgood' has greater resistance to anthracnose and is faster growing.

Platanus occidentalis   American plane, sycamore

Comments: This tree drops twigs very readily, giving clean-up problems following wind storms, but the effect of the flaking bark far outweighs this disadvantage.

Hardiness: Canadian zone 5b; U.S. zone 4.

Availability: **S** in Canada; **A** in U.S.

Height: 80' (24 m). *Spread:* 80' (24 m).

Propagation: Seed.

Soil preferences: Deep and moist.

Location: Sun.

Good points: Button-like brown fruits add interest in fall but the real beauty is in the bark, which lifts off in plates to show the paler, greenish inner bark.

Bad points: Anthracnose fungus causes late leafing out and twig dieback; it is more likely on trees under stress. Good sanitation is essential and spraying may be necessary.

Uses: Specimen; shade tree.

Populus spp.   Poplar, aspen

Poplars are not recommended for most gardens due to their twig and branch litter, their susceptibility to a large number of pests and diseases, and their water-seeking roots that can block sewer lines. They have a limited use on large properties as windbreaks and shelterbelts, and especially as nurse trees to shelter more desirable species.

They are fairly short-lived and often send up a thicket of suckers when the tops are removed. Many are very hardy and are planted where other trees won't grow. Following are the most readily available poplars, with brief descriptions.

Bolleana poplar (*Populus alba* 'Pyramidalis') is an upright form that lives longer than the Lombardy poplar; zone 3 Canada and U.S.

Carolina poplar (*P.* x *canadensis* 'Eugenei') is very fast growing with a pyramidal form and dark green leaves; zone 2 Canada, zone 3 U.S.

Cottonwood *(P. deltoides)* 'Siouxland' is a male form that does not make the objectionable cotton and has a narrower shape than the species; zone 3 Canada and U.S.

Lombardy poplar *(P. nigra* 'Italica'), although often planted for its very narrow shape and fast growth, is subject to a canker that causes serious dieback of the upper branches; zone 4 Canada, zone 3 U.S.

Northwest poplar is a hardy hybrid of several species that was selected for its relatively fast growth and disease resistance; zone 2 Canada and U.S.

Quaking aspen *(P. tremuloides)* is a prolific tree that quickly inhabits abandoned farms and pastures. The leaves move in the slightest breeze, giving it its common name. It has good fall color but is disease-prone; zone 1 Canada and U.S.

Swedish aspen *(P. tremula* 'Erecta') makes a good replacement for the Lombardy poplar as it seems disease-resistant; zone 2 Canada, zone 3 U.S.

Theves poplar *(P. nigra* 'Thevestina') is an improved and hardier form of the Lombardy poplar, but not as narrow in shape and still quite canker-prone; zone 2 Canada and U.S.

Tower poplar *(P. x canescens* 'Tower') is a narrow, seedless form that doesn't sucker; zone 2 Canada and U.S.

***Prunus* spp.**   **Cherry, cherry plum**

These cherries and cherry plums are the tree-like members of this genus. Shrubby cherries and flowering almonds can be found in the "Shrubs" section of this chapter.

Prunus cerasifera   **Cherry plum**

Comments: Although the species is rarely grown, several named forms are available. They are small trees grown mostly for their purple foliage.

Hardiness: Canadian zone 4-5; U.S. zone 4.

Availability: **A.**

Height: 15-20' (4.5-6 m). *Spread:* 15-20' (4.5-6 m).

Propagation: Cuttings in mist.

Soil preferences: Well drained.

Location: Sun.

Good points: These trees suit small gardens. Pink flowers appear as the leaves unfurl and the purple foliage is eye-catching all summer.

Bad points: They are subject to many pests and diseases. All the cherry plums and almonds suffer from aphids on the new growth, several leaf spots, and tent caterpillars. They also get black knot (see *P. padus* for control). Use this tree in moderation; if your neighbor has one, plant something else.

Uses: Specimen tree.

Cultivars: 'Atropurpurea', 'Newport' and 'Thundercloud' differ slightly in the depth of color, hardiness and ultimate size.

Prunus maackii   **Amur chokecherry**

Comments: Pyramidal when young, this medium-sized tree becomes rounded with age. A tree for all seasons, it has something to commend it year-round. Being native to Korea and Manchuria's Amur peninsula, it is very hardy.

Hardiness: Canadian zone 2b; U.S. zone 3b.

Availability: **M.**

Height: 30' (9 m). *Spread:* 25' (7.5 m).

Propagation: Cuttings in summer.

Soil preferences: Well drained.

Location: Sun.

Good points: Numerous small clusters of white flowers in late spring give rise in August to black fruits that attract birds. There is good shade from bright green foliage but best of all is the bark: cinnamon brown, peeling in strips like a birch—great for winter interest.

Bad points: It is attacked by the usual pests and diseases, but not as badly as many cherries, especially in the north.

Uses: Specimen; shade tree.

Prunus padus   **European bird cherry**

Comments: A popular tree grown for its 6-inch-long (15-cm) pendulous sprays of fragrant white flowers. In Europe it flowers about May 1, hence its other common name of Mayday tree. The native pincherry is the North American counterpart.

Hardiness: Canadian zone 2; U.S. zone 3b.

Availability: **M**.

Height: 30' (9 m). *Spread:* 25' (7.5 m).

Propagation: Seed or summer cuttings.

Soil preferences: Well drained.

Location: Sun.

Good points: One of the first trees to leaf out, it is a harbinger of spring. Spring flowers produce small black fruits that birds love.

Bad points: It is very susceptible to black knot disease, a fungus that attacks many plums and cherries. Black, rope-like swellings grow on the branches, which become girdled and die. Eventually the entire tree is killed. Prune out any infected areas as soon as noticed, cutting well past the visible fungus. Sterilize the pruning tools with weak Javel water or rubbing alcohol between cuts to avoid carrying contamination into clean wood.

Uses: Specimen tree.

Cultivars: 'Colorata' bears pink flowers and leaves that are bronzy when young. *P. padus* var. *commutata* flowers earlier with larger individual flowers.

Prunus sargentii   **Sargent's cherry**

Comments: A beautiful tree with pink flowers that open before the leaves and so are very visible. It also has good bronzy-red fall color.

Hardiness: Canadian zone 5b; U.S. zone 4b.

Availability: **F**.

Height: 30' (9 m). *Spread:* 25' (7.5 m).

Propagation: Seed for the species; grafting for the cultivar.

Soil preferences: Well drained, slightly acidic.

Location: Sun.

Good points: In addition to the flowers and fall color, this tree has gorgeous reddish bark with horizontal white flecks. It is worth planting for this alone.

Bad points: Few. Sargent's cherry is not as prone to problems as most cherries.

Uses: Specimen tree.

Cultivars: 'Rancho' is a narrow, upright form, ideal for smaller properties and more widely available.

Prunus serrulata   **Japanese flowering cherry**

Comments: The species is rarely available since the many named forms are more spectacular. Where they will survive, these rival crab apples for their display.

Hardiness: Canadian zone 6; U.S. zone 5.

Availability: **M**.

Height: 25' (7.5 m). *Spread:* 20' (6 m). These are average sizes for the cultivars.

Propagation: Grafting.

Soil preferences: Well drained.

Location: Sun.

Good points: Spectacular at flowering time, they also have fairly good fall color—certainly better than most crab apples. The wide range of cultivars means there are many different shapes to choose from with either white or pink blooms.

Bad points: Flowering cherries are prone to several diseases.

Uses: Specimen tree.

Cultivars: 'Kiku-shidare-sakura' (often listed as 'Shidare-sakura') is a weeping form with deep pink, double flowers. 'Kwanzan' (also called 'Kanzan' and 'Hisakura') has double, deep pink flowers, and is one of the hardiest and most readily available forms. The new leaves have a reddish tinge and the fall color is orangish. 'Mt. Fuji' has large, single to semi-double white flowers. This cultivar is wider than tall at maturity and the branches may hang to the ground.

Prunus virginiana   **Chokecherry**

Comments: This is a very tough native tree with red to purple fruit that is fit for jellies and preserves only (just think about how it came by its common name—the fruit is very bitter and dries the mouth).

Hardiness: Canadian zone 2 ; U.S. zone 3a.

Availability: **M.**

Height: 25' (7.5 m). *Spread:* 20' (6 m).

Propagation: Seed.

Soil preferences: Well drained.

Location: Sun to light shade.

Good points: This grows as a small tree with a rounded head that will survive in the worst locations. At the University of Alberta in Edmonton, I saw a chokecherry growing—and thriving—in a tiny courtyard, tight against a building, with almost no soil to keep it alive.

Bad points: It is very susceptible to tent caterpillar. The species tends to sucker badly, but the named forms are grafted onto non-suckering bird cherry.

Uses: Specimen tree.

Cultivars: 'Shubert' has foliage that opens green and then darkens to a brownish-purple. 'Canada Red' is very similar to 'Shubert' and may be the same. *P. virginiana* var. *melanocarpa* has black fruit, rather than purple.

Ptelea trifoliata   **Hoptree**

Comments: This large, shade-tolerant, native small tree or shrub grows as an understory plant in woods from Ontario to Florida.

Hardiness: Canadian zone 4; U.S. zone 3.

Availability: **H.**

Height: 15' (4.5 m). *Spread:* 12' (3.5 m).

Propagation: Seed or cuttings.

Soil preferences: Moist.

Location: Sun to medium shade.

Good points: While the flowers are not showy, the flat, yellowish, hop-like fruits, up to 1 inch (2.5 cm) across and carried in clusters, are most noticeable in fall. It is subject to very few pests and diseases.

Bad points: None.

Uses: Borders; specimen.

Pyrus spp.   **Ornamental pear**

Closely related to edible pears, the ornamental species do not have a usable fruit but are grown for their flowers and foliage.

Pyrus calleryana   **Callery pear**

Comments: The species is rarely grown but the named forms are gaining popularity as flowering trees with good fall color. Plant B & B trees in spring.

Hardiness: Canadian zone 5b; U.S. zone 5.

Availability: **M.**

Height: 25' (7.5 m). *Spread:* 20' (6 m).

Propagation: Stratified seed for the species; grafting is best for the cultivars since cuttings are difficult to root.

Soil preferences: Most.

Location: Sun.

Good points: Fairly rapid growth makes this a good tree for new developments, but overplanting could cause problems if it gets too popular. White flowers in spring cover the tree while fall color varies from yellow to red but is generally good. It is quite resistant to fire blight.

Bad points: Late frost may damage flower buds, especially when an early warm spell starts the buds into growth.

Uses: Specimen tree; mixed border.

Cultivars: 'Aristocrat' is a broadly pyramidal form. 'Bradford' was the first named form but is now showing problems as plants mature: the branches tend to arise from a small area of the trunk and, when mature, the trunk cannot take the strain and the tree falls apart. 'Chanticleer' (or 'Cleveland Select') is a narrow form that may be slightly hardier. 'Redspire' is another pyramidal type that is said to color better in the fall.

Pyrus salicifolia   Willow-leaved pear

Comments: I first became aware of this tree on seeing a magnificent specimen at the Cambridge Botanic Garden in England. It has a large spreading shape with slightly weeping branches.
Hardiness: Canadian zone 5; U.S. zone 4.
Availability: **S**.
Height: 20' (6 m). *Spread:* 20' (6 m).
Propagation: Seed.
Soil preferences: Most.
Location: Sun.
Good points: Small white clusters of flowers in spring open just before the leaves, which are a silvery-green above, almost white beneath, making this tree stand out all summer.
Bad points: Unfortunately it is prone to fire blight.
Uses: Specimen; shade tree.
Cultivars: 'Silver Cascade' and 'Silver Frost' may be identical and have more pendulous branches than the species.

Pyrus ussuriensis   Ussurian pear

Comments: This grows into a fairly dense tree with an oval head and glossy green leaves; the fruit is small, hard, and slightly decorative after the leaves have fallen. I have noticed considerable variation in the quantities of flower and the intensity of fall color in a batch of plants grown from seed. This is another plant nurseries should be selecting with care.
Hardiness: Canadian zone 2b; U.S. zone 3.
Availability: **A**.
Height: 40' (12 m). *Spread:* 30' (9 m).
Propagation: Stratified seed.
Soil preferences: Most.
Location: Sun.
Good points: This pear has white flowers in spring and a good, dark red fall color. Good resistance to fire blight.
Bad points: None.
Uses: Specimen tree.

Quercus spp.   Oak

Although they are reputed to be slow growing, oaks can make a respectable-sized tree in a comparatively short time. Many have good fall color and the shingle oak is particularly attractive in winter. Oak leaves are slow to break down and are the best choice for insulating slightly tender plants over winter. They are also acidic and make a good mulch for acid-loving plants such as rhododendrons.

In general, oaks can be divided by their leaves into two main types: the white oak group with rounded lobes and the red oak group with leaves deeply cut into pointed segments.

Quercus alba   White oak

Comments: The white oak is more adaptable to soil type than many oaks, but it resents compaction. Building near stands of white oaks can lead to a gradual decline in the trees unless great care is taken.
Hardiness: Canadian zone 2b; U.S. zone 2.
Availability: **F**.
Height: 50' (15 m). *Spread:* 50' (15 m).
Propagation: Seed.
Soil preferences: Deep, well drained.
Location: Sun.

Good points: This is a majestic tree but it is slow growing. Plant it for the next generation.

Bad points: Leaf galls are very unsightly some years, and the small acorns can be a job to clean up.

Uses: Specimen; shade tree.

Quercus bicolor **Swamp white oak**

Comments: In nature, this species is found along stream banks and flood plains, while the white oak is found in dryer locations.

Hardiness: Canadian zone 4b; U.S. zone 3?

Availability: **H.**

Height: 50' (15 m). *Spread:* 50' (15 m).

Propagation: Seed.

Soil preferences: Acidic and wet (but it is adaptable).

Location: Sun.

Good points: It transplants fairly well as B & B plants.

Bad points: It gets chlorosis on non-acid soils.

Uses: Shade tree.

Quercus coccinea **Scarlet oak**

Comments: This member of the red oak group has typical deeply cut leaves with very pointed lobes.

Hardiness: Canadian zone 4; U.S. zone 4.

Availability: **F.**

Height: 70' (21 m). *Spread:* 40' (12 m).

Propagation: Seed.

Soil preferences: Dry and acidic.

Location: Sun.

Good points: Scarlet oak is the best choice for fall color.

Bad points: It is difficult to transplant; use container-grown plants for best success. Like most of the red oak group, this species suffers from galls and a chlorosis (yellowing of the leaves) on alkaline soils due to the poor availability of iron. This can be corrected by

spraying with a soluble form of iron, but it is better to plant in the right soil type initially.

Uses: Specimen; shade tree.

Quercus imbricaria **Shingle oak**

Comments: At first glance (or even at second glance) this does not look like an oak. The leaves look more like a willow: long, pointed and with a smooth edge.

Hardiness: Canadian zone 4b; U.S. zone 4.

Availability: **F.**

Height: 50' (15 m). *Spread:* 50' (15 m).

Propagation: Stratified seed.

Soil preferences: Deep, well drained.

Location: Sun.

Good points: This oak transplants easily and grows moderately quickly. The leaves turn brown in fall, then hang on the tree all winter to be pushed off by the newly opening buds in spring. I have not noticed any chlorosis on trees growing in slightly alkaline soils.

Bad points: The old leaves are messy in spring. It can suffer badly from scale.

Uses: Specimen; shade tree.

Quercus macrocarpa **Burr oak**

Comments: A large native tree of the white oak group, this is also known as the mossycup oak because of the fringe of hairs on the cup holding the acorn.

Hardiness: Canadian zone 2; U.S. zone 2.

Availability: **M.**

Height: 70' (21 m). *Spread:* 70' (21 m).

Propagation: Seed.

Soil preferences: Most.

Location: Sun.

Good points: This is a good choice for city conditions, if you have enough room. It is comparatively slow growing.

Bad points: It is difficult to transplant and may be slow to establish. It is also susceptible to various leaf galls, although they are seldom serious. They are unsightly and special care should be taken to clean up the leaves in bad years.

Uses: Specimen; shade tree.

Quercus palustris   Pin oak

Comments: More upright in habit than many of the oaks, this is one of the red oak group.
Hardiness: Canadian zone 4; U.S. zone 4.
Availability: **M**.
Height: 60' (18 m). *Spread:* 30' (9 m).
Propagation: Seed.
Soil preferences: Wet and acidic.
Location: Sun.
Good points: It transplants readily, grows away well and has good fall color most years. It will grow well where water collects in spring.
Bad points: It becomes chlorotic on non-acidic soils and may get leaf galls.
Uses: Specimen; shade tree.

Quercus robur   English oak

Comments: Another large tree in the white oak group, this is too large for many city properties, but is good in the country.
Hardiness: Canadian zone 5; U.S. zone 4.
Availability: **M**.
Height: 60' (18 m). *Spread:* 60' (18 m).
Propagation: Seed.
Soil preferences: Well drained.
Location: Sun.
Good points: Both the species and the cultivar are readily available. The cultivar is the best choice for city gardens and grows moderately fast.
Bad points: The English oak does not suffer from leaf galls nearly as much as native species, but may have bad mildew problems.
Uses: Specimen; shade tree. The cultivar is good as a screen.

Cultivars: 'Fastigiata' is an upright form growing as tall as the species but only about 15 feet (4.5 m) wide that can fit into all but the smallest garden. It comes true from seed so there is some variation in width. If you want to plant it on a small property, visit a nursery and select the plant with the most upright branches.

Quercus rubra   Red oak

Comments: If size will not become a problem and the soil is acidic, this is a good choice for city conditions.
Hardiness: Canadian zone 3; U.S. zone 3.
Availability: **M**.
Height: 60' (18 m). *Spread:* 60' (18 m).
Propagation: Seed.
Soil preferences: Sandy and acidic.
Location: Sun.
Good points: It transplants well, has reddish new foliage in spring and very good fall color.
Bad points: It gets chlorosis if grown in alkaline soils (see *Q. coccinea*).
Uses: Specimen; shade tree.

Robinia pseudoacacia   Black locust

Comments: This very adaptable tree will grow in most soils, including poor sandy gravel, since it is able to obtain some of the nitrogen it needs from the air. The wood is very hard and is used for fence posts. When cut down, the tree will regrow from the base.
Hardiness: Canadian zone 4; U.S. zone 3.
Availability: **S** to **F**.
Height: 35' (10.5 m). *Spread:* 20' (6 m).
Propagation: Scarified seed.
Soil preferences: Any but wet.
Location: Sun.
Good points: The small leaflets on the compound leaves allow grass to grow well. Fragrant white flowers hang in dense clusters in late

spring and attract bees, making this a good honey plant.

Bad points: Locust borer attacks and can kill trees under stress, but I have seen trees with many borer holes still growing and flowering.

Uses: Shade tree; land reclamation.

Cultivars: 'Frisia' leaves are a good yellow and don't turn green with age. 'Umbraculifera' makes an umbrella-shaped head, good for shade, but it has few flowers.

Salix spp.   Willow

Although willows are almost as bad as poplars for blocking sewer pipes, the large ones have a place in park-like settings and the small ones (see "Shrubs" later in this chapter) make good hedges. Their immature catkins are the pussy willow you can cut for forcing in spring, although some species have larger buds than others and *S. caprea*, the goat willow, is the best.

Salix alba   White willow

Comments: White willow is a large tree with upright branches that form a broad fan shape. The cultivars are more commonly grown. Prune in summer or fall. This species of willow (or its cultivars) is the best choice for making willow-water (see "Making cuttings" in chapter 8).

Hardiness: Canadian zone 4; U.S. zone 4.

Availability: **M**.

Height: 70' (21 m). *Spread:* 50' (15 m).

Propagation: Cuttings.

Soil preferences: Moist.

Location: Sun.

Good points: This is a good tree for wet soils.

Bad points: The wood is brittle and subject to wind damage.

Uses: Specimen tree, especially near water.

Cultivars: 'Tristis' (golden weeping willow) is the tree we think of when we hear the word willow.

The twigs (not the leaves) are bright yellow. 'Vitellina' is like the species in shape but has yellow stems. It may be slightly hardier.

Salix pentandra   Laurel willow

Comments: This is a good tree for wet locations in colder regions.

Hardiness: Canadian zone 1b; U.S. zone 2.

Availability: **M**.

Height: 40' (12 m). *Spread:* 40' (12 m).

Propagation: Cuttings.

Soil preferences: Wet.

Location: Sun.

Good points: It has shiny, dark green leaves; in spring the yellow catkins are quite attractive.

Bad points: Leaf spots can cause problems some years but are seldom serious if you clean up the fallen foliage.

Uses: Specimen tree for wet spots.

Cultivars: 'Prairie Cascade' is a hybrid between this and another species that was developed on the Canadian prairies; it is just as hardy, but has a weeping shape.

Sophora   Pagoda tree,
japonica   scholar tree

Comments: A large spreading tree with small leaflets, it flowers in summer with long trusses of creamy white blooms. Transplant B & B or container-grown plants for best success.

Hardiness: Canadian zone 5b; U.S. zone 4.

Availability: **F**.

Height: 60' (18 m). *Spread:* 70' (21 m).

Propagation: Seed.

Soil preferences: Well drained.

Location: Sun.

Good points: Pagoda tree withstands pollution and poor soils well, so it's good for city parks, but rather large for most gardens. The late flowering is an asset and the clusters of fruit give fall interest.

Bad points: None, except clearing up the fallen fruit after you have finished raking leaves.

Uses: Specimen; shade tree.

Cultivars: 'Regent', selected for fast growth and a more upright habit, may be slightly hardier.

Sorbus spp.   Mountain ash

These showy trees have several different leaf shapes, but the clusters of red fruit are the main attraction. Also known as rowanberry, the fruit can be used for a preserve. All the species can be stricken with fire blight to varying degrees (see *Malus* for description and control).

Sorbus alnifolia   Korean mountain ash

Comments: The leaves of this mountain ash are simple, rather than compound, and resemble a beech leaf. Plant B & B trees and prune in early spring if needed.

Hardiness: Canadian zone 4; U.S. zone 4.

Availability: **F**.

Height: 40' (12 m). *Spread:* 25' (7.5 m).

Propagation: Stratified seed.

Soil preferences: Well drained.

Location: Sun.

Good points: The bright green foliage turns orange to golden in fall and the white flowers give berries that last into winter.

Bad points: This species is somewhat susceptible to fire blight but less so than the European mountain ash *(S. aucuparia)*.

Uses: Specimen; shade tree.

Sorbus   American
americana   mountain ash

Comments: This tree is the North American counterpart of the European mountain ash *(S. aucuparia)*, but is not as widely grown in gardens for some reason. The showy mountain ash *(S. decora)* is similar, more northerly in distribution, and has larger fruit.

Hardiness: Canadian zone 3; U.S. zone 3.

Availability: **M**.

Height: 30' (9 m). *Spread:* 20' (6 m).

Propagation: Stratified seed.

Soil preferences: Moist.

Location: Sun.

Good points: The showy fruit brings birds into the garden. This species may be less affected by fire blight than some species, but tent caterpillars love it.

Bad points: This is not a good choice where summers are hot. Sawfly larvae (inchworms) can rapidly defoliate a tree. Spray with insecticidal soap at the first signs.

Uses: Specimen tree.

Sorbus   European mountain
aucuparia   ash, rowan

Comments: A good tree for cooler country locations, it does not grow well in compacted soils or heat. Plant B & B or container-grown specimens.

Hardiness: Canadian zone 3; U.S. zone 3.

Availability: **M**.

Height: 30' (9 m). *Spread:* 20' (6 m).

Propagation: Stratified seed.

Soil preferences: Well drained.

Location: Sun.

Good points: Orange to red fruit in fall follows flat heads of white flowers. Fruit must vary in taste, since birds will strip one tree but leave another, close by, until really cold weather strikes.

Bad points: Fire blight is particularly troublesome on this species and has almost wiped out mountain ashes in some areas. Borers can be a problem with stressed trees. There are several other problems but none are serious.

Uses: Specimen; shade tree.

Cultivars: 'Black Hawk' is a columnar form with orange fruit. 'Cardinal Royal' was named for the color of the fruit; the leaves are silvery beneath. 'Fastigiata' is a very upright form. 'Pendula' is the reverse, a weeping form whose branches touch the ground; a mature tree is 20 feet (6 m) by 25 feet (7.5 m). 'Rossica' (Russian mountain ash) is an upright, hardy form with a slightly different leaf shape and less prone to fire blight.

Sorbus	**Swedish mountain ash,**
intermedia	**Swedish whitebeam**

Comments: The leaves on this species are partly cut, with broad lobes, and are green above and silvery below. It is more attractive in summer than other mountain ashes because of this.

Hardiness: Canadian zone 3; U.S. zone 3.
Availability: **S**.
Height: 25' (7.5 m). *Spread:* 20' (6 m).
Propagation: Stratified seed.
Soil preferences: Well drained.
Location: Sun.
Good points: This tree does not seem as subject to fire blight. The silvery undersides of the leaves are revealed in a light breeze. The berries are orange-red and hang on well into winter—birds permitting. This is a good tree that should be planted more.
Bad points: Few—except possibly fire blight.
Uses: Specimen tree.

Sorbus x	**Oakleaved**
thuringiaca	**mountain ash**

Comments: This hybrid has leaves that are intermediate between simple and compound, having a few free leaflets at the base with the upper part lobed.

Hardiness: Canadian zone 5; U.S. zone 4.
Availability: **M**.
Height: 25' (7.5 m). *Spread:* 20' (6 m).
Propagation: Cuttings.

Soil preferences: Well drained.
Location: Sun.
Good points: This species has survived when nearby European mountain ashes have died from fire blight. The orange-copper fall color can mask the fruit until the leaves drop.
Bad points: An attack of sawfly larvae can quickly strip the foliage.
Uses: Specimen; shade tree.
Cultivars: 'Fastigiata' is a more upright form, at least for the first 20 years or so. It will become broader with age but the shape can be kept slender with careful pruning.

Styrax japonicus   **Snowbell**

Comments: This attractive small tree has never become popular for some reason. Transplant B & B plants.

Hardiness: Canadian zone 6; U.S. zone 5.
Availability: **S** in Canada; **A** in U.S.
Height: 25' (7.5 m). *Spread:* 30' (9 m).
Propagation: Cuttings.
Soil preferences: Acidic, well drained.
Location: Sun to light shade.
Good points: The white, bell-shaped flowers are more spreading than those of silverbells *(Halesia).* Fruits look like small gray-green pears and, like the flowers, hang below the foliage, which is shiny, deep green, on the upper side of the branches and turns yellow in fall.
Bad points: None.
Uses: Specimen tree.

Tilia spp.   **Linden, basswood**

These shade trees are much used for street planting, especially in Europe. Tea made from the blossoms is said to be helpful in ensuring a good night's sleep. The flowers are rich in nectar, making them good bee plants.

Tilia americana
American linden, basswood

Comments: This large-leaved tree is better suited to country estates than city gardens.

Hardiness: Canadian zone 2b; U.S. zone 2.

Availability: **M**.

Height: 60' (18 m). *Spread:* 40' (12 m).

Propagation: Seed.

Soil preferences: Deep, well drained.

Location: Sun.

Good points: It is a stately tree that transplants easily and has a rounded outline when mature.

Bad points: There are several pests and diseases, but none are fatal. The dense shade it casts makes grass-growing beneath it difficult, especially when trees are young and have low branches.

Uses: Specimen tree.

Cultivars: 'Redmond' is more pyramidal in shape.

Tilia cordata
Little-leaf linden

Comments: At one time this was widely planted as a street tree because it had few problems. Overplanting and monoculture changed minor problems into major ones and borers now limit the use of this plant.

Hardiness: Canadian zone 3; U.S. zone 3.

Availability: **M**.

Height: 60' (18 m). *Spread:* 40' (12 m).

Propagation: Seed; grafting for the named forms.

Soil preferences: Moist.

Location: Sun.

Good points: Its small leaves allow grass to thrive beneath this species. Small yellow flowers are very showy on 'June Bride' but are not as noticeable on the other hybrids.

Bad points: It is prone to aphids and borer when widely planted.

Uses: Shade tree.

Cultivars: 'Glenleven' is fast growing with an open habit. 'Greenspire' has a more narrow form better for small properties. 'June Bride' is pyramidal in shape; it's not readily available but worth searching out for the abundance of fragrant flowers.

Tilia tomentosa
Silver linden

Comments: This species is worth looking for now that it is becoming available. It shows up well in the landscape.

Hardiness: Canadian zone 5; U.S. zone 4.

Availability: **F**.

Height: 50' (15 m). *Spread:* 30' (9 m).

Propagation: Stratified seed.

Soil preferences: Well drained.

Location: Sun.

Good points: The leaves turn in the wind to reveal their silvery undersides and the flowers are very fragrant. Bark is smooth and beech-like when young, adding winter interest.

Bad points: Bees may be stupefied by the flower scent and drop on unsuspecting people beneath the tree.

Uses: Specimen; shade tree.

Cultivars: 'Sterling' has a broad pyramidal shape and extra-silvery leaves.

Ulmus spp.
Elm

This tree was once the symbol of small-town America, but the elm-shaded streets and lawns are a thing of the past. Dutch elm disease has decimated the elm population in much of the country, although in parts of the prairies and the midwest, isolated from the beetle that spreads the disease, elms still flourish.

The American elm *(Ulmus americana)* is very susceptible to Dutch elm disease and its use should be restricted. A young tree will thrive for a time, until the bark gets furrowed enough to attract the bark beetles, then the disease strikes and the tree is doomed. There are a few supposedly resistant strains of American elm, but their availability is very limited at present.

Some of the hybrid elms, using species that are immune to Dutch elm disease, are becoming available, but their mature height and shape is still unclear. 'Homestead' (zone 5 in Canada, 4 in U.S.) is more pyramidal. 'Jacan' (zone 3 in Canada, 3 in U.S.) is vase-shaped. 'Pioneer' (zone 5 in Canada, 4 in U.S.) has a globe to oval outline.

The other common elm, the weeping Camperdown elm, is also prone to Dutch elm disease. They seemed to be thriving when all the American elms were dying round them, but eventually they too turned yellow and died.

Ulmus pumila   Chinese elm, Siberian elm

Comments: Pumila means dwarf—a misnomer for this tree. It is resistant to Dutch elm disease but is not very desirable.

Hardiness: Canadian zone 3; U.S. zone 3.
Availability: **M**.
Height: 50' (15 m). *Spread:* 40' (12 m).
Propagation: Seed.
Soil preferences: Any.
Location: Sun.
Good points: It will grow (and grow) almost anywhere. It gives fast shade on new developments.

Bad points: Brittle and dirty, it sheds twigs and branchlets with reckless abandon. It seeds freely and every seed germinates.
Uses: Hedge (which needs very frequent clipping); windbreak.

Zelkova serrata   Japanese zelkova

Comments: This is a large tree, somewhat similar to elm in shape and often recommended as a replacement, as it is fairly resistant to Dutch elm disease. Transplant B & B stock and prune for shape in fall.
Hardiness: Canadian zone 5b?; U.S. zone 5.
Availability: **A**.
Height: 50' (15 m). *Spread:* 50' (15 m).
Propagation: Stratified seed.
Soil preferences: Well drained.
Location: Sun.
Good points: Deep green leaves turn yellow in fall. The young bark is reddish with white spots, and the older bark may flake off to show a paler inner bark.
Bad points: None serious.
Uses: Specimen; shade tree.
Cultivars: 'Green Vase' was selected for its shape and fast growth. 'Village Green' is an upright form with greater resistance to Dutch elm disease and elm leaf and bark beetles. The foliage turns reddish in fall.

SHRUBS

If trees are the bones of garden design, shrubs must surely be the flesh that covers the bones. Shrubs come in a great array of sizes, shapes and colors. They can give a succession of flower from spring thaw to freeze-up and can then add winter interest to the garden. The majority of shrubs are deciduous; those that keep their leaves are noted. Coniferous shrubs are described later under "Conifers" and some small shrubs, best as ground covers, are under "Ground Covers."

Acer spp.   Maple

The majority of maples are trees and are covered in that section, but two that are grown mostly as shrubs are described here.

Acer palmatum   Japanese maple

Comments: This is one of the plants that tempts me to move a little farther south where it will survive. The Japanese maple and the closely related fullmoon maple *(Acer japonicum)* are beautiful shrubs or small trees with a wide range of forms and colors and are important landscape plants where they are hardy. Plant only B & B or container-grown stock.

Hardiness: Canadian zone 6; U.S. zone 5.

Availability: **M** to **H**.

Height: 20' (6 m). *Spread:* 20' (6 m).

Propagation: Stratified seed for species and varieties; cuttings or grafting for cultivars.

Soil preferences: Well drained.

Location: Dappled shade is best.

Good points: Plants have two leaf forms—regular or deeply dissected—and may be green, red or purple. In general, those with regular leaves grow upright while plants with dissected leaves are weeping. Good fall color on a wonderfully versatile plant.

Bad points: Few. Colored forms may bleach if planted in strong sun, but plants are not harmed.

Uses: Specimen shrub or small tree; borders; accent plant.

Cultivars: There are dozens of cultivars; the following half-dozen of each form are ones I would grow if I could.

Regular leaves *(Acer palmatum)* 'Atropurpureum' has leaves of a purple-red. It is probably the hardiest form and will survive one zone colder than given above, with some tip kill. 'Bloodgood' is a darker red with good fall color. 'Burgundy Lace' is a dark wine red all summer. 'Butterfly' has gray-green leaves edged with cream and a touch of pink. 'Osakazuki' has bright green leaves turning brilliant red in fall. 'Oshia-beni' has orange-red new leaves that turn a bronzy-green with age, and scarlet fall color.

Feathery leaves *(A. palmatum* var. *dissectum)* 'Atropurpureum' has deep purple fern-like foliage. (This is a different 'Atropurpureum' from the one with regular leaves.) 'Crimson Queen' has reddish-purple leaves with the leaves divided into slender lobes. 'Ever Red' is deep red at first, becoming bronzy. 'Garnet' is deep red and faster growing. 'Seiryu' has leaves that are red when young, becoming bright green. 'Viridis' is bright green with a good red fall color.

Acer tataricum ssp. *ginnala*   Amur maple

Comments: This useful small tree or large shrub is attractive all summer long. It is listed as *Acer ginnala* in most catalogs. I prefer the tatarian maple *(A. tataricum)*, which has many leaves without the characteristic three-pronged shape, since most tatarian maple trees have a better, brighter fruit color than Amur maples. They need careful propagating by nurseries to select the brightest forms.

Transplanting shock

1. This tree was transplanted as a large specimen. Sixteen months later the early fall color and twig dieback show it has not yet recovered.

Leaf spots and mildew

2. The holes left by some leaf beetles (here on high bush-cranberry viburnum) can be hard to tell from later stages of leaf spots.

3. Mildew also attacks many trees and shrubs, especially lilac.

Caterpillars

4. In spring, tent caterpillars (seen here), and in fall, webworm, spin their nests and munch on foliage.

Aphids

5. The woolly aphid is easier to spot than the aphid.

Early-flowering trees

Crab apples and hawthorns are some of the first trees to bloom.

6. 'Paul's Scarlet' hawthorn at the University of Guelph Arboretum, Ontario (p. 80)

7. Columnar Siberian crab apple at the Dominion Arboretum in Ottawa, Ontario (p. 87)

Summer-flowering trees

8. Few trees flower in summer but 'June Bride' little-leaf linden gives color as well as shade (p. 102).

Trees with colored foliage

Even when not in flower, some trees provide color interest.

9. This Swedish whitebeam, in a garden in Cold Spring, New York, has silvery foliage (p. 101).

10. 'Tricolor' European beech has leaves of many pinkish tones. This one is at Smith College, Massachusetts (p. 82).

Shapely trees

11. Some plants, like this mature weeping mulberry at George Eastman House, Rochester, New York, are striking without flowers or fancy foliage (p. 90).

Evergreen trees

Conifers provide winter interest in the garden. These two will do well in small gardens for many years.

12. Swiss stone pine keeps its branches down to the ground (p. 158).

13. The weeping form of Nootka false cypress, here at Swarthmore College near Philadelphia, is surprisingly hardy (p. 150).

Fruiting trees

In early fall many trees have interesting fruit.

14. The black berries on the Amur corktree smell of turpentine (p. 91).

15. Crab apple fruit is usually red or yellow but varies greatly in size. Pictured here is 'Indian Magic' (p. 90).

Trees in the fall

Many trees give fall color.

16. 'Morgan' red maple colors well every year (p. 70).

17. The yellow foliage of the katsura tree (p. 78)

Winter bark

When the leaves are gone, bark can still add winter interest.

18. Children playing have polished the almost horizontal branch on a mature Amur corktree at the Arnold Arboretum near Boston (p. 91).

19. This lacebark pine, at the Morris Arboretum near Philadelphia, has multicolored bark (p. 158).

20. Spring in Longwood gardens in Pennsylvania shows off the flaking bark on this 'Heritage' river birch (p. 75).

Spring-flowering shrubs

21. Forsythia 'Northern Gold' is one of the hardiest (p. 118).

22. 'Regent' saskatoon has flowers, fruit and fall color (p. 105).

23. The rose daphne is free-flowering and tough (p. 114).

Flowering cherries

Cherries come in a variety of forms.

24. The double form of flowering almond can be a small tree or a shrub (p. 132).

25. Flowers on purple-leaved sand cherry are often hidden by the opening leaves (p. 130).

Azaleas

26. This azalea in a private garden in Grimsby, Ontario, is the variety 'Narcissiflora' (p. 134). It will bloom well even where temperatures reach -25°F (-32°C).

Viburnums

Viburnum flowers have a variety of shapes.

27. The round globes of European snowball (p. 147).

28. Outside flowers are often much more showy than centre ones.

Lilacs

29. Lilacs come in a wide range of sizes and colors. This hybrid 'Minuet' stays a fairly small bush, good for small gardens (p. 145).

Late-summer shrubs

Shrubs that give late summer interest are harder to find.

30. Recently introduced, Chinese heptacodium flowers in early October at Ottawa, Ontario. It can also be grown as a small tree (p. 85).

Low evergreens

Evergreens play a major part in the landscape.

31. The yellow color of this 'Reingold' cedar accentuates the surrounding plants in this display at the University of Wisconsin (p. 165).

32. Spreading junipers and stones make a tidy, work-free edging to this garden in Boulder, Colorado (p. 171).

Shrubs in the fall

Our gardens would be
dull without the fall color
of shrubs.

33. Many viburnums turn a copper color in fall.

34. Serviceberry turns an orange-red (p. 105).

35. 'Sparkleberry' holly has bright fruit (p. 122).

36. The red chokeberry can also brighten the garden
(p. 106).

A hawthorn hedge

37/38. A hedge of cockspur hawthorn looks good winter and summer and is impenetrable (p. 80).

Other hedges

39. Informal hedges, like this 'Abbotswood' potentilla, do not need clipping on a regular basis (p. 130).

40. This tapestry hedge at White Flower farm in Connecticut uses two different forms of Sawara false-cypress (p. 151).

Ground cover for sun

41. 'Vancouver Gold' woadwaxen in my own garden in Ottawa, Ontario, grows well in full sun (p. 169).

Small-flowered clematis

Some of the lesser-known, small-flowered clematis
42. This Russian virgin's bower is in my garden in Ottawa (p. 180).

43. 'Duchess of Albany' scarlet clematis at the University of Wisconsin is an attractive vine (p. 180).

Attractive vines

44. 'Elegans' porcelain vine, grown mainly for its variegated leaves, is seen here at Sonnenburg House, near Rochester, New York (p. 176).

45. This scarlet trumpet honeysuckle is at Evergreen Farm, Kemptville, Ontario (p. 181).

Vigorous vines

Vigorous vines need
strong support

46/47. Kolomikta vine at
Montreal Botanic Gardens
and in close-up (p. 176)

Wisteria

48. A white form of the Japanese wisteria at Wavehill in Riverdale, New York (p. 183)

49. The hardiest wisteria variety, 'Lawrence', in flower at the Dominion Arboretum, Ottawa, Ontario (p. 183)

Hardiness: Canadian zone 1b; U.S. zone 2.
Availability: **M**.
Height: 20' (6 m). *Spread:* 20' (6 m).
Propagation: Stratified seed.
Soil preferences: Most.
Location: Sun to light shade.
Good points: Creamy white fragrant flowers in spring produce fruit that becomes reddish in midsummer. It is pollution-tolerant and has excellent fall color. It makes a good tree for smaller gardens, and can be grown as an attractive shrubby windbreak.
Bad points: Few.
Uses: Specimen; border; screen.
Cultivars: 'Flame' was selected for fruit color and brilliant fall foliage.

Aesculus parviflora   **Bottlebrush buckeye**

Comments: This is the most readily available shrubby form of this genus, which also contains several trees. In time, it makes a tall shrub with creamy yellow flowers that are very attractive to butterflies, especially swallowtails. Due to its eventual size it may not be appropriate for small city gardens.
Hardiness: Canadian zone 4; U.S. zone 4.
Availability: **F**.
Height: 9' (2.7 m). *Spread:* 15' (4.5 m).
Propagation: Seed, sown when fresh.
Soil preferences: Well drained, slightly acidic.
Location: Sun to light shade.
Good points: The flowers are in loose, upright candles in midsummer and the dark green leaves show off other plants well. It can be cut back almost to the ground if it gets too large.
Bad points: It tends to sucker slowly.
Uses: Specimen shrub; large mixed border.

Amelanchier spp.   **Serviceberry**

Some of the serviceberries are trees and are covered in that section. The following are more shrubby, although you may occasionally find them pruned to a single stem.

Amelanchier   **Saskatoon,**
alnifolia   **Juneberry**

Comments: Growing at the most westerly range of this genus, this species gave its name to a town in Saskatchewan. It is more shrubby than other species, but it can be trained into a small tree. When mixed with buffalo fat, the fruit made pemmican, a staple native food.
Hardiness: Canadian zone 2b; U.S. zone 2.
Availability: **M**.
Height: 10' (3 m). *Spread:* 8' (2.4 m).
Propagation: Stratified seed.
Soil preferences: Moist.
Location: Sun.
Good points: Saskatoon has very bright fall color and good fruit production; several selections have been made for superior fruiting.
Bad points: Cedar-apple rust attacks occasionally if junipers are growing nearby.
Uses: Border; screen; specimen.
Cultivars: 'Regent' is a compact form with good flowers and denser foliage growing about 7 feet (2.1 m) tall.

Amelanchier   **Downy serviceberry,**
arborea   **shadblow, Juneberry**

Comments: This may also be *A. canadensis*, as there is confusion over the correct name, and plants offered under either name are probably the same. The young leaves are very hairy and look gray-green.
Hardiness: Canadian zone 3b; U.S. zone 3.
Availability: **M**.
Height: 20' (6 m). *Spread:* 15' (4.5 m).

Propagation: Stratified seed or cuttings.

Soil preferences: Well drained.

Location: Sun.

Good points: Good flowers, early fruit and great fall color make this plant well worth garden space.

Bad points: Cedar-apple rust can be bad on this species some years.

Uses: Specimen; border.

Amorpha fruticosa   False indigo

Comments: A largish shrub that grows well in poor, sandy soils and is useful for controlling erosion.

Hardiness: Canadian zone 2b; U.S. zone 2.

Availability: **S.**

Height: 15' (4.5 m). *Spread:* 10' (3 m).

Propagation: Seed.

Soil preferences: Most, including very dry.

Location: Sun.

Good points: 6-inch-long (15-cm) spikes of small indigo-blue flowers with yellow stamens are very attractive close up and last for several weeks in midsummer. It can be cut back to the ground in early spring if it becomes overgrown.

Bad points: Seed may be invasive if the conditions are right.

Uses: Border; screen.

Aralia   Hercules club,
spinosa   devil's walking stick

Comments: This is an exotic-looking shrub with large fern-like leaves and spiny stems that is native from Pennsylvania to Florida. The Japanese angelica tree *(Aralia elata)* is similar, but grows twice as large and has leaves over a yard (1 m) long. It is more readily available but not quite as hardy.

Hardiness: Canadian zone 4b; U.S. zone 4.

Availability: **S.**

Height: 15' (4.5 m). *Spread:* 10' (3 m).

Propagation: Seed or division.

Soil preferences: Most.

Location: Sun to light shade.

Good points: The small white flowers are produced over a long period, while the purple fruit attracts the birds. Its exotic appearance makes this shrub a conversation piece.

Bad points: None.

Uses: Specimen; border.

Aronia arbutifolia
and A. melanocarpa   Chokeberry

Comments: There are two slightly different chokeberries, red-fruited and black-fruited. Both form bushy, upright shrubs with good fall color and attractive fruit. As with the chokecherry, the fruit cannot be eaten out of hand, but this is worse—I did a taste comparison!

Hardiness: Canadian zone 4; U.S. zone 4b.

Availability: **F.**

Height: 6-8' (2.4 m). *Spread:* 5' (1.5 m).

Propagation: Stratified seed or softwood cuttings.

Soil preferences: Most soils, but black-fruited does better on wet soils.

Location: Sun to light shade.

Good points: Frothy white flowers in spring turn into attractive fruit, especially the red-fruited, which brings the birds. Good orange to red and magenta fall color that lasts well.

Bad points: It has a somewhat open form if planted singly.

Uses: Mass planting of the species; specimen shrub of the cultivars; worth trying as a hedge.

Cultivars: Red-fruited 'Brilliantissima' has shiny berries. Black-fruited 'Autumn Magic' is a recent University of British Columbia introduction with spectacular fall color.

Berberis spp.   Barberry

Growing most barberries has been banned in Canada for many years because some species are an alternate host to a rust disease on wheat. However, these restrictions are now under review and may be relaxed somewhat, particularly in non-wheat-growing regions. Check with your local Agriculture and Agri-Foods Canada, Plant Protection Division office, to learn which barberries you can grow. In the U.S., barberries are very popular plants but there are some restrictions in certain states. Check with your County Agent if you live where wheat is a major crop.

Berberis julianae   Wintergreen barberry

Comments: An evergreen variety with showy flowers in early summer.
Hardiness: U.S. zone 5b.
Availability: **F** in U.S.
Height: 6' (1.8 m). *Spread:* 4' (1.2 m).
Propagation: Seed; cuttings.
Soil preferences: Slightly acidic and well drained.
Location: Part shade to full sun.
Good points: The yellow flowers are small but showy, and it makes a good informal hedge.
Bad points: It is very spiny and needs protection from drying winter winds, especially at the limits of hardiness.
Uses: Specimen plant; informal hedge.

Berberis x mentorensis   Mentor barberry

Comments: This is a cross between the Japanese and wintergreen barberries that was raised in Mentor, Ohio, hence the common name.
Hardiness: U.S. zone 5.
Availability: **F** in U.S.
Height: 5' (1.5 m). *Spread:* 6' (1.8 m).
Propagation: Cuttings.
Soil preferences: Well drained.
Location: Part shade to sun.

Good points: The small yellow flowers are not as showy as the wintergreen barberry, but neither is it as viciously spiny. It has good orange-red fall color.
Bad points: None.
Uses: Specimen plant; people-proof hedge.

Berberis thunbergii   Japanese barberry

Comments: The Japanese barberry is the most widely grown of all the barberries and has many interesting forms and cultivars. The species itself has green leaves but the variety *atropurpurea* has red to purple foliage.
Hardiness: U.S. zone 4.
Availability: **A** in U.S.
Height: 6' (1.8 m). *Spread:* 7' (2.1 m).
Propagation: Seed; cuttings.
Soil preferences: Well drained.
Location: Sun.
Good points: It leafs out early in spring and has small, bright yellow, pendulous flowers followed by bright red berries that last well into winter.
Bad points: The small, very sharp spines make it unpleasant to handle.
Uses: Hedge or barrier (the spines make it most effective); specimen and foundation plant.
Cultivars: 'Crimson Pygmy' is a red-leaved dwarf form. 'Rosy Glow' has pink-tinged new foliage that turns green with time. 'Aurea' has yellow foliage. There are many other named forms available in the U.S.

Buddleja spp.   Butterfly bush

As the common name suggests, these shrubs are most attractive to butterflies and, once the flowers open, there are always butterflies dancing around the flower spikes. You will probably find this spelled *Buddleia* on nursery tags.

Buddleja alternifolia   **Fountain buddleia**

Comments: This good small shrub should be grown more. Unlike the more common *B. davidii*, it flowers on the old wood and should be pruned after flowering, rather than in spring.

Hardiness: Canadian zone 4b; U.S. zone 4.

Availability: **S**.

Height: 6' (1.8 m). *Spread:* 6' (1.8 m).

Propagation: Seed or softwood cuttings.

Soil preferences: Well drained.

Location: Sun.

Good points: Arching branches bear pink-lavender flowers in June amid gray-green foliage. The arching shape gives an interesting winter silhouette and it can be trained on a single stem into a small tree.

Bad points: None.

Uses: Specimen shrub; mixed border.

Cultivars: 'Argentea' has silvery leaves but it is seldom available.

Buddleja davidii   **Butterfly bush**

Comments: Like bush clover *(Lespedezia)*, this shrub is valuable for its late flowering. It is a glorious weed in Britain, where it grows in the tops of old walls, along railway embankments and on road verges. Residents probably curse it though.

Hardiness: Canadian zone 5b-6; U.S. zone 5.

Availability: **A**.

Height: 10' (3 m). *Spread:* 8' (2.4 m).

Propagation: Seed for the species; semi-ripe cuttings for cultivars.

Soil preferences: Well drained.

Location: Sun.

Good points: A useful late-flowering shrub that should be cut back hard in spring to promote new growth. It is not quite hardy for me, but plants are not expensive and will flower the first year so I grow it as an annual. In a mild winter the roots may survive in Canadian zone 5.

Bad points: It tends to be weedy when conditions suit it.

Uses: Massing; mixed border; wildlife gardens.

Cultivars: There are many named forms in shades of blue-lilac, pink, purple and white.

Buxus hybrids   **Boxwood**

Comments: These are generally low-growing evergreen shrubs and are much used farther south. For northern climates, hybrids of the Korean and common boxwoods are the best choice. Korean box *(Buxus koreana)* turns a yellowish color in winter, but is the hardiest.

Hardiness: Canadian zone 5; U.S. zone 4.

Availability: **A**.

Height: 2-5' (60-150 cm). *Spread:* 3' (90 cm).

Propagation: Cuttings in a plastic tent.

Soil preferences: Well drained.

Location: Sun to part shade.

Good points: Ideal for dwarf hedges or as small foundation plants, they are attractive in winter where the climate is not too severe.

Bad points: Boxwoods desiccate badly in winter, especially at the limits of hardiness, so provide protection from winds.

Uses: Clipped formal hedge; dwarf topiary; foundation planting.

Cultivars: 'Green Gem' is ball-shaped and olive green. 'Green Mountain' is the most readily available form and pyramidal in shape. 'Green Mound' makes a dark green hummock. 'Green Velvet' is very slow growing and suitable for larger rock gardens.

Calycanthus floridus   **Carolina allspice**

Comments: A native shrub with rather strange brownish-red flowers that dry well for use in winter arrangements. Found in the wild from Virginia to Florida, it is surprisingly hardy.

Hardiness: Canadian zone 5; U.S. zone 4.
Availability: **F**.
Height: 6' (1.8 m). *Spread:* 6' (1.8 m).
Propagation: Fresh seed or softwood cuttings.
Soil preferences: Moist.
Location: Sun to shade.
Good points: Scattered, artificial-looking, dark red flowers with narrow petals open from late spring to late summer. The dark green foliage has a spicy fragrance, especially when crushed, and turns yellow in fall.
Bad points: The flowers are not very showy; don't plant it for floral effect.
Uses: Specimen; plant close to a sitting area where the foliage scent can be appreciated.

Caragana spp.   **Peashrub**

These tough, hardy shrubs and small trees are much used as shelterbelts on the prairies, and as foundation plants elsewhere. They survive on poor soils.

Caragana arborescens   **Siberian peashrub**

Comments: A tough plant much used as a shelter belt, it can be cut back almost to ground level when it becomes overgrown and will quickly regrow.
Hardiness: Canadian zone 2; U.S. zone 2.
Availability: **M**.
Height: 15' (4.5 m). *Spread:* 15' (4.5 m).
Propagation: Seed.
Soil preferences: Almost any.
Location: Sun.
Good points: A very tough plant with yellow flowers in late spring; it will thrive in dry and poor soils.
Bad points: The explosive seed pods spread seeds far and wide, and then they germinate.
Uses: Screen; shelter belt; hedge; specimen.
Cultivars: 'Lorbergii' is a form with the leaflets reduced almost to threads. 'Pendula' is a weeping form that is grafted onto an upright stem. 'Walker' is a cross between 'Lorbergii' and 'Pendula'—a strongly weeping plant with thread-like leaves. Like 'Pendula' they are grafted and plants can be obtained at various heights.

Caragana aurantiaca   **Orange peashrub**
Caragana frutex   **Russian peashrub**
Caragana pygmea   **Dwarf peashrub**

Comments: All three species are low-growing plants useful as hedging and foundation plants in harsh climates or on poor soils.
Hardiness: Canadian zone 2b; U.S. zone 2.
Availability: **M**.
Height: Dwarf and orange peashrub to 4' (1.2 m); Russian peashrub to 6' (1.8 m).
Spread: 4' (1.2 m).
Propagation: Seed.
Soil preferences: Any but wet.
Location: Sun.
Good points: Very adaptable, they will take poor soils and salt and survive in windswept locations and similar harsh sites. Yellow (or orange) flowers appear in late spring.
Bad points: These shrubs tend to be weedy and seed freely, but are not as bad as the Siberian peashrub.
Uses: Foundation; low screen; hedge.
Cultivars: C. frutex 'Globosa' is a dwarf form only 2 feet (60 cm) tall that is good as a low hedge.

Cephalanthus occidentalis   **Buttonbush**

Comments: Native from New Brunswick to Florida and Mexico, buttonbush grows best in wet areas, but it will also do well on dryer soils. The fruit looks like small round buttons.
Hardiness: Canadian zone 5; U.S. zone 4.
Availability: **S** to **H**.

Height: 12' (3.5 m). *Spread:* 15' (4.5 m).
Propagation: Softwood cuttings.
Soil preferences: Moist to wet.
Location: Sun.
Good points: Small white, pincushion-like flowers are borne on the ends of branches in midsummer and become persistent brown, circular fruit that shows up well against the glossy green foliage.
Bad points: It becomes floppy with age; cut back almost to soil level to renew.
Uses: Wet area; mass planting.

Chaenomeles spp.   **Flowering quince**

Comments: Selections of the common quince *(C. speciosa)*, and several cultivars of the cross between it and the Japanese quince *(C. japonica)* are sold, but only a few are readily available. Plant only B & B or container-grown stock.
Hardiness: Canadian zone 5-5b; U.S. zone 4.
Availability: **A.**
Height: 6' (1.8 m). *Spread:* 6' (1.8 m).
Propagation: Cuttings.
Soil preferences: Most, except very alkaline.
Location: Sun to very light shade.
Good points: Spring flowers are in a range of colors from bright red to white. Fruit, which can be made into jam and preserves, is better after a frost, or can be left on the plant for winter decoration. This plant makes a good wall shrub and a crashproof informal hedge. At the limits of its range, plant it where good snow cover can be expected.
Bad points: Few, but the thorns are vicious on most cultivars.
Uses: Border; foundation; wall shrub; hedge.
Cultivars: 'Cameo' has double apricot-pink flowers and is thornless. 'Crimson & Gold' has red flowers with a pronounced yellow center; it is the hardiest form. 'Jet Trail' has white

flowers freely born on a spreading plant. 'Rubra' is an older, dark red form. 'Texas Scarlet' has about the brightest red flowers on a spreading plant and makes a good wall shrub. 'Toyo Nishiki' is more upright, with red, pink and white flowers on the same plant.

Clethra alnifolia   **Summersweet**

Comments: Native to the eastern seaboard, this shrub flowers when few other shrubs are blooming. Its natural habitat is moist woods, but it does well in dryer locations in the garden, not getting quite as tall. Transplant B & B or container-grown specimens.
Hardiness: Canadian zone 4b; U.S. zone 4.
Availability: **A.**
Height: 6' (1.8 m). *Spread:* 5' (1.5 m).
Propagation: Cuttings.
Soil preferences: Moist, acidic.
Location: Light shade.
Good points: Long panicles of fragrant white flowers bloom in July over bright green leaves that turn golden in the fall; it is salt-tolerant and so is good for city planting.
Bad points: It is subject to mites, especially on dry soils.
Uses: Border; specimen.
Cultivars: 'Paniculata' has bigger flower trusses on a more vigorous plant. 'Pink Spire' buds and flowers are pink, fading slightly as they open. 'Rosea' buds and flowers are pale pink fading to near white, while the leaves are a much darker green.

Colutea arborescens   **Bladder senna**

Comments: I don't know why this plant is not better known. The flowers, while small, are produced over a long period, and the inflated seed pods are tinged pink.
Hardiness: Canadian zone 5; U.S. zone 4.
Availability: **H.**

Height: 8' (2.4 m). *Spread:* 6' (1.8 m).
Propagation: Scarified seed.
Soil preferences: Sandy.
Location: Sun.
Good points: The pea-like orange and red flowers are carried on short spikes from midsummer to late fall. They are still opening in September when the seed pods are most attractive (and fun to pop!).
Bad points: It needs renewal pruning to keep it shapely.
Uses: Specimen shrub. It would probably make a good windbreak.

Cornus spp.   Dogwood

This genus also contains trees and ground covers, described elsewhere in this chapter. The shrub forms are versatile plants that grow in sun or shade, and some like wet feet.

Cornus alba   Tatarian dogwood

Comments: This is the European version of our red osier. The variegated forms are most useful since they do not lose their variegation in shade, unlike most other plants. Twig color is more muted early in the winter.
Hardiness: Canadian zone 2; U.S. zone 2.
Availability: **M**.
Height: 8' (2.4 m). *Spread:* 5' (1.5 m).
Propagation: Cuttings; layering.
Soil preferences: Moist, well drained.
Location: Sun to medium shade.
Good points: This shrub has a fairly tidy shape that doesn't spread like the red osier.
Bad points: Plants may suffer from scale.
Uses: Screen; border; foundation; informal hedge.
Cultivars: 'Argenteo-marginata', often called 'Elegantissima' in catalogs, has leaves with a cream margin and good red twigs on young growth. 'Gouchaultii' has leaf margins of yellow and pink, with pink-tinged leaf centers

and twigs that are oxblood red. 'Sibirica' has bright red stems and pale blue fruit. 'Spaethii' is similar to 'Gouchaultii' but without the pink tinge and with a more pronounced yellow. It is smaller at maturity.

Cornus mas   Cornelian cherry

Comments: This is the first dogwood to flower— midwinter in mild climates.
Hardiness: Canadian zone 4; U.S. zone 4.
Availability: **A**.
Height: 20' (6 m). *Spread:* 15' (4.5 m).
Propagation: Stratified seed or cuttings.
Soil preferences: Most, except wet.
Location: Sun to light shade.
Good points: The branches are covered in small yellow flowers before the leaves. Unlike most dogwoods, it is the flowers that are attractive, not the bracts. The red fruit in fall is edible and rich in vitamin C.
Bad points: None.
Uses: Border; screen.

Cornus racemosa   Gray dogwood

Comments: This is a good plant for difficult locations where little else can be made to grow.
Hardiness: Canadian zone 2b; U.S. zone 2.
Availability: **M**.
Height: 10' (3 m). *Spread:* 10' (3 m).
Propagation: Stratified seed.
Soil preferences: Any, including gravel.
Location: Sun to part shade.
Good points: It has white flowers in late spring and white fruit that attract birds, while the reddish fall color is good, but not brilliant. The chief benefit is its ability to grow in the poorest soils.
Bad points: None.
Uses: Border; screen.

Cornus stolonifera   **Red osier dogwood**

Comments: This plant had a name change a few years ago which hasn't reached all the nurseries yet, so you may find it labeled *C. sericea*. It is a useful shrub, especially for the winter effect of the twigs. Cut it back almost to the ground in spring occasionally to promote new growth with the brightest color. It was used to make baskets, hence the name osier.

Hardiness: Canadian zone 2; U.S. zone 2.

Availability: **M**.

Height: 8' (2.4 m). *Spread:* 10' (3 m).

Propagation: Cuttings; layering.

Soil preferences: Moist (but adaptable).

Location: Sun to light shade.

Good points: White flowers in early summer produce white to steel-blue fruit that birds love. It spreads by stolons—prostrate stems (like a strawberry)—and is good for retaining banks. It has good fall color.

Bad points: May get scale infestations.

Uses: Hedge; ground cover; erosion control.

Cultivars: 'Cardinal' is the best red-stemmed selection. 'Flaviramea', the yellow-twigged form, is very effective against red brick. 'Isanti' is a shorter form with good twig color. 'Kelseyi', a dwarf form to 30 inches (75 cm), is the best ground cover but does not have as good winter twig color.

Corylus spp.   **Filbert, hazel**

A group of large shrubs (and one small tree) some of which are used commercially for nut production in warmer climates. Some of the shrubs are very decorative and worth a place in the garden.

Corylus americana   **American filbert**

Comments: This native shrub has edible nuts but they are small and do not compare with the European filbert for crackability or yield.

Hardiness: Canadian zone 4; U.S. zone 4.

Availability: **A**.

Height: 10' (3 m). *Spread:* 10' (3 m).

Propagation: Seed.

Soil preferences: Most (including poor soils).

Location: Sun.

Good points: The decorative catkins open in early spring, before the leaves, and can be forced into early bloom indoors. This species grows well in poor soils, including gravel, but is much smaller in these conditions.

Bad points: None.

Uses: Screen; stabilizing bank; wildlife food.

Corylus   **European filbert,**
avellana   **European hazel**

Comments: Some forms of this have been selected for their superior nut production, others for their horticultural appeal.

Hardiness: Canadian zone 5; U.S. zone 4.

Availability: **A**.

Height: 15' (4.5 m). *Spread:* 10' (3 m).

Propagation: Seed or grafting.

Soil preferences: Most.

Location: Sun.

Good points: The species itself is rarely grown, but the two cultivars listed are worth looking for and are good garden plants.

Bad points: Grafted plants may produce suckers from the roots and can revert to the species if these are not pruned off.

Uses: Specimen shrub.

Cultivars: 'Aurea' is a yellow-leaved form that is hard to find. 'Contorta', known as Harry Lauder's walking stick, is readily available. It has strangely twisted and contorted branches much used for Japanese-style flower arrangements.

Cotinus coggygria Smokebush, smoketree

Comments: The visual impact of this large shrub comes from the hairs on the flower and fruit stalks that give the appearance of smoke. Some of the cultivars with purple foliage are attractive all summer long.

Hardiness: Canadian zone 5; U.S. zone 4.
Availability: **M**.
Height: 15' (4.5 m). *Spread:* 20' (6 m).
Propagation: Cuttings.
Soil preferences: Well drained.
Location: Sun.
Good points: The smoke effect is best in late summer and early fall. The purple-leaved forms have a pinkish look. In my opinion, the species has a better fall color (glowing yellow) than the named forms.
Bad points: Few. Pruning the purple-leaved forms hard in spring gives brighter foliage, but at the expense of flowers—and smoke.
Uses: Specimen; border; screen.
Cultivars: 'Royal Purple' has the best (darkest) purple foliage and keeps its color all summer long.

Cotoneaster spp.   Cotoneaster

This group of small shrubs and ground covers (see "Ground Covers" later in chapter) is grown for the bright berries. It is pronounced cot-own-ee-aster, not coton-easter.

Cotoneaster lucidus   Hedge cotoneaster

Comments: Much used for hedging, this good, upright, deciduous plant is worthy of more general use. Buy container-grown or B & B plants.
Hardiness: Canadian zone 2; U.S. zone 3.
Availability: **A**.
Height: 8' (2.4 m). *Spread:* 6' (1.8 m).
Propagation: Scarified seed or cuttings.

Soil preferences: Most, except very heavy.
Location: Sun to light shade.
Good points: Shiny, dark green foliage becomes reddish in fall. Pink flowers give black fruit that lasts into winter and feeds the birds.
Bad points: None.
Uses: Hedging; border.

Cytisus spp.   Broom

Comments: The descriptions below apply to both the common, or Scotch, broom and the Warminster broom. European catalogs list a multitude of cultivars with brighter flowers, but few are available here. Pity! The varieties available have cream or yellow flowers in spring.
Hardiness: Canadian zone 5b; U.S. zone 5.
Availability: **S**.
Height: 5' (1.5 m). *Spread:* 5' (1.5 m).
Propagation: Seed, cuttings.
Soil preferences: Sandy.
Location: Sun.
Good points: The plants are very attractive in flower, have a good form when not, and are salt-tolerant.
Bad points: Older plants die suddenly for no apparent reason, but self-sown seedlings will grow as replacements. The explosive seed pods spread seed and this can be a problem, especially in milder regions.
Uses: Shrub border; brooms go well with heaths and heathers.
Cultivars: 'Allgold' and 'Warminster' are yellow, 'Moonlight' is cream.

Daphne spp.   Daphne

Named for a nymph in Greek mythology, the following three species are the easiest to grow and find of the many in the genus.

Daphne x *burkwoodii*   Burkwood daphne

Comments: A hybrid with rose daphne as one parent, it is later flowering (May-June) but equally fragrant.

Hardiness: Canadian zone 4; U.S. zone 4.

Availability: **A**.

Height: 4' (1.2 m). *Spread:* 5' (1.5 m).

Propagation: Cuttings.

Soil preferences: Not heavy and wet.

Location: Sun.

Good points: A mound-shaped shrub with fragrant pink-tinged flowers, it is attractive even when out of flower.

Bad points: The berries are poisonous.

Uses: Specimen; foundation; mixed border.

Cultivars: 'Carol Mackie' has leaves with a narrow white margin. 'Somerset' is the most commonly found form with green leaves. 'Arthur Burkwood' is slightly shorter; plants without a name are probably this cultivar.

Daphne   Rose daphne,
cneorum   garland flower

Comments: This daphne is a low-growing plant with evergreen foliage. It is very fragrant, and fills the air with the perfume of its flowers in midspring.

Hardiness: Canadian zone 2b; U.S. zone 2.

Availability: **M**.

Height: 1' (30 cm). *Spread:* 3' (90 cm).

Propagation: Stratified seed.

Soil preferences: Sandy, poor, well drained.

Location: Sun to light shade.

Good points: The rose-pink flowers smother the plant and even when not in bloom the shape is attractive.

Bad points: Established plants are noted for dying rapidly for no apparent reason. Mine did.

Uses: Large rock garden; front of a border.

Cultivars: 'Ruby Glow' has flowers of a darker pink.

Daphne mezereum   February daphne

Comments: Although it will not bloom in February for most of us, it is one of the first shrubs to flower. Plant only container-grown stock.

Hardiness: Canadian zone 4; U.S. zone 3b.

Availability: **M**.

Height: 4' (1.2 m). *Spread:* 4' (1.2 m).

Propagation: Seed.

Soil preferences: Well drained to sandy and poor.

Location: Sun.

Good points: Fragrant, rose-purple flowers tell us spring has arrived. It can be cut and forced indoors for extra-early bloom.

Bad points: Seed is poisonous, and it sets seed freely.

Uses: Specimen; foundation; mixed border.

Cultivars: 'Alba' has flowers of an off-white shade.

Deutzia spp.   Deutzia

This group of small to medium shrubs is closely related to mock orange. They have daintier, somewhat bell-shaped white flowers, but are not fragrant and are slightly later-flowering.

Deutzia gracilis   Slender deutzia

Comments: This species grows with somewhat arching branches, so allow room for it to spread.

Hardiness: Canadian zone 5b; U.S. zone 4.

Availability: **M**.

Height: 4' (1.2 m). *Spread:* 6' (1.8 m).

Propagation: Cuttings.

Soil preferences: Slightly acidic.

Location: Sun.

Good points: It is very free-flowering with upright clusters of white blooms.

Bad points: Winter twig dieback makes frequent renewal pruning necessary.

Uses: Specimen; foundation; informal hedge.

Deutzia x lemoinei   **Lemoine's deutzia**

Comments: A hybrid with the slender deutzia as one parent, this is the hardiest deutzia.

Hardiness: Canadian zone 5; U.S. zone 4.

Availability: **A**.

Height: 5' (1.5 m). *Spread:* 5' (1.5 m).

Propagation: Cuttings.

Soil preferences: Slightly acidic.

Location: Sun.

Good points: Clusters of white flowers appear in late spring.

Bad points: It may get winter twig dieback.

Uses: Specimen; foundation; shrub border.

Cultivars: 'Compacta' grows only 4 feet (1.2 m) tall and is slightly hardier. Do not confuse this with the Nikko deutzia (*D. crenata* 'Nikko'), which is only 2 feet (60 cm) high and very free-flowering.

Deutzia scabra   **Fuzzy deutzia**

Comments: This is the last to flower of the three deutzias commonly available.

Hardiness: Canadian zone 6; U.S. zone 5.

Availability: **A**.

Height: 6' (1.8 m). *Spread:* 8' (2.4 m).

Propagation: Cuttings.

Soil preferences: Slightly acidic.

Location: Sun.

Good points: Its copious white flowers are tinged pink on the outside.

Bad points: Gets winter twig dieback at the limits of its range and may need annual pruning.

Uses: Specimen; foundation; shrub border.

Cultivars: 'Godsall Pink' has double flowers of a strawberry-ice-cream pink. 'Pride of Rochester' is also double, but a paler pink.

Dirca palustris   **Leatherwood**

Comments: This small shrub is native to most of the eastern seaboard, from New Brunswick to Florida. It has very pliable shoots that were used by native people and early settlers for baskets and lashings.

Hardiness: Canadian zone 4; U.S. zone 4.

Availability: **H**.

Height: 4' (1.2 m). *Spread:* 4' (1.2 m).

Propagation: Stratified seed.

Soil preferences: Moist and acidic.

Location: Sun to light shade.

Good points: Yellow flowers appear in early spring before the light green leaves, which turn yellow in the fall.

Bad points: None.

Uses: Border; naturalizing.

Elaeagnus spp.   **Hardy olive**

This group of plants is grown for its silvery foliage, fragrant flowers and fall fruit, which is also silvery. All are good on poor soils, as they have a symbiotic relationship with nitrogen-fixing bacteria that can convert the nitrogen in the air into a form usable by plants.

Elaeagnus angustifolius   **Russian olive**

Comments: This is a much-used large shrub or small tree that makes a wonderful silver accent plant.

Hardiness: Canadian zone 2; U.S. zone 2.

Availability: **M**.

Height: 15' (4.5 m). *Spread:* 12' (3.5 m).

Propagation: Stratified seed.

Soil preferences: Light.

Location: Sun.

Good points: It is very adaptable and salt-tolerant. Bright yellow flowers perfume the air in late spring. The edible, if rather mealy, fruit is used as a food in its native Russia.

Bad points: The wood is somewhat brittle and can be damaged in storms. There are small spines on the branches, but these are not a major hazard.

Uses: Specimen; border; screen.

Elaeagnus commutata **Silverberry**

Comments: A native shrub found over much of the more northerly and eastern parts of North America that has silvery foliage and fruit.
Hardiness: Canadian zone 2; U.S. zone 2.
Availability: **M.**
Height: 10' (3 m). *Spread:* 10' (3 m).
Propagation: Seed (or dig up suckers).
Soil preferences: Poor.
Location: Sun.
Good points: This shrub is a good choice for soil conservation and windbreaks. The silvery-yellow flowers are very fragrant.
Bad points: It suckers freely (a good point when used to stabilize soil).
Uses: Screen; border.

Elaeagnus umbellatus **Autumn olive**

Comments: Leaves are silvery on the underside, green above. The fruit is not as tasty as that of Russian olive.
Hardiness: Canadian zone 5; U.S. zone 4.
Availability: **A.**
Height: 12' (3.5 m). *Spread:* 15' (4.5 m).
Propagation: Stratified seed.
Soil preferences: Poor.
Location: Sun.
Good points: Pale yellow, fragrant flowers give rise to fruit that is silvery at first, red when ripe.
Bad points: It can become weedy; birds eat the fruit and spread the seed.
Uses: Specimen; screen.
Cultivars: 'Cardinal' has brighter fruit; it was introduced for soil conservation as it is more drought-tolerant.

Enkianthus **Redvein**
campanulatus **enkianthus**

Comments: Related to heaths and heathers, this forms an attractive, medium-sized shrub.
Hardiness: Canadian zone 5b; U.S. zone 4.

Availability: **A.**
Height: 10' (3 m). *Spread:* 6' (1.8 m).
Propagation: Seed.
Soil preferences: Acidic.
Location: Sun to light shade.
Good points: It bears numerous small, light pink, bell-shaped flowers in late spring and has good fall color.
Bad points: None.
Uses: Specimen shrub; companion plant for heaths and heathers.

Euonymus spp. **Euonymus**

Euonymus have a variety of common names, such as hearts-a-bustin'-with-love and fishwood, but these tend to be very regional. Fruit capsules burst open to reveal a colored interior and often bright, contrasting seeds. One tree of this genus is listed in the "Deciduous Tree" section of this chapter and some low plants are listed under "Ground Covers."

Euonymus **Winged euonymus,**
alatus **burningbush**

Comments: A small to medium shrub with a wide-spread habit.
Hardiness: Canadian zone 3; U.S. zone 3.
Availability: **M.**
Height: 10' (3 m). *Spread:* 15' (4.5 m).
Propagation: Stratified seed.
Soil preferences: Well drained.
Location: Sun.
Good points: The corky ridges on the bark add winter interest and give rise to the common name. It has good reliable fall color and attractive fruit after leaf drop.
Bad points: Few; not as likely to get scale.
Uses: Border; screen; hedge; foundation.
Cultivars: 'Compactus' is smaller and makes a better hedge, but the bark wings are not as pronounced, so there is less winter effect.

Euonymus nanus   **Dwarf**
var. *turkestanicus*   **euonymus**

Comments: It makes an attractive hedge but in harsh climates it may only last a few years before developing gaps.
Hardiness: Canadian zone 2; U.S. zone 2.
Availability: **M**.
Height: 3' (.9 m). *Spread:* 3' (.9 m).
Propagation: Cuttings.
Soil preferences: Well drained.
Location: Sun.
Good points: Fruit is pink outside, orange inside, but it is grown mainly for its brilliant red fall color; the summer leaves are gray-green.
Bad points: It is very susceptible to scale, especially in warmer regions.
Uses: Border; hedge; foundation.

Exochorda x macrantha   **Pearlbush**

Comments: The single cultivar is by far the most popular of all the pearlbushes, partly because it is more refined, but mostly because of its free-flowering habit.
Hardiness: Canadian zone 5; U.S. zone 4.
Availability: **A**.
Height: 5' (1.5 m). *Spread:* 5' (1.5 m).
Propagation: Cuttings.
Soil preferences: Well drained.
Location: Sun.
Good points: Masses of white flowers cover somewhat arching branches in spring.
Bad points: The plant is of little interest for the rest of the year.
Uses: Border; screen; foundation.
Cultivars: 'The Bride' has larger and more numerous flowers.

Forsythia spp.   **Forsythia**

This plant was named for William Forsyth, head gardener to King George III at Kensington Palace, and should be pronounced like his name, not for-sith-ia. The bright yellow flowers make it one of our best-known spring-flowering shrubs.

Forsythia x intermedia   **Border forsythia**

Comments: This shrub is hardier than the zone given below, but the flower buds are only hardy to the zone listed and flowers are the main reason to grow it.
Hardiness: Canadian zone 6; U.S. zone 5.
Availability: **A**.
Height: 10' (3 m). *Spread:* 10' (3 m).
Propagation: Cuttings.
Soil preferences: Well drained.
Location: Sun.
Good points: Spring flowers of bright yellow put on an outstanding display. Branches can be cut in late winter and forced into early bloom indoors.
Bad points: It needs frequent renewal pruning to prevent it from becoming a jungle.
Uses: Border; large specimen.
Cultivars: 'Lynwood' (or 'Lynwood Gold') is a more upright and free-flowering selection. 'Spectabilis' is an old variety, but still one of the best for quantity of blooms. 'Spring Glory' has large flowers, freely produced.

Forsythia ovata   **Early forsythia**

Comments: Flowers are smaller than on other forsythias, but open earlier.
Hardiness: Canadian zone 5b; U.S. zone 4.
Availability: **M**.
Height: 6' (1.8 m). *Spread:* 5' (1.5 m).
Propagation: Cuttings.
Soil preferences: Well drained.
Location: Sun.
Good points: This is often the first shrub to flower in spring.
Bad points: The rapid growth makes annual pruning a must on established plants.
Uses: Border; specimen; informal hedge.

Cultivars: 'Ottawa' has flower buds that are hardier and plants will bloom reliably in zone 4 at least. 'Tetragold' has larger flowers and is even earlier.

| **Forsythia** | **Weeping forsythia,** |
| **suspensa** | **goldenbells** |

Comments: Its arching habit makes this plant distinctive. It forms a dense thicket if not pruned, which makes it useful as an informal hedge on large properties.
Hardiness: Canadian zone 5b; U.S. zone 4.
Availability: **A.**
Height: 8' (2.4 m). *Spread:* 8' (2.4 m).
Propagation: Cuttings.
Soil preferences: Well drained.
Location: Sun.
Good points: This large shrub is most attractive when in bloom.
Bad points: The spreading form means it takes up a lot of room.
Uses: Border; informal hedge.

Hybrid forsythia

Several other forsythias are readily available that are hybrids of the various species. They have been selected for their improved flower bud hardiness, chiefly by breeders in colder regions.

'Arnold Dwarf' is a low ground cover that flowers only sparsely and is no hardier than the rest. 'Beatrix Farrand', introduced for its darker flowers, is also not hardier. 'Happy Centennial' is a free-flowering dwarf that forms a mat about 12 inches (30 cm) high by 4 feet (120 cm) across; it is hardy to zone 4 at least and will probably replace 'Arnold Dwarf' in time. 'Meadowlark', 'Northern Gold' and 'Northern Sun' are fairly recent introductions selected for their flower hardiness. They are worth trying in Canadian zone 4, U.S. zone 3b.

| **Fothergilla** spp. | **Fothergilla** |

These shrubs have spreading branches and a mounded shape and are native to the southeastern United States. Dr. John Fothergill was an English physician who specialized in growing American plants, then new and exotic, in the mid-1700s.

| **Fothergilla gardenii** | **Dwarf fothergilla** |

Comments: This attractive shrub should be more widely grown.
Hardiness: Canadian zone 5b; U.S. zone 4.
Availability: **A** to **S**.
Height: 3' (.9 m). *Spread:* 4' (1.2 m).
Propagation: Softwood cuttings.
Soil preferences: Acid and humusy.
Location: Sun to light shade.
Good points: Fragrant white flowers open in spring on a nicely rounded bush; it has good fall color.
Bad points: None.
Uses: Border; screen; hedge.
Cultivars: 'Blue Mist' has leaves with a bluish tinge, but they don't color as well in the fall. It may not be quite as hardy.

| **Fothergilla major** | **Large fothergilla** |

Comments: Similar to the dwarf fothergilla but taller and slower growing.
Hardiness: Canadian zone 5b; U.S. zone 4.
Availability: **A** to **S**.
Height: 8' (2.4 m). *Spread:* 6' (1.8 m).
Propagation: Softwood cuttings.
Soil preferences: Acidic.
Location: Sun.
Good points: The fragrant flowers appear before the leaves and the fall color is bright.
Bad points: None.
Uses: Border; screen; hedge; specimen.

Hamamelis **spp.**   **Witch hazel**

This is a group of very interesting shrubs that flower when little else is in bloom and have small clusters of blooms with bright, strap-like petals. The liniment is extracted from the common witch hazel.

Hamamelis mollis   **Chinese witch hazel**

Comments: This species grows into a large shrub or small tree that has the typical witch hazel flowers. Transplant B & B stock and prune in spring if needed.

Hardiness: Canadian zone 6; U.S. zone 5.

Availability: **F**.

Height: 20' (6 m). *Spread:* 20' (6 m).

Propagation: Stratified seed.

Soil preferences: Well drained, acidic.

Location: Sun.

Good points: It bears fragrant yellow flowers in late winter and early spring (February-March where this species is hardy) and has good yellow fall color.

Bad points: The flowers may be damaged by late frosts.

Uses: Specimen tree or shrub.

Cultivars: The following are hybrids of this species and the Japanese witch hazel *(H. japonica)*. Propagate them by cuttings. 'Arnold Promise' has fragrant yellow flowers with petals about 1 inch (2.5 cm) long; the base of the flower is reddish. It flowers in late winter and the flowers last a long time. 'Diane' has dull red, slightly fragrant flowers; the foliage turns yellow and red in fall. 'Jelena' has petals that are red at the base and yellow at the top, so the plant seems orange from a distance; it has good fall color. 'Ruby Glow' flowers are copper-colored with a red sheen and a wine-red base.

Hamamelis vernalis   **Vernal witch hazel**

Comments: This is the earliest of the witch hazels to bloom, although it has the smallest flowers. Plant B & B or container-grown plants. It makes a rounded shrub.

Hardiness: Canadian zone 5b; U.S. zone 4.

Availability: **H** in Canada; **A** in U.S.

Height: 8' (2.4 m). *Spread:* 10' (3 m).

Propagation: Stratified seed.

Soil preferences: Moist.

Location: Sun to mid-shade.

Good points: Flowering starts in January and can continue for a month. The petals roll up in cold weather and seem to escape injury. Flowers vary from yellow to orange, depending on the plant, and are quite fragrant.

Bad points: None.

Uses: Specimen; screen; border.

Cultivars: Several have been selected for early flowering or better color, but they are very hard to locate.

Hamamelis   **Common**
virginiana   **witch hazel**

Comments: Bright yellow flowers bloom from October to hard frost. It makes a good hedge, flowering even when trimmed. Reputedly twigs of this species are the best of all shrubs for water divining.

Hardiness: Canadian zone 4b; U.S. zone 4.

Availability: **M**.

Height: 10-15' (3-4.5 m). *Spread:* 10' (3 m).

Propagation: Stratified seed.

Soil preferences: Moist.

Location: Sun to shade.

Good points: It has very good yellow fall color and the flowers continue the show once the leaves fall. The flowers look exceptionally good against an early snowfall, and are not usually damaged.

Bad points: Fall foliage detracts from the beauty of the flowers for a while. There are leaf spots but these are not serious.

Uses: Specimen; screen; woodland; hedge.

Hibiscus syriacus   **Rose of sharon**

Comments: These shrubs are valued for their late flowering and the size of the blooms. Flowering is on the new wood, so prune in spring when needed.

Hardiness: Canadian zone 6; U.S. zone 5.

Availability: **A**.

Height: 10' (3 m). *Spread:* 8' (2.4 m).

Propagation: Seed or cuttings.

Soil preferences: Most except very wet.

Location: Sun.

Good points: Large, bright flowers open from August to frost. This is a good plant for late color in the shrub border.

Bad points: Japanese beetles may strip the foliage of this plant.

Uses: Border; screen.

Cultivars: 'Ardens' is a semi-double, light mauve. 'Blue Bird' is blue with a red center. 'Diana' is a large white with pleated petals. 'Jeanne d'Arc' is a semi-double white. 'Red Heart' is white with a red center.

Hippophae rhamnoides   **Sea buckthorn**

Comments: The "oides" part of the species name means "like," so the name means it looks like a *Rhamnus,* the common buckthorn. Plant container-grown stock only. It withstands salt, so is suitable for planting near the coast or roadways. Male and female flowers are produced on separate plants, so grow several to ensure fruit.

Hardiness: Canadian zone 2b; U.S. zone 3.

Availability: **M**.

Height: 15' (4.5 m). *Spread:* 10' (3 m).

Propagation: Stratified seed or layering.

Soil preferences: Sandy, not rich.

Location: Sun to light shade.

Good points: The soft gray foliage is a good foil for other plants. Clusters of bright orange berries on female plants persist for most of the winter.

Bad points: It is difficult to establish, especially in rich or heavy soils.

Uses: Female plants as a specimen shrub (with a male in a less conspicuous place); mixed border; hedge.

Hydrangea spp.   **Hydrangea**

Flowering varies from species to species, so pruning methods vary also. The flower heads often consist of showy but sterile outer flowers with conspicuous petals, and fertile inner flowers without petals.

Hydrangea arborescens Smooth hydrangea

Comments: This is quite similar to the peegee hydrangea, but the flowers are in flat heads rather than cones. The two cultivars are the most commonly grown forms.

Hardiness: Canadian zone 2b; U.S. zone 2.

Availability: **M**.

Height: 5' (1.5 m). *Spread:* 5' (1.5 m).

Propagation: Cuttings.

Soil preferences: Well drained.

Location: Sun to light shade.

Good points: This is an adaptable, reliable shrub. I once had a plant that the mailman walked over every winter once the snow had fallen. By spring it was trampled flat but still recovered and flowered in July. This is not the recommended pruning method, but the plant survived.

Bad points: Few. It is best treated as a perennial in the north and cut back almost to the ground in spring.

Uses: Border; informal hedge.

Cultivars: 'Annabelle' has globe-shaped flower heads, 8 inches (20 cm) across and made up mainly of sterile flowers, so they are very showy. 'Grandiflora' (hills of snow) is an old cultivar with loose, globular, flower heads. 'Annabelle' is an improvement.

Hydrangea macrophylla — **Florist's hydrangea, bigleaf hydrangea**

Comments: Cultivars of this species are grown as pot plants (especially at Easter). Flower color of some cultivars can be controlled by the soil pH. Acid soils give blue flowers; almost neutral to alkaline, pink.

Hardiness: Canadian zone 6; U.S. zone 6.

Availability: **M**.

Height: 6' (1.8 m). *Spread:* 6' (1.8 m).

Propagation: Cuttings.

Soil preferences: Moist, humusy, acidic.

Location: Sun to light shade.

Good points: It has very showy flowers in large trusses and a variety of colors. It flowers on the previous year's wood, so prune immediately after flowering.

Bad points: None.

Uses: Shrub border; mixed border.

Cultivars: 'Nikko Blue' is the only widely available form. There are many other named forms but this seems to be the hardiest. It gives its best color on acid soils; instead of turning pink on alkaline soils, it becomes a grayish-blue.

Hydrangea paniculata 'Grandiflora' — **Peegee hydrangea**

Comments: The common name comes from the first letter of the species and its cultivar. It is available both as a shrub and a small tree and the shrub form can be cut back hard if it becomes overgrown. Flowers are on new growth, so prune early in spring.

Hardiness: Canadian zone 3b; U.S. zone 3.

Availability: **M**.

Height: 15' (4.5 m). *Spread:* 10' (3 m).

Propagation: Cuttings.

Soil preferences: Well drained.

Location: Sun to light shade.

Good points: Showy, inverted, white cones of bloom turn pink and then brown. The flowers persist in this brown state all winter and, while they are not very attractive, they do give some winter color in snowy climates.

Bad points: This shrub is fast growing and needs frequent pruning. If the shoots that grow after pruning are left unthinned, flowering is reduced. It is very common and overplanted in some areas.

Uses: Specimen (tree form); border.

Hydrangea quercifolia — **Oakleaved hydrangea**

Comments: I really like this shrub and wish it was hardy for me. It too flowers on the old wood, so prune (if required) after flowering.

Hardiness: Canadian zone 5b; U.S. zone 5.

Availability: **S**.

Height: 6' (1.8 m). *Spread:* 8' (2.4 m).

Propagation: Seed.

Soil preferences: Well drained.

Location: Sun to light shade.

Good points: White flowers are in upright clusters and the oak-like leaves turn a reddish-brown in fall. Even at the northern limit of its range, where flower buds may be killed, it is worth growing this plant for the foliage alone.

Bad points: None.

Uses: Specimen; border.

Cultivars: 'Snow Queen' has more sterile flowers in each spike so it is more showy; the flower clusters age to a pink shade, rather than turning brown as they do in the species.

Ilex spp.   Holly

In warmer climates hollies are evergreen trees with spiny leaves and bright red berries. To most of us these are only found on Christmas cards, but they can be almost weedy where they grow well. The types we can grow are smaller and shrubby, but still interesting. All these hollies have male and female flowers on separate plants, so you need to plant both to get berries.

Ilex x meserveae   Blue holly

Comments: A cross between the English and a native American holly, this is much hardier, but has the English holly type of foliage. These are the hardiest of all the evergreen hollies but the foliage can winter-burn badly at the limits of its range.

Hardiness: Canadian zone 5b; U.S. zone 5.

Availability: **M**.

Height: 8-10' (3 m). *Spread:* 8' (2.4 m).

Propagation: Cuttings.

Soil preferences: Well drained.

Location: Sun to light shade.

Good points: This is the best berried holly for northern climates—but not too far north.

Bad points: It needs a sheltered location or protection from drying winds.

Uses: Border; hedge.

Cultivars: 'Blue Boy', 'Blue Prince', 'Blue Stallion' are male clones. 'Blue Angel', 'Blue Girl', 'Blue Maid', 'Blue Princess' are female clones. 'China Boy' and 'China Girl' have a different parentage and are slightly hardier.

Ilex verticillata   Winterberry

Comments: This deciduous native holly grows well in moist soils. In nature it does not fruit well every year, but in a good year it is most eye-catching, especially in sunlight.

Hardiness: Canadian zone 3b; U.S. zone 3.

Availability: **A**.

Height: 6' (1.8 m). *Spread:* 4' (1.2 m).

Propagation: Seed.

Soil preferences: Moist to wet, but adaptable.

Location: Sun to medium shade.

Good points: The clusters of bright red berries are highly visible after leaf fall.

Bad points: Berries may soon disappear if the birds are hungry.

Uses: Border (both sexes are needed for fruit).

Cultivars: 'Winter Red' sets copious fruits that persist for a long time. 'Apollo' and 'Sparkleberry' are male and female hybrids of winterberry and another native holly that were selected for good pollination. They seem adaptable and I have observed plants of 'Sparkleberry' consistently covered with fruit every fall, growing in regular, dry soil.

Itea virginica   Sweetspire

Comments: This is another native shrub that seems very adaptable to different growing conditions. In the wild it grows mostly beside streams, but it seems very drought-tolerant in cultivation.

Hardiness: Canadian zone 6; U.S. zone 5.

Availability: **H** in Canada; **A** in U.S.

Height: 6' (1.8 m). *Spread:* 6' (1.8 m).

Propagation: Seed or cuttings.

Soil preferences: Moist.

Location: Sun to medium shade.

Good points: Fragrant white spikes of flower appear in early to midsummer. It's a good plant for wet locations, with bright red fall color.

Bad points: None.

Uses: Border; screen.

Cultivars: 'Henry's Garnet' has longer flower spikes (up to 6 inches/15 cm) and better fall color on a shorter (and possibly hardier) plant.

Kalmia latifolia   **Mountain laurel**

Comments: A native plant that varies considerably in flower color in the wild, it transforms the Appalachian mountains when in flower. Its name commemorates Pehr Kalm, a student of Linnaeus, the father of modern plant nomenclature. Transplant B & B or container-grown plants.

Hardiness: Canadian zone 5b; U.S. zone 4.

Availability: **A** to **H**.

Height: 10' (3 m). *Spread:* 10' (3 m).

Propagation: Seed; cuttings (difficult, but may root if a vaporizer is used).

Soil preferences: Acidic, moist, but well drained.

Location: Sun to shade.

Good points: Wonderful flowers in a range of pink/white/red combinations are produced in the cultivars. Mountain laurel flowers are best in sun, but the plants grow better in shade. New leaves are a yellow-green, darkening with time and persisting over winter, although there is some edge burn at the limits of the range. It is a good companion plant in front of rhododendrons or behind heaths and heathers.

Bad points: A few diseases and pests will attack this plant but none are serious.

Uses: Specimen; border; foundation.

Cultivars: There are now close to 50 named forms which are generally smaller than the species. Those listed are the most readily available at the time of writing, but this may change. All the forms I have seen are worth garden space. 'Bullseye' has dark red buds opening cream. 'Elf' is a dwarf with pink buds that open white. 'Minuet' is similar to 'Elf' but with a maroon band inside the flower. 'Olympic Fire' has dark red buds that open pink. 'Ostbo Red', with bright red buds that open pink, is the most commonly grown cultivar. 'Pink Charm' has dark pink buds that open to a paler pink.

Kerria japonica   **Japanese kerria**

Comments: A very popular shrub in England and one of the first I learned to recognize when I started training. Plant B & B or container-grown stock.

Hardiness: Canadian zone 5; U.S. zone 4.

Availability: **M**.

Height: 6' (1.8 m). *Spread:* 6' (1.8 m).

Propagation: Cuttings.

Soil preferences: Well drained (although I first encountered it growing on London clay).

Location: Light to medium shade.

Good points: Bright yellow flowers open in spring and occasionally through the summer and the bright green stems are attractive in winter.

Bad points: It tends to form a thicket and needs frequent renewal pruning.

Uses: Border; foundation.

Cultivars: The cultivars are not quite as hardy: zone 5b in Canada, zone 4b in U.S. 'Plena' has double flowers like miniature yellow roses and is the most common form. 'Picta' has single flowers, with white-edged leaves.

Kolkwitzia amabilis   **Beautybush**

Comments: This shrub is wonderful when in flower but has no other redeeming features. It is rather straggly the rest of the summer and has no fall color.

Hardiness: Canadian zone 5; U.S. zone 4.

Availability: **M**.

Height: 8' (2.4 m). *Spread:* 8' (2.4 m).

Propagation: Cuttings in early summer.

Soil preferences: Well drained.

Location: Full sun.

Good points: Arching sprays of trumpet-shaped pink flowers almost hide the foliage in late spring.

Bad points: It needs regular renewal pruning to keep it flowering well.

Uses: Plant at the back of the border so other plants can take over when it has finished flowering.

Cultivars: 'Pink Cloud' has a brighter color.

Lespedezia bicolor   Bush clover

Comments: I like this shrub, if only because it flowers in late summer, a time when few other shrubs provide color. The foliage is similar to peashrub, to which it is related.

Hardiness: Canadian zone 5; U.S. zone 4.

Availability: **S.**

Height: 8' (2.4 m). *Spread:* 5' (1.5 m).

Propagation: Softwood cuttings.

Soil preferences: Well drained.

Location: Sun.

Good points: Rose-purple flowers are carried in spikes on the open, arching branches in late summer and fall. To rejuvenate, cut back hard in early spring and, since it flowers on the new wood, it will still bloom the same summer.

Bad points: At the limit of its range, its top may be winter-killed, but it will grow again from the rootstock.

Uses: Specimen; shrub border.

Leucothoe fontanesia   Fetterbush

Comments: A member of the heather family, this shrub grows well in acid soil conditions. Use container-grown plants.

Hardiness: Canadian zone 6; U.S. zone 5.

Availability: **A.**

Height: 5' (1.5 m). *Spread:* 5' (1.5 m).

Propagation: Seed or cuttings.

Soil preferences: Acidic and humusy.

Location: Light to medium shade.

Good points: Dark green evergreen leaves contrast with the waxy white flowers in spring. It grows well with rhododendrons.

Bad points: It may get leaf spot in humid weather.

Uses: Front of the border; specimen shrub in the heather bed.

Cultivars: 'Rainbow' has new leaves tinged with white, pink or yellow, becoming green as they age.

Ligustrum spp.   Privet

Privet is the major hedging plant in Britain, but it doesn't rate as highly here. It takes clipping very well and can be kept to almost any height.

Ligustrum amurense   Amur privet

Comments: Most plants from the Amur peninsular are quite hardy; this one is the exception.

Hardiness: Canadian zone 6; U.S. zone 5.

Availability: **A.**

Height: 12' (3.5 m) *Spread:* 10' (3 m).

Propagation: Cuttings.

Soil preferences: Well drained.

Location: Sun.

Good points: It makes a good hedge that can be kept quite low and is grows well under city conditions.

Bad points: Several diseases and pests attack this plant, but few are serious.

Uses: Hedging.

Ligustrum obtusifolium   Regel
var. regelianum   privet

Comments: This is grown mainly as a shrub, rather than used for hedging, and can be used as a tall ground cover.

Hardiness: Canadian zone 5b; U.S. zone 5.

Availability: **F.**

Height: 4' (1.2 m). *Spread:* 6' (1.8 m).

Propagation: Cuttings.

Soil preferences: Well drained.

Location: Sun.

Good points: Arching branches and shiny, dark green leaves make this a good choice for the shrub border.

Bad points: Mildew may attack this privet in some summers.

Uses: Border; ground cover.

Ligustrum x vicaryi   Golden privet

Comments: A cross between the golden form of the oval-leaved privet (*L. ovalifolium* 'Aureum') and the common privet, this is the most commonly grown of the yellow privets.

Hardiness: Canadian zone 6; U.S. zone 5.

Availability: **M**.

Height: 10' (3 m). *Spread:* 8' (2.4 m).

Propagation: Cuttings.

Soil preferences: Well drained.

Location: Sun.

Good points: It keeps its golden color all summer long, providing it is in full sun.

Bad points: This hybrid is slower growing, although this is a plus once the hedge is the size you want it.

Uses: Hedge.

Ligustrum vulgare   Common privet

Comments: This is probably the most common hedging plant in the U.K. It has white flowers with a strange smell that are rich in nectar.

Hardiness: Canadian zone 5b; U.S. zone 4.

Availability: **M**.

Height: 10' (3 m). *Spread:* 8' (2.4 m).

Propagation: Cuttings.

Soil preferences: Well drained.

Location: Sun.

Good points: This privet clips well and can be kept to almost any size as long as you trim it three times each summer.

Bad points: An anthracnose twig blight can seriously affect this species, especially in regions with high summer humidity.

Uses: Hedging.

Cultivars: 'Cheyenne' is a hardier selection. 'Lodense' is a dwarf form that only grows about 3 feet (.9 m) tall and is the best for low hedges.

Lindera benzoin   Spicebush

Comments: Spicebush is another underused native shrub with aromatic leaves. It is often cut down to the snowline at the limits of its hardiness. Plant B & B or container-grown specimens. It will survive in medium shade but becomes a bit open and ratty.

Hardiness: Canadian zone 5b; U.S. zone 4.

Availability: **H** in Canada; **F** in U.S.

Height: 8' (2.4 m). *Spread:* 10' (3 m).

Propagation: Stratified seed.

Soil preferences: Moist.

Location: Sun to medium shade.

Good points: It bears attractive yellow flowers, best seen close up, in spring, and the fragrant foliage turns a bright yellow in fall. The edible red fruit lasts well into winter, birds permitting.

Bad points: None.

Uses: Border; foundation.

Lonicera spp.   Honeysuckle

This group of small to large shrubs and vines (see "Climbers" later in this chapter) is used extensively in gardens. They are grown for their flowers, strongly fragrant in a couple of the climbers, and for their fruit. Some have become weeds. I remember driving along Interstate 81 in North Carolina and the air was deliciously perfumed with the scent of Japanese honeysuckle, a noxious weed in that area. Birds love the fruit of honeysuckles but don't digest the seeds. Seedlings spring up freely wherever the birds drop them, often inside other shrubs.

Shrubby honeysuckles grow into dense thickets that need frequent renewal pruning. The wood is hard and you will need to use loppers on branches you would expect to cut easily with pruners. Many honeysuckles suffer from attacks by the Russian aphid, which feeds on new growth and produces a tassel effect. A virus carried by the aphid may also be involved.

Lonicera caerulea   **Bearberry honeysuckle**

Comments: This is the only species with fruit worth eating. The rest are not poisonous, but don't taste good.
Hardiness: Canadian zone 2; U.S. zone 3.
Availability: **M**.
Height: 4' (1.2 m). *Spread:* 4' (1.2 m).
Propagation: Stratified seed or cuttings.
Soil preferences: Most.
Location: Sun.
Good points: This dense shrub with yellowish flowers has blue-bloomed berries that can be eaten out of hand but are best made into pies.
Bad points: None serious.
Uses: Hedge; border.
Cultivars: *L. caerulea* var. *edulis* has the best-tasting fruit.

Lonicera korolkowii   **Blueleaf honeysuckle**

Comments: Small blue-green leaves clothe a slender, more open shrub.
Hardiness: Canadian zone 4; U.S. zone 3.
Availability: **M** (cv).
Height: 10' (3 m). *Spread:* 10' (3 m).
Propagation: Cuttings.
Soil preferences: Most.
Location: Sun.
Good points: The pink to white flowers turn into bright red fruit that shows up well against the foliage.
Bad points: It is harder to transplant than most honeysuckles and suffers from aphid damage.
Uses: Border; hedge.
Cultivars: 'Freedom' is resistant to the Russian aphid. 'Zabelii' has dark pink flowers followed

by red berries in late summer. It is listed as a variety of the Tatarian honeysuckle in some catalogs.

Lonicera tatarica   **Tatarian honeysuckle**

Comments: Although this is still widely grown, its free-seeding habit and the tassel effect caused by the Russian aphid make it less desirable where other shrubs can be used.
Hardiness: Canadian zone 3; U.S. zone 2.
Availability: **M**.
Height: 10' (3 m). *Spread:* 8' (2.4 m).
Propagation: Cuttings.
Soil preferences: Most.
Location: Sun to light shade.
Good points: White, pink or red flowers in late spring are followed by red or yellow berries that the birds love—unfortunately, since they then spread seed everywhere.
Bad points: New growth may be disfigured by the tassel effect from Russian aphids feeding in spring. The aphids can be controlled with insecticidal soap, but this takes vigilance and several sprays.
Uses: Border; screen; hedge.
Cultivars: There are many, but the following are the most common. 'Arnold Red' has the darkest red flowers. 'Hack's Red' has red flowers with a purple tinge. 'Rosea' is pink.

Lonicera x *xylostoides*   **Clavey's dwarf**
'Clavey's Dwarf'   **honeysuckle**

Comments: A cross between the Tatarian and fly honeysuckles, this cultivar is the only form grown.
Hardiness: Canadian zone 2; U.S. zone 3.
Availability: **M**.
Height: 4-8' (1.2-2.4 m). *Spread:* 6-8' (1.8-2.4 m).
Propagation: Cuttings.
Soil preferences: Most.
Location: Sun.

Good points: A rounded, slow-growing shrub, it can be kept low with an occasional clipping. Flowers are greenish-cream and the fruit is red.

Bad points: This hybrid is susceptible to aphids but doesn't become as badly disfigured as the tatarian honeysuckle.

Uses: Foundation; hedge; border.

Magnolia spp.   Magnolia

This is one of the best known of all garden plants. Even keen gardeners in colder climates know of, and could probably recognize, magnolias. Although associated with southern plantations, some species are quite hardy. There are many new hybrids with mixed parentage and of unknown hardiness beginning to appear. Buy these only from a reputable nursery that will be there the following spring, and get a one-year warranty on the hardiness.

All magnolias should be planted as B & B or container-grown stock in spring—often in flower. Prune immediately after flowering if needed.

Magnolia x *loebneri*   Loebner magnolia

Comments: This hybrid resulted from a cross made in Germany by Max Loebner with the star magnolia *(M. stellata)* as one parent. Plants flower while still young.

Hardiness: Canadian zone 5(b?); U.S. zone 4.

Availability: **A** to **F**—depending on the cultivar.

Height: 20' (6 m). *Spread:* 15' (4.5 m).

Propagation: Softwood cuttings.

Soil preferences: Slightly acidic.

Location: Sun.

Good points: Early spring flowers are freely produced and up to 4 inches (10 cm) across and the foliage is attractive all summer.

Bad points: The flower buds may be killed by a late frost.

Uses: Specimen; border.

Cultivars: 'Ballerina' has very fragrant white flowers with a light pink center and up to 30 petals. 'Leonard Messel' is pink outside and white inside with a dark pink line down the center of each of the 12 petals. 'Merril' is pure white and very free-flowering with 15 petals.

Magnolia x *soulangeana*   Saucer magnolia

Comments: This is a very showy shrub when in bloom. Flower buds may be killed at the limits of its range in an extra-hard winter, but established plants will generally survive. There may be a few scattered flowers in the fall, given an Indian summer.

Hardiness: Canadian zone 5; U.S. zone 4.

Availability: **M.**

Height: 20' (6 m). *Spread:* 20' (6 m).

Propagation: Softwood cuttings.

Soil preferences: Well drained, slightly acidic.

Location: Sun to light shade.

Good points: Large cup-shaped flowers, white inside, eventually open almost flat and may be 9 inches (23 cm) across. It blooms in early spring, just before the Loebner magnolia, most years.

Bad points: There are several leaf diseases, but they are seldom serious.

Uses: Specimen shrub; shade plant when mature.

Cultivars: 'Alexandrina' blooms early with flowers that are a purply-pink outside. 'Lennei' is late flowering with a more upright habit; petals are a dark purple on the outside and are almost as wide as they are long. 'Rustica Rubra' has petals that are a dark pinkish-red outside.

Magnolia *stellata*   Star magnolia

Comments: This magnolia is normally a smaller, less massive shrub with more stems. Twelve to fifteen narrow petals on each flower give a starburst effect.

Hardiness: Canadian zone 5; U.S. zone 4.
Availability: **A** to **S**.
Height: 8' (2.4 m). *Spread:* 8' (2.4 m).
Propagation: Cuttings.
Soil preferences: Slightly acidic.
Location: Sun to light shade.
Good points: Fragrant white flowers open in early spring at about the same time, or slightly before, the saucer magnolia. Good summer foliage turns yellow in fall.
Bad points: None.
Uses: Specimen; border.
Cultivars: 'Royal Star' has pink buds that open to almost double flowers with twice the number of petals and is later to flower. 'Waterlily' flowers are cup-shaped at first with a pink exterior. The petals are longer and narrower.

Mahonia aquifolium   Oregon grape

Comments: Usually a fairly low-growing evergreen shrub, this plant does best on sites sheltered from drying winter winds. Exposed shoots often desiccate in winter at the limits of its range. Plant B & B or container-grown stock. The creeping mahonia *(M. repens)* is an even more dwarf species that spreads slowly underground and makes a better ground cover, but it is not easy to find.
Hardiness: Canadian zone 5; U.S. zone 4.
Availability: **M**.
Height: 5' (1.5 m). *Spread:* 5' (1.5 m).
Propagation: Layering; stratified seed.
Soil preferences: Moist and acidic; but it is adaptable and I have seen it growing well on alkaline soils.
Location: Dappled shade.
Good points: The holly-like spring foliage is a bright pinkish-green, darkening with age. It bears spikes of bright yellow flowers in spring above the foliage and then clusters of grape-like edible fruit. Foliage turns a bronzy

purple in early winter in cold regions, but is not shed.
Bad points: Picking up old leaves can be a painful experience. Plants need some protection, such as a circle of snow fence, from drying winter winds in cold regions.
Uses: Border; foundation; ground cover.

Myrica pennsylvanica   Bayberry

Comments: This native shrub has aromatic leaves and is very tolerant of salt and poor soils. It tends to sucker slowly and form thickets. Plant container-grown stock (or B & B at a pinch), as it does not transplant readily.
Hardiness: Canadian zone 2; U.S. zone 3.
Availability: **A**.
Height: 6' (1.8 m). *Spread:* 6' (1.8 m).
Propagation: Stratified seed.
Soil preferences: Sandy and poor (will not grow on heavy or rich soils).
Location: Sun to part shade.
Good points: Waxy berries persist through winter into the following spring (on female plants only). The plant is semi-evergreen and the wax on the berries is the source of candle fragrance. It is pest- and disease-free.
Bad points: Male and female flowers are on separate plants so you need to plant several to be sure of getting berries.
Uses: Mass plantings, especially where road or sea salt is a problem.

Philadelphus spp.   Mock orange

Comments: The majority of mock orange sold are named forms, either of a single species, or, more commonly, with complex parentage. Study the list of cultivars carefully to be sure you don't get an 8-footer (2.4 m) when you need a dwarf form. Of the more than 70 cultivars, those listed in the table are the easiest to find.

Mock orange variety	Size	Zone	Comments
'Aureus'	8 ft (2.4 m)	C 3/US 3	Golden leaves hide the flowers.
'Buckley's Quill'	4 ft (1.2 m)	C 4/US 3	Double flowers with narrow petals.
'Galahad'	5 ft (1.5 m)	C 3/US 3	Single, very fragrant flowers.
'Minnesota Snowflake'	8 ft (2.4 m)	C 3b/US 3	Double flowers, very popular.
'Snowbelle'	6 ft (1.8 m)	C 3/US 3	Semi-double pendulous flowers.
'Snowdwarf'	2 ft (60 cm)	C 3b/US 3	A recent dwarf introduction.
'Virginal'	8 ft (2.4 m)	C 3b/US 3	More open growth with double flowers.
'Waterton'	6 ft (1.8 m)	C 2b/US 2	Dense bush with single flowers.

Hardiness: Canadian zone 2b-4; U.S. zone 2-3.
Availability: **M**.
Height: 2-10' (.6-3 m). *Spread:* 4-8' (1.2-2.4 m).
Propagation: Cuttings.
Soil preferences: Most.
Location: Sun.
Good points: It bears white flowers in early summer, mostly with a strong fragrance. The gray-green foliage is not striking but makes a good foil for brighter plants.
Bad points: Mock orange are fairly fast growing and need renewal pruning every couple of years to stop them from becoming a jungle. Giving an over-tall plant a haircut removes the flower buds, so it is better to replace it with a more suitable variety.
Uses: Border; foundation; informal hedge (dwarf cultivars); screen.
Cultivars: The hardiness zones are given for Canada, followed by the U.S. *See table above.*

Physocarpus opulifolius   Ninebark

Comments: This is a very adaptable, but rather unrefined shrub. It may be a little large for city properties, but the dwarf form makes a good low hedge. Cut it back hard in late winter if it gets overgrown.
Hardiness: Canadian zone 2b; U.S. zone 2.
Availability: **M**.

Height: 8' (2.4 m). *Spread:* 8' (2.4 m).
Propagation: Seed or cuttings.
Soil preferences: Most.
Location: Sun.
Good points: The yellow forms have a place in the mixed border and its hardiness makes it useful in harsh climates.
Bad points: Flowers are a creamy color but not very showy; fruit is brown but hangs on into the winter. For most of us there are better shrubs, but this has a place in far northern gardens.
Uses: Border; screen; hedge.
Cultivars: 'Dart's Gold' is a shorter yellow form growing 3 feet (90 cm) tall that keeps its golden color until late summer. 'Luteus' is the original yellow form that turns green fairly quickly. 'Nanus', a dwarf form, grows only 2 feet (60 cm) tall and can be clipped as a low formal hedge or left unclipped as an informal one.

Pieris   Japanese pieris,
japonica   lily-of-the-valley shrub

Comments: This lovely evergreen shrub is related to the heaths and heathers and needs similar conditions. Plant B & B or container-grown plants.
Hardiness: Canadian zone 5b; U.S. zone 5.

Availability: **A.**
Height: 10' (3 m). *Spread:* 8' (2.4 m).
Propagation: Cuttings.
Soil preferences: Acidic; well drained but humusy.
Location: Light shade.
Good points: New foliage is a bronzy-red turning to green. Flowers are white, waxy and hang in clusters, rather like lily-of-the-valley.
Bad points: Winter winds and sun can scorch the foliage, so the site needs careful selection. Lacebugs and mites cause serious damage some years.
Uses: Shady border; specimen plant.
Cultivars: 'Forest Flame' may be a hybrid of *P. japonica* and the Himalayan pieris, *P. formosa.* Bright red new foliage turns pink, then white and finally green. 'Mountain Fire' has orange-red new growth. 'Valley Rose' has flowers of a pale pink. 'Valley Valentine' has maroon buds that open to rose-pink flowers.

Potentilla fruticosa   Potentilla, cinquefoil

Comments: I prefer the German common name, finger-bush, which describes the foliage. The newer red- and pink-flowered forms introduced from Europe in recent years bloom yellow in heat, only showing their true color with cooler weather. Do not cut back or you will get no flowers until the second summer.
Hardiness: Canadian zone 1-3; U.S. zone 2.
Availability: **M.**
Height: 1-4' (30-120 cm).
Spread: 2-5' (60-150 cm).
Propagation: Softwood cuttings.
Soil preferences: Most, including poor and dry.
Location: Sun to light shade.
Good points: Cinquefoils are very free-flowering from mid-June to hard frost. The flowers are bright and the plants little troubled by problems.
Bad points: None.

Uses: Foundation planting; shrub or mixed border; informal hedge.
Cultivars: Of the more than 50 named forms, the following are my favorites of those readily available. Several are called by more than one name in nurseries. *See table opposite.*

Prinsepia sinensis   Cherry prinsepia

Comments: This rather overlooked shrub is one of the first to leaf out in spring and last to shed in fall. Cut back hard in spring if it becomes overgrown.
Hardiness: Canadian zone 2b; U.S. zone 3.
Availability: **F.**
Height: 5' (1.5 m). *Spread:* 8' (2.4 m).
Propagation: Seed.
Soil preferences: Not fussy, it will grow in clay or sand.
Location: Sun.
Good points: It produces small clusters of yellow flowers in spring and edible red fruit in fall. A dense shrub, it does well as a hedge: the small spines stop people pushing through.
Bad points: None. It is very disease- and pest-resistant.
Uses: Hedge; screen; border.

**Prunus   Purple-leaved sand
x cistena   cherry**

Comments: This hybrid has the purple-leaved cherry plum as one parent. It can look good against a pale background, but tends to be overplanted.
Hardiness: Canadian zone 3; U.S. zone 3b.
Availability: **M.**
Height: 6' (1.8 m). *Spread:* 5' (1.5 m).
Propagation: Cuttings.
Soil preferences: Well drained.
Location: Sun.
Good points: This is a reasonably hardy, bushy shrub that makes a good contrast plant. The

Potentilla variety	Color	Height	Comments
'Abbotswood'	white	3 ft (90 cm)	Large flowers.
'Coronation Triumph'	yellow	4 ft (120 cm)	Free-flowering.
'Daydawn'	gingery	2 1/2 ft (75 cm)	Best color when cool.
'Elizabeth' ('Sutters Gold')	yellow	3 ft (90 cm)	Grayish foliage.
'Gold Drop' ('Farreri')	yellow	2 ft (60 cm)	Darker flowers.
'Goldfinger'	gold	3 ft (90 cm)	Upright, later flowering.
'Katherine Dykes'	pale yellow	3 ft (90 cm)	Arching form.
'Moonlight' ('Maanleys')	mid-yellow	4 ft (120 cm)	Flowers have darker centers.
'Princess' ('Pink Queen')	pink	2 1/2 ft (75 cm)	Blooms are white in heat.
'Red Ace'	red	2 1/2 ft (75 cm)	Flowers are yellow in heat.
'Snowbird'	white	3 ft (90 cm)	Plentiful small flowers.
'Tangerine'	yellow	2 ft (60 cm)	Flowers reddish when cool.

edible fruits are hard to find in the foliage, although the birds seem to manage.

Bad points: Branches die back after a hard winter, even where it should be perfectly hardy. The flowers open after the leaves and are not very noticeable.

Uses: Specimen shrub; hedge (but tends to be a bit open); foundation planting against pale siding; shrub border for contrast.

Prunus tenella   Dwarf Russian almond

Comments: A free-flowering, low shrub that puts on a good display every year. The nuts are said to contain prussic acid, and eating too many could be fatal, but they are so hard to open this is rather academic. It flowers on the old wood, so prune lightly.

Hardiness: Canadian zone 2; U.S. zone 3.
Availability: **A**.
Height: 4' (1.2 m). *Spread:* 4' (1.2 m).
Propagation: Seed or cuttings under mist.
Soil preferences: Well drained.
Location: Sun to light shade.

Good points: It flowers very early with masses of bright pink blossoms that are really eye-catching and look good with forsythia.

Bad points: It is reputed to sucker badly, but I have never found this to be the case. Like forsythia, it is a bit bland once flowering is done, and there is no fall color.

Uses: Mixed border; foundation plant.

Cultivars: 'Fire Hill' is a brighter pink but not quite as hardy.

Prunus   Nanking cherry, Peking
tomentosa   cherry, Manchu cherry

Comments: This versatile shrub has pink or whitish flowers in early spring and edible red fruits. I grew it as a hedge, keeping it clipped to 3 feet (90 cm), and it still flowered and fruited.

Hardiness: Canadian zone 2; U.S. zone 3.
Availability: **M**.
Height: 9' (2.7 m). *Spread:* 12' (3.5 m).
Propagation: Stratified seed or cuttings.
Soil preferences: Most.

Location: Sun.

Good points: As well as the flowers and fruit, its light brown, flaking bark gives winter interest. The foliage is a dull green and makes a good background for perennials. Underplant with spring squill *(Scilla sibirica)*, which blooms at the same time.

Bad points: This species is very attractive to mice, which girdle the stems in winter. Protect young plants with a repellent; older plants will usually regrow from the roots.

Uses: Screen; hedge; mixed border; foundation.

Prunus triloba   Flowering almond

Comments: The single-flowered species is seldom offered, the double form, 'Multiplex', being much more popular. This is available as a shrub or grafted on a stem as a small tree. It has proved fairly short-lived in Ottawa— about 10 years.

Hardiness: Canadian zone 2b; U.S. zone 3b.

Availability: **M**.

Height: Shrub: 12' (3.5 m); tree: depending on the height of the stem but generally 15-20' (4.5-6 m).

Spread: 10' (3 m).

Propagation: Cuttings in mist.

Soil preferences: Most.

Location: Sun.

Good points: Spectacular in flower, when the branches are clothed in small pink powderpuffs. The tree form can be useful in small gardens.

Bad points: Late frosts kill the flower buds some years. A plant in my own garden suckered badly, but I know of other trees that have not done this. It has no ornamental value other than the flowers.

Uses: Screen; border; small specimen tree.

Cultivars: 'Mutiplex' (also listed as 'Plena') is the popular double form.

Pyracantha spp.   Firethorn

Comments: These small shrubs, often trained against a wall as espaliers, are grown mainly for their brilliantly colored fruit. Plant container-grown specimens only. There are many named hybrids but few are readily available commercially.

Hardiness: Canadian zone 6; U.S. zone 5.

Availability: **S** to **A**.

Height: 6' (1.8 m). *Spread:* 10' (3 m).

Propagation: Cuttings in mist.

Soil preferences: Dry to well drained.

Location: Sun.

Good points: Glossy green leaves show off clusters of white flowers in late spring. Bright red or orange fruit persists well into winter.

Bad points: When it grows well, it can get out of hand and need frequent pruning; watch out for the thorns.

Uses: Border; wall shrub; people-proof hedge.

Cultivars: 'Lalandei' has orange-red fruits and is one of the hardiest (Canadian zone 5b). 'Mohave' has very bright berries, may be evergreen in southern areas, and is disease-resistant.

Rhamnus frangula   Alder buckthorn

Comments: This rather weedy large shrub or small tree will give some autumn color. It grows in difficult situations and has some merit for binding slopes or growing where little else will establish. The common buckthorn *(Rhamnus cathartica)* is a real weed although it is a good food plant for birds. Unfortunately, the seeds pass through undigested and are deposited with abandon. They germinate readily and can be a big problem, especially when they grow up inside other, desirable, shrubs.

Hardiness: Canadian zone 3b; U.S. zone 2.

Availability: **S** in Canada; **F** in U.S.

Height: 10' (3 m). *Spread:* 8' (2.4 m).

Propagation: Seed for the species; the cultivar by cuttings.

Soil preferences: Well drained.

Location: Sun to light shade.

Good points: There are not many for the species, but the cultivar has some merit where a narrow shrub is required.

Bad points: Like the common buckthorn, this can also be weedy, although to a lesser extent.

Uses: A plant for difficult locations; the cultivar is useful for hedging.

Cultivars: 'Columnaris' has an upright form and only grows about 4 feet (1.2 m) wide.

Rhododendron **spp.**	**Rhododendron and azalea**

The two sourcebooks mentioned at the beginning of the plant listings contain page after page of rhododendron species and hybrids; however, as their use is restricted to the milder parts of North America, I will not go into great detail on the cultivar descriptions.

As well, there are many books specializing in rhododendron culture that contain descriptions of hundreds of cultivars. Readers who would like to try these plants should refer to Suggested Reading at the end of the book.

Although I am no expert, I did grow rhododendrons for several years because they were such a challenge in Ottawa. I was living in a garden with high overhead shade that suited these plants well; when I moved to a shade-free garden I stopped growing rhododendrons. In general terms, both rhododendrons and azaleas (about which more later) need a well-drained, humusy, acidic soil in light shade. They do not tolerate prolonged droughts or sites with strong winter winds.

On soils with a high pH they show severe chlorosis—the leaves turn bright yellow with green veins. Spraying with chelated iron will give a temporary quick cure. Feeding with sulphate of iron will give slower, but longer-lasting results. Do not use aluminum sulphate or aluminum toxicity may result after a while. Powdered sulphur will alter the soil pH more permanently, but it is slow acting. Where the natural soil is alkaline, raised beds are the only solution.

These are such spectacular plants that you may be willing to go the extra mile to cater to their needs, particularly if you have dappled shade already. A single raised bed, filled with a woodland-type soil mix will provide the right conditions for rhododendrons. Do not raise the bed too much: rhododendrons are quite shallow-rooted and in cold climates frost can penetrate from the front of the bed, making the soil colder than normal. A mounded bed is better than one with a retaining wall.

Although both rhododendrons and azaleas are spring-flowering, there is a considerable range of flowering times and you could have different varieties in bloom for several weeks. Having a special bed with acidic soil also gives you the opportunity to grow some of the companion plants (like enkianthus and pieris), so the bed is attractive when the rhododendrons have finished blooming.

A deep mulch of oak leaves in fall will help protect the plants over winter and increase the acidity of the bed. If you live in an area where a good, reliable snowfall can be expected, there will be less winter damage if you surround the bed with a circle of snow fence to help trap the snow. You could even carefully shovel some snow between the plants after the first fall to help improve their chances.

A few rhododendrons are hardy to zone 4 but these may make poor specimens at the limit of their range, growing into a long stick with a tuft of leaves at the top. These hardy rhododendrons are large plants, but they can be pruned to keep them low and spreading so they are less winter-damaged. In winter, the leaves hang vertically and roll into a cigar shape during cold weather to conserve moisture. When they unroll in spring, they may have brown edges and a dead area close to the midrib if the temperatures were very low.

The American Rhododendron Society has its own hardiness ratings for these plants and you may find nursery tags marked in this way. They use a rating of H-1 to H-7 and the lower the number the colder temperatures the plant will tolerate. Plants rated H-1 will not be injured at -25°F (-31°C); H-2 means hardy to -15°F (-26°C); H-3, to -5°F (-20.5°C) and so on, with H-7 plants being hardy only to 32°F (0°C).

Rhododendron	**Iron-clad**
catawbiense	**hybrids**

Comments: This is a group of very tough plants that will survive quite low temperatures (at least -40°) although the flower buds are killed below about -25°F (-30°C). They are mostly selections of this native species, growing about 8 feet (2.4 m) tall, and have mauvish-purple or white flowers. Look for 'Album', 'Boursault', 'Grandiflorum', 'Lees Dark Purple' and 'Roseum Elegans'.

Other very hardy hybrids of mixed parentage worth trying are 'America', with deep red flowers; 'Blue Ensign', which is lavender with a darker blotch; 'Dora Amateis', white; 'English Roseum', a light pink; 'Nova Zembla', magenta red; 'Purpureum Elegans', dark violet; and 'Vulcan', a dark red. If temperature is not a limiting factor, you have literally hundreds of cultivars to choose from, given the right soil conditions.

To most people, the word rhododendron conjures up a vision of a great ball of flowers up to 9 inches (23 cm) across on a plant with large, dark green leaves. If you are willing to settle for smaller flowers, there is a much hardier strain, but they don't look like the accepted rhododendron hybrids. 'PJM' makes a small rounded bush a little over 3 feet (1 m) tall with small, evergreen leaves that turn a rich plum color in cold weather. Flowers are small, bright mauvish-pink and open with the daffodils. It is hardy to zone 4 and I predict if you can grow daffodils you can grow 'PJM' without winter injury, as long as the soil is right. Other clones, with similar parentage and slightly different colors, are now beginning to appear.

Azaleas

Generally, rhododendrons are evergreen while azaleas are deciduous (although there are also evergreen azaleas), and rhododendrons are usually larger (although there are some very large azaleas and some dwarf rhodendrons). Because the hardier azaleas lose their leaves and don't suffer the same winter damage, they make a more attractive plant than rhododendrons in harsh climates.

Plants in the Northern Lights series, introduced by the University of Minnesota, seem very hardy and are becoming increasingly available. Look for such varieties as 'Golden Lights' and 'White Lights'. They are reputedly hardy to -40° and grow about 5 feet (1.5 m) tall.

Others that have done well with an average winter low of -25°F (-31°C) include several of the Exbury and Knap Hill hybrids from England such as 'Cecile', pink with yellow markings; 'Gibralta', orange; 'Homebush', double pink; 'Satan', scarlet; 'Tunis', crimson; 'White Swan', white with a yellow throat and fragrant; and 'Narcissiflora', which is not a Knap Hill but is bright yellow, very fragrant and worth searching for. These are mostly smaller than the Northern Lights and will reach 4 feet (1.2 m) at maturity with 'Narcissiflora' growing a little taller.

Rhus spp.   Sumac

This group of shrubs and vines has a variety of uses. The genus includes such wonderful garden plants as poison ivy and poison oak! All the sumacs have male and female flowers on separate plants. See also *R. aromatica*, the fragrant sumac, under "Ground Covers."

Rhus typhina   Staghorn sumac

Comments: In the east this native plant is much maligned, while in England it is a most desirable plant that does not sucker as it does in its native range. The common name comes from the velvety covering on new shoots in winter and its antler-like branch structure.
Hardiness: Canadian zone 3; U.S. zone 3.
Availability: **M**.
Height: 20' (6 m). *Spread:* You name it.
Propagation: Suckers.
Soil preferences: Not wet.
Location: Sun to light shade.
Good points: This is a useful, soil-holding plant where its spread will not interfere. In the garden, mowing generally keeps the suckers in check. It is one of the first plants to color (brilliantly) in fall, especially when under stress or on dry soils.
Bad points: Stems can die off suddenly for no obvious reason, but suckers will generally take over.
Uses: Specimen; large border; soil conservation.
Cultivars: 'Laciniata' has individual leaflets that are divided into narrow, fern-like fronds.

Ribes spp.   Currants

Related to the edible currants, these shrubs are grown for their flowers. They do produce fruit, but it is not tasty and cannot be used.

Ribes alpinum   Alpine currant

Comments: This upright shrub is much used for hedging. The flowers are small and bright yellow and the fruit is white.
Hardiness: Canadian zone 2; U.S. zone 2.
Availability: **M**.
Height: 6' (1.8 m). *Spread:* 6' (1.8 m).
Propagation: Stratified seed or softwood cuttings.
Soil preferences: Most; does well in alkaline soils.
Location: Sun to deep shade.
Good points: An excellent hedging plant with shredding bark that gives winter interest. It is shade-tolerant and stands up well to city pollution.
Bad points: Leaf diseases cause early leaf drop some years, especially in humid regions. Currants cannot be planted in some parts of the U.S. where white pine blister rust occurs, although this species is not the alternate host.
Uses: Hedging.
Cultivars: 'Green Mound' is smaller and more spreading. 'Schmidt' is a dwarfer, upright selection.

Ribes aureum   Golden currant

Comments: Many books say this shrub is interchangeable with the clove, or buffalo, currant *(R. odoratum)* but the fragrance is very different. Golden currant is sweet-smelling; buffalo currant distinctly clovish and much harder to find commercially.
Hardiness: Canadian zone 2; U.S. zone 2.
Availability: **M**.
Height: 6' (1.8 m). *Spread:* 8' (2.4 m).
Propagation: Softwood cuttings.
Soil preferences: Most.
Location: Sun to light shade.
Good points: An untidy shrub, it is worth growing at the back of the border for its showy, fragrant flowers and for the reddish fall color.

Bad points: This is the alternate host for white pine blister rust so planting it is banned in parts of the eastern U.S. It also suffers from leaf problems in the humid east, but is good in dry climates.

Uses: Shrub border.

Rosa spp.   Rose

While the culture of modern hybrid roses is outside the scope of this book, there is a place for some of the species, the old-fashioned roses, and the new hardy roses in a shrub border or as specimens. In general, the species and hybrids are not as plagued by pests and diseases as hybrid tea and floribunda roses. A few of these are covered here, but for more detailed information, consult the list in Suggested Reading at the end of the book.

Species and old-fashioned roses

Both the Austrian copper (*Rosa foetida* 'Bicolor') and the Persian yellow (*R. foetida* 'Persiana') roses are good border subjects, hardy to zone 3 Canada, zone 2 U.S. They are most eye-catching in flower, have bright red fruit in fall and grow 6 to 8 feet (1.8 to 2.4 m) tall.

The yellow rose of Texas *(R. x harisonii)*, better known as Harison's yellow, flowers over a longer period but lacks the bright fruit. It is hardy to zone 2 (Canada or U.S.), grows almost 6 feet (1.8 m) high and makes a good upright informal hedge.

The redleaf rose, (now called *R. glauca* but probably still listed as *R. rubrifolia* in local nurseries) is also hardy to zone 2 and has single pink flowers and dark red foliage. It has attractive, egg-shaped fruits in fall that can be used to make rose-hip preserves or wine. If you leave them on the plant, you will probably get the odd seedling growing. It grows as an open bush about 5 feet (1.5 m) tall.

Rosa rugosa   Rugosa roses

Rugosa roses have mid-green, somewhat pleated foliage, pink to white flowers and orange-red hips. They flower in early summer and again later on. There have been many selections made over the years and some of the Explorer series are in this group. Unless otherwise noted, rugosa roses grow around 5 feet (1.5 m) tall. Following are the chief ones. 'Agnes' is double, fragrant, pale yellow; zone 3. 'Blanc Double de Coubert' is double white; zone 2. 'Charles Albanel' is a good pink-flowered ground cover growing only 20 inches (50 cm) tall; zone 2. 'David Thompson' has light pink, double flowers; zone 3. The Grootendorst family of roses were introduced by a Dutch nursery of that name and are hardy to zone 2. 'F.J. Grootendorst' is dark pink; 'Grootendorst Supreme' is red; and 'Pink Grootendorst' is light pink. They are more robust and can reach 7 feet (2.1 m). 'Hansa' has fragrant, double red flowers; zone 3. 'Henry Hudson' is another low-growing form that grows a little over 2 feet (60 cm) tall; it has white to blush-pink flowers; zone 3. 'Therese Bugnet' (pronounced boo-nay) is an older variety that is very fragrant with double pink flowers; zone 2.

Modern shrub roses

There are many hybrid shrub roses of mixed parentage, including some of the Parkland Series from Agriculture Canada in Morden and the Explorer Series from Ottawa, which are easy to find. The following are the most common of this type. 'Adelaide Hoodless' (Parkland), named for the founder of the Woman's Institute, has semi-double red flowers and blooms twice; 3 feet (90 cm); zone 2. 'Bonica' was the first shrub rose to win an All-America Rose Selection award and is a pale pink double with flushes of bloom all summer; 5 feet (1.5 m); zone 5 in Canada, zone 4 in U.S. 'Carefree Beauty' is a semi-double medium pink that blooms all summer; 4 feet (1.2 m); zone 5 in

Canada, zone 4 in U.S. 'Champlain' (Explorer) is a favorite of mine, with flowers that are bright red, slightly fragrant and freely produced all summer. It grows about 3 feet (1 m) high and wide and makes a good low hedge; zone 3 in Canada, zone 2 in U.S. 'Cuthbert Grant' (Parkland) is an upright shrub with dark red, fragrant flowers; 5 feet (1.5 m); zone 3 in Canada, zone 2 in U.S. 'John Franklin' (Explorer) has large clusters of bright red, slightly fragrant flowers; 4 feet (1.2 m); zone 3 in Canada, zone 2 in U.S. 'Morden Blush' (Parkland) is pink to white (depending on the temperature); 3 feet (90 cm); zone 2. 'Morden Cardinette' (Parkland) has double red flowers; 18 inch (45 cm); zone 2. 'Morden Centennial' (Parkland) is pink; 3 feet (90 cm); zone 2.

David Austin roses

These are modern shrub roses, developed in England, that look like the old-fashioned roses you see in prints. Their hardiness is not yet fully known but is probably in the zone 4-5 range. If you try these, buy them locally and get a guarantee.

I have not tried many of them as yet but some of the best seem to be the following. 'Abraham Darby' is pink, flushed with apricot and fragrant; 5 feet (1.5 m). 'Gertrude Jekyll' is darker pink and very fragrant; 4 feet (1.2 m). 'Graham Thomas' has good yellow, fragrant blooms; 4 feet (1.2 m). 'L.D. Braithwaite' has brilliant red blooms and is also fragrant; 3 1/2 feet (1 m). 'Swan' is white, somewhat fragrant, and has very double flowers; 4 feet (1.2 m).

Salix spp.　　　　　　　　　　**Willow**

The large willows were covered in the "Deciduous Trees" section; these species are smaller and not as likely to cause problems with their roots.

Salix caprea　　　　　　　**Goat willow**

Comments: Grow this for the furry spring catkins (pussy willow), that open bright yellow with pollen. It makes a rounded shrub or small tree.
Hardiness: Canadian zone 4b; U.S. zone 4.
Availability: **M**.
Height: 20' (6 m). *Spread:* 15' (4.5 m).
Propagation: Cuttings.
Soil preferences: Moist.
Location: Sun.
Good points: Its early flowers are one of the first signs of spring. Branches can be cut and forced indoors.
Bad points: Leaf spots are more serious on this species and can cause premature leaf drop.
Uses: Border; specimen.
Cultivars: 'Pendula' is a trailing form that either forms a mound or can be top-grafted to weep properly.

Salix matsudana　　　　　　**Corkscrew**
'Tortuosa'　　　　　　　　　　　**willow**

Comments: This cultivar is about the only form of *S. matsudana* ever sold. It can be grown as a tree or shrub.
Hardiness: Canadian zone 5; U.S. zone 4.
Availability: **A**.
Height: 20' (6 m). *Spread:* 10' (3 m).
Propagation: Cuttings.
Soil preferences: Moist.
Location: Sun.
Good points: Its twisted and gnarled branches are a flower-arranger's delight, and it is an interesting conversation piece even if you never arrange a flower. Cut back hard occasionally, as the new growth is the most contorted. Fast growing.
Bad points: It is occasionally attacked by leaf spots, but these are seldom serious.
Uses: Specimen plant.

Salix purpurea **Arctic willow**

Comments: This shrub grows up to 9 feet (2.7 m) tall. The most commonly grown forms are the two cultivars below.

Hardiness: Canadian zone 3; U.S. zone 3.

Availability: **M**.

Height: 9' (2.7 m). *Spread:* 3' (.9 m).

Propagation: Cuttings.

Soil preferences: Moist.

Location: Sun.

Good points: This is a good choice for weaving baskets, as the branches are flexible.

Bad points: It gets several leaf spots and pests, but few are serious.

Uses: Hedging; specimen.

Cultivars: 'Gracilis', a pendulous form usually grafted onto a stem, makes a good small weeping tree. 'Nana' is dwarfer, with blue-green foliage, and is used for hedging.

Sambucus **spp.** **Elder**

Elders are large, rather coarse shrubs that are fast growing and give quick cover in a new garden. They are generally not long-lived.

Sambucus canadensis **American elder**

Comments: This native elder was much grown in the past for its fruit that was used in pies, jams and wine.

Hardiness: Canadian zone 3; U.S. zone 3.

Availability: **M**.

Height: 12' (3.5 m). *Spread:* 10' (3 m).

Propagation: Seed or cuttings.

Soil preferences: Well drained.

Location: Sun to light shade.

Good points: The large, flat-topped, creamy flower heads have an unusual scent that is supposed to repel flies. The resulting fruit is black, copiously produced, and can weigh the branches down.

Bad points: It is rather coarse for small gardens, seeds freely and can become a weed.

Uses: Border.

Cultivars: 'Aurea' has golden leaves and red fruit.

Sambucus nigra **European elder**

Comments: This large shrub also has black fruit and is the best choice for wine-making.

Hardiness: Canadian zone 3; U.S. zone 3.

Availability: **A**.

Height: 20' (6 m). *Spread:* 15' (4.5 m).

Propagation: Seed or cuttings.

Soil preferences: Almost any.

Location: Sun.

Good points: Several of the named forms are worth growing, if you have room.

Bad points: It tends to become weedy and the smell of the foliage and flowers is disagreeable to some.

Uses: Border; behind other shrubs.

Cultivars: 'Aurea' has golden foliage. 'Laciniata' has leaves that are divided into narrow leaflets. 'Marginata' has foliage edged in cream; it is not as easy to find.

Sambucus racemosa **European red elder**

Comments: This red-fruited elder has some of the best cultivars.

Hardiness: Canadian zone 3; U.S. zone 3.

Availability: **M**.

Height: 12' (3.5 m). *Spread:* 10' (3 m).

Propagation: Seed or cuttings.

Soil preferences: Most.

Location: Sun.

Good points: The colored forms grow rapidly and have a bright effect. Cut them back hard in spring once they are established to promote brightly colored new growth.

Bad points: The foliage may burn in hot climates.

Uses: Border; specimen.

Cultivars: 'Plumosa Aurea' has divided foliage; the yellow new growth turns green with age. 'Sutherland Golden' has lacy foliage that stays yellow all summer.

Securinega suffruticosa · Spoil axe

Comments: This almost-unknown plant is in the same family as poinsettia. It forms an upright shrub that becomes arching with age and has very hard wood. It attracts attention, particularly in fall, and deserves to be grown more.
Hardiness: Canadian zone 4; U.S. zone 4.
Availability: **H**.
Height: 8' (2.4 m). *Spread:* 6' (1.8 m).
Propagation: Seed.
Soil preferences: Well drained.
Location: Sun.
Good points: Light green, finely divided leaves give a fresh look in summer and become yellow in fall. The yellowish flowers are not showy but the long strings of green fruit add interest.
Bad points: None.
Uses: Specimen; border.

Shepherdia argentia · Buffalo berry

Comments: This prairie-native shrub has pale foliage that makes a good contrast for other, smaller shrubs. Male and female flowers are on separate plants so plant more than one.
Hardiness: Canadian zone 1; U.S. zone 2.
Availability: **M**.
Height: 15' (4.5 m). *Spread:* 12' (3.5 m).
Propagation: Stratified seed or cuttings.
Soil preferences: Poor, dry and alkaline.
Location: Sun.
Good points: Buffalo berry will grow in most soils except wet ones. The foliage is silvery on both sides and the orange to red fruit can be used for preserves.

Bad points: The wood is somewhat brittle so plants may be damaged in ice storms.
Uses: Accent plant; hedging.

Sorbaria sorbifolia · False spirea

Comments: This upright, suckering shrub makes a good ground cover for banks and wild gardens. It can escape and go semi-wild.
Hardiness: Canadian zone 2; U.S. zone 2.
Availability: **M**.
Height: 5' (1.5 m). *Spread:* Infinite.
Propagation: Seed or cuttings.
Soil preferences: Most, but grows taller in wettish conditions.
Location: Sun to light shade.
Good points: The white flower trusses in midsummer are attractive and look similar to a somewhat fluffy lilac spray. The leaves are like those of a mountain ash; they open early but fall with no color change. This plant can be chopped back almost to ground level in spring if it gets too bushy; it grows well in dappled shade.
Bad points: It can become invasive if neglected.
Uses: Screen; ground cover.

Spiraea spp. · Spirea

This is a very versatile group of shrubs, many of which are grown for their flowers; the modern, dwarf forms are finding great acceptance as foliage plants.

Modern plant nomenclature now lumps the bumalda and Japanese spireas together under *S. japonica*, but they mostly have complex parentage and you will normally find them in catalogs as they are listed here.

Spiraea x arguta · Garland spirea

Comments: This is one of the first spireas to bloom.
Hardiness: Canadian zone 3; U.S. zone 3.

Availability: **F**.
Height: 5' (1.5 m). *Spread:* 6' (1.8 m).
Propagation: Cuttings.
Soil preferences: Most.
Location: Sun.
Good points: This shrub has flat clusters of small white flowers in early spring on somewhat arching branches.
Bad points: It may suffer from mildew in wet summers.
Uses: Border; foundation.
Cultivars: 'Compacta' is a lower-growing form useful for the front of a border and readily available.

Spiraea x bumalda   Bumalda spirea

Comments: This hybrid of two Japanese species originated in Switzerland—see how plants get around! The various named forms of this and the Japanese spirea are among the most popular shrubs. Recent breeding work means you can expect to see many more varieties, in different colors, appear on the market in the next few years. Prune in spring.
Hardiness: Canadian zone 3; U.S. zone 3.
Availability: **M**.
Height: 2-5' (60-150 cm).
Spread: 2-4' (60-120 cm).
Propagation: Cuttings.

Soil preferences: Most, except wet.
Location: Sun.
Good points: Flat clusters of pink flowers up to 4 inches (10 cm) across bloom in midsummer. Removing the old flowers will give a second show later, and there is good fall color most years. The differing height of the cultivars means you can find one to fit most locations.
Bad points: There are several pests and diseases that can attack these plants, but I have never found them to be a problem.
Uses: Border; foundation; informal hedge.
Cultivars: See table below.

Spiraea japonica   Japanese spirea

Comments: These mostly small, mound-forming shrubs are grown for both their foliage and flowers.
Hardiness: Canadian zone 2b; U.S. zone 2.
Availability: **M**.
Height: Varies according to cultivar.
Spread: Varies according to cultivar.
Propagation: Cuttings.
Soil preferences: Most.
Location: Sun to light shade.
Good points: This shrub is grown for the flat heads of pink flowers; in the colored forms, the leaves don't turn green in bright sun.

Bumalda spirea variety	Size	Comments
'Anthony Waterer'	4 ft (1.2 m)	Pink-tinged new foliage; repeat bloom.
'Coccinea'	4 ft (1.2 m)	Much darker flower than 'Anthony Waterer'.
'Crispa'	3 ft (90 cm)	Darker, puckered foliage; grows wider than tall.
'Froebelli'	5 ft (1.5 m)	Taller, but similar to 'Anthony Waterer'.
'Goldflame'	3 ft (90 cm)	New leaves are orange, turning yellow then green; flowers are not conspicuous.
'Limemound'	3 ft (90 cm)	Lime-green leaves are tinged pink when young.

Bad points: It can suffer from several diseases, such as mildew and leaf spot, but they are generally rare.

Uses: Border; foundation; ground cover.

Cultivars: 'Golden Princess' is a new British introduction with bronzy new foliage becoming yellow; it may not be quite as hardy and gets 2 1/2 feet (75 cm) high. 'Goldmound' has yellow foliage that is brightest in spring but stays good all summer: it grows about 2 1/2 feet (75 cm) tall. 'Little Princess' has green leaves and dark pink flowers on a 2-foot (60-cm) plant. 'Shirobana' has green leaves and flowers of rose, pink and white, often in the same cluster; it is not quite as hardy and grows to 3 feet (90 cm) high.

Spiraea nipponica   Nippon spirea

Comments: This is known best by the two cultivars listed below. Prune immediately after flowering when necessary.

Hardiness: Canadian zone 3; U.S. zone 3.

Availability: **M**.

Height: See cultivar descriptions below.

Spread: See cultivar descriptions below.

Propagation: Cuttings.

Soil preferences: Most.

Location: Sun.

Good points: The foliage, dark green above and bluish beneath, is hidden by the flat heads of white flowers in early summer.

Bad points: It may occasionally get mildew.

Uses: Border; foundation; informal hedge.

Cultivars: 'Halward's Silver' is a dwarf form growing 3 feet (90 cm) high and wide, with a densely branched form that becomes covered with flowers. 'Snowmound' is a good replacement for the popular bridalwreath *(S. x vanhouttei)* with a more compact habit, but similar flowers; it grows to 4 feet (1.2 m) tall and 6 feet (1.8 m) wide.

Spiraea trichocarpa   Korean spirea

Comments: Closely related to the nippon spirea *(S. nipponica)*, this blooms just after bridalwreath *(S. x vanhouttei)* and thus extends the season. Prune plants immediately after flowering.

Hardiness: Canadian zone 3; U.S. zone 3.

Availability: **A**.

Height: 6' (1.8 m). *Spread:* 8' (2.4 m).

Propagation: Cuttings.

Soil preferences: Most.

Location: Sun.

Good points: Clusters of small cream flowers with yellow centers are borne on the top of the branches in early summer. This is a tough shrub that will survive in poorer conditions than other, similar, white-flowered spireas.

Bad points: It may occasionally get mildew.

Uses: Border; foundation.

Cultivars: 'Snow White' is an improved form with paler leaves and larger, whiter flowers.

Spiraea trilobata   Three-lobed spirea

Comments: The lobes on the foliage make this spirea distinctive when not in flower, but the blooms are obviously those of a spirea. When necessary, prune immediately after flowering.

Hardiness: Canadian zone 2b; U.S. zone 2.

Availability: **M**.

Height: 4' (1.2 m). *Spread:* 4' (1.2 m).

Propagation: Cuttings.

Soil preferences: Most.

Location: Sun.

Good points: This is probably the hardiest of the white-flowered spireas and is the most attractive when not in bloom. It has large clusters of white flowers on the top of arching branches early in the season.

Bad points: Again, mildew is about the only problem.

Uses: Border; foundation.

Spiraea x vanhouttei — Bridalwreath spirea, Van Houtte spirea

Comments: This sometimes overplanted spirea has an attractive arching habit. Renewal prune in spring immediately after flowering when needed.

Hardiness: Canadian zone 3; U.S. zone 3.
Availability: **M**.
Height: 5' (1.5 m). *Spread:* 7' (2.1 m).
Propagation: Cuttings.
Soil preferences: Most.
Location: Sun.
Good points: In late spring, small white flowers in flat clusters 1 to 2 inches (2.5 to 5 cm) across are abundantly produced and often hide the foliage, which may turn red in the fall. This shrub is a good choice for town gardens, being pollution-tolerant.
Bad points: Mildew can be bad some years.
Uses: Border; specimen; foundation.

Staphylea trifolia — Bladdernut

Comments: This unusual native shrub grows at the edge of woods from Quebec to Oklahoma and makes a shapely bush in cultivation.

Hardiness: Canadian zone 4; U.S. zone 3.
Availability: **H**.
Height: 12' (3.5 m). *Spread:* 10' (3 m).
Propagation: Stratified seed.
Soil preferences: Moist but well drained.
Location: Sun to shade.
Good points: The bladders (fruit) persist into winter and contain loose seeds that rattle in the wind and add interest.
Bad points: Flowers are plentiful, but being greenish-white they are not showy.
Uses: Winter interest. Plant close to a path where the seed pods can be heard.

Symphoricarpos spp. — Snowberry

Mostly native shrubs from eastern Canada and the northern U.S. with inconspicuous flowers but showy fruit that lasts well into winter. In areas with early snow, the white-fruited forms blend into the background while those with colored fruit stand out.

Symphoricarpos albus — Snowberry

Comments: This is a good shrub for winter interest where snow comes late or not at all.

Hardiness: Canadian zone 3; U.S. zone 3.
Availability: **M**.
Height: 5' (1.5 m). *Spread:* 4' (1.2 m).
Propagation: Cuttings.
Soil preferences: Most.
Location: Sun to shade.
Good points: This shrub grows and fruits well in shade. It makes a good ground cover on slopes, as it suckers slowly.
Bad points: Anthracnose and several other diseases, but they are seldom serious.
Uses: Border; foundation; ground cover.

Symphoricarpos orbiculatus — Coralberry, Indian currant

Comments: I had never realized the value of this shrub until one fall it caught my attention in a restaurant parking lot. I have been a fan ever since. Prune in spring.

Hardiness: Canadian zone 2b; U.S. zone 2.
Availability: **M**.
Height: 5' (1.5 m). *Spread:* 6' (1.8 m).
Propagation: Cuttings.
Soil preferences: Not fussy.
Location: Sun to light shade.
Good points: Arching branches have gray-green leaves that turn a dull red in fall, with the upper surface changing first. The red fruits are in clusters like small raspberries, except that the end berry is usually the largest.

Bad points: There are several pests and diseases, of which anthracnose is probably the most serious.

Uses: Border; screen; tall ground cover.

Cultivars: Coralberry is one parent of a hybrid snowberry, *S.* x *chenaultii*, of which the form 'Hancock' is readily available. A good ground cover growing 18 inches (45 cm) tall, it is widely used in Europe.

Syringa spp.   Lilac

This large group of shrubs is best known for the common lilac and its multitude of named forms (see *S. vulgaris*). Many an old homestead site can still be located by the peony, 'Golden Glow' rudbeckia and lilac bush that have survived over the years, even when the house has returned to the earth. By selecting from the different groups, you can have lilacs in flower for several weeks in spring.

All lilacs are best planted as container-grown or B & B plants, although many of the hybrids are sold prepackaged in spring. If you trim off the old flowers immediately below the truss once they have faded, the size and quantity of the next year's flowers will be improved. Renewal pruning every few years is usually enough unless the plant is very overgrown.

Syringa x hyacinthiflora   American lilac

Comments: A cross between the common lilac (*S. vulgaris*) and the early lilac (*S. oblata*), this is very similar in appearance to the French hybrids.

Hardiness: Canadian zone 2b; U.S. zone 2.

Availability: **F** to **S**.

Height: 10' (3 m). *Spread:* 8' (2.4 m).

Propagation: Cuttings taken as soon as the flowers fade.

Soil preferences: Not wet.

Location: Sun.

Good points: They are early-flowering, before the French hybrids; they start the lilac season and have a good perfume.

Bad points: See *Syringa vulgaris*.

Uses: Specimen; border; screen.

Cultivars: 'Ester Staley', 'Pocahontas', and 'Sister Justina' all have single flowers and are magenta, purple and white respectively.

Syringa x prestoniae   Preston lilac

Comments: This is a cross between the late and the nodding lilacs (*S. villosa* x *S. reflexa*), first made at Ottawa and named for the originator, Miss Isabella Preston. It is a useful plant for extending the flowering season.

Hardiness: Canadian zone 2; U.S. zone 2.

Availability: **M** to **A**.

Height: 10' (3 m). *Spread:* 8' (2.4 m).

Propagation: Cuttings.

Soil preferences: Not wet.

Location: Sun.

Good points: It flowers after the French hybrids with long, nodding trusses containing hundreds of small, single flowers with a pleasing scent. The colors are more muted and the leaves are slightly hairy. This hybrid is not as prone to leaf miner.

Bad points: The scent is not as strong as on many French hybrids.

Uses: Screen; specimen; hedge.

Cultivars: 'Coral' and 'James Macfarlane' are pink, while 'Donald Wyman' and 'Royalty' are shades of purple.

Syringa reticulata   Japanese tree lilac

Comments: A much larger shrub that is often trained as a small tree, it seems able to withstand salt and can be used as a street tree.

Hardiness: Canadian zone 2; U.S. zone 2.

Availability: **M**.

Height: 25' (7.5 m). *Spread:* 20' (6 m).

Propagation: Cuttings.
Soil preferences: Not wet.
Location: Sun.
Good points: Creamy white flowers, with a strange perfume that some people don't like, bloom when all the other lilacs are over; a speckled bark adds winter interest. This species is resistant to mildew and borers.
Bad points: Few.
Uses: Specimen shrub or tree.
Cultivars: 'Chantilly Lace' has leaves with a yellow margin but it is hard to find as yet. 'Ivory Silk' is usually grown as the tree form; it has a rounded head and starts to flower while still a young plant.

Syringa	**French hybrids,**
vulgaris	**common lilac**

Comments: The first really popular hybrids came from Lemoine Nurseries in France, thus all the forms of common lilac became known as French hybrids. Many new cultivars have since been raised world-wide. Try to buy plants on their own roots (from cuttings) or grafted onto ash seedlings; plants grafted onto lilac suckers can lead to two different colors on one plant if shoots come from the roots. Cultivars are sometimes top-grafted to form a small tree.
Hardiness: Canadian zone 2; U.S. zone 2.
Availability: **M**.
Height: 12' (3.5 m). *Spread:* 8' (2.4 m).
Propagation: Cuttings taken as soon as the flowers fade.
Soil preferences: Not wet.
Location: Sun.
Good points: Fragrant single or double flowers bloom in a range of colors. This is one of the showiest plants when in bloom.
Bad points: After blooming it is dull for the rest of the year and has no fall color. Plants can

sucker badly and form thickets. Mildew is a problem some years, as are leaf miners, while borers can cause stems to wilt and die. Wet soil in spring can cause flower buds to abort, or even kill plants.
Uses: Specimen; screen; hedge; mixed plantings.
Cultivars: There are several hundred named forms but these are the most readily available: 'Belle de Nancy' is double and pinkish. 'Charles Joly' is double purple. 'Katherine Havemeyer' is another double pink. 'Ludwig Spath' is a popular single purple. 'Michel Buchner' is double lilac. 'Miss Ellen Wilmott' is double white. 'Mme Lemoine' is also double white. 'President Grevy' is double with bluish flowers. 'President Lincoln' is a single violet. 'Sensation' is different, having single purple blooms with a white edge to the petals. 'Primrose' is a single cream that can be yellow while in bud. Also worth looking for are 'Dappled Dawn', a single magenta with variegated leaves, and 'Agincourt Beauty', a single violet with the largest individual flowers of all.

Syringa spp.	**Other lilacs**

The species above are the "big four" lilacs, but there are several others that are worth considering for the garden.
Rouen (Chinese) lilac *(S. x chinensis)*. The common name comes from the French town where this was first discovered. It has no connection with China, but it does have masses of small pinkish-white fragrant flowers about the same time as the Preston lilacs (late in the season). The plant forms a mid-sized, rounded bush up to 10 feet (3 m) tall.
Dwarf Korean lilac *(S. meyeri)*. This makes a small bushy shrub to 8 feet (2.4 m), has pink flowers and makes a good hedge or specimen plant.
Korean lilac *(S. patula)*. Another smallish lilac, it grows about 9 feet (2.7 m) tall. 'Miss Kim' is the most readily available cultivar. It has pale pink

flowers over a long period and good fall color, unusual in a lilac.

Persian lilac *(S. x persica).* This has arching branches and will reach about 8 feet (2.4 m) tall and wide. It has showy, bright pink flowers and makes a good informal hedge or a screen.

Late lilac *(S. villosa).* One of the parents of the Preston lilacs, this is a large plant, up to 12 feet (3.5 m) tall, with pink flowers. It is useful for the back of a border and also makes a good, tall, flowering hedge, in which case trim shortly after blooming to give time for flower buds to form for the next year.

'Minuet'. Similar to Preston lilacs when in flower, this is a denser plant growing about 8 feet (2.4 m) high. It is readily available and flowers freely.

Tamarix ramosissima   **Tamarix,**
(pentandra)   **tamarisk**

Comments: Tamarix is tolerant of sandy soils and salt, making it useful for both seaside and city planting. It flowers on the new wood, so it can be cut back hard in spring when overgrown. Doing some renewal pruning each spring keeps plants shorter and flowering better. Plant container-grown stock.

Hardiness: Canadian zone 4; U.S. zone 4.

Availability: **A.**

Height: 10-12' (3-3.5 m). *Spread:* 6-8' (1.8-2.4 m).

Propagation: Seed or cuttings.

Soil preferences: Sandy and acidic, but adaptable.

Location: Sun.

Good points: The feathery foliage is light and airy; the flowers are pale pink and small, but form large panicles in June, July and occasionally thereafter.

Bad points: Powdery mildew is bad some years.

Uses: Specimen; border.

Cultivars: 'Pink Cascade' has a blue tinge to the foliage and brighter flowers. 'Rubra' or 'Summerglow' (same plant) has rosy pink flowers.

Viburnum spp.   **Viburnum**

This is a very diverse group of shrubs that flower from midwinter (in mild regions) to late summer, and whose showy fruit, in a multitude of shades, gives color late into winter. Flowers are white, or occasionally pink, and are among the most fragrant of any shrub. Like hydrangea, the flower heads often have showy sterile flowers on the outside and small fertile flowers in the center.

Viburnum x   **Burkwood's**
burkwoodii   **viburnum**

Comments: The smaller Korean spice viburnum *(V. carlesii)* is one parent of this hybrid, which accounts for the clove-like scent.

Hardiness: Canadian zone 6; U.S. zone 5.

Availability: **M.**

Height: 10' (3 m). *Spread:* 8' (2.4 m).

Propagation: Cuttings in mist.

Soil preferences: Well drained.

Location: Sun to light shade.

Good points: Pink buds open white and are delightfully fragrant in spring. Leaves are dark green above, gray-green beneath and turn dark red in fall.

Bad points: Several leaf spots and insects (including scale) occasionally infest this shrub, but they are seldom very serious.

Uses: Specimen; border; screen.

Cultivars: 'Mohawk' has darker pink buds which are showy for several weeks before the flowers open, and it has better disease resistance.

Viburnum x   **Fragrant snowball**
carlcephalum   **viburnum**

Comments: This is another fragrant hybrid with the Korean spice viburnum as one parent. From the other parent comes the large flower heads.

Hardiness: Canadian zone 6; U.S. zone 5.

Availability: **M.**

Height: 10' (3 m). *Spread:* 8' (2.4 m).
Propagation: Cuttings.
Soil preferences: Most.
Location: Sun to light shade.
Good points: The pink buds open to give dense clusters of white flowers up to 5 inches (13 cm) across. Dark green leaves turn a brick red in fall.
Bad points: Leaf spots and mildew attack this species occasionally.
Uses: Screen; border.
Cultivars: 'Cayuga' is smaller in size, the flowers are a pinkish-red and the plant has improved disease resistance.

Viburnum carlesii   Korean spice viburnum

Comments: This forms an egg-shaped bush with plentiful white flowers that have a distinctive spicy scent. It has been used in breeding several hybrids because of this.
Hardiness: Canadian zone 5b; U.S. zone 4.
Availability: **A**.
Height: 6' (1.8 m). *Spread:* 6' (1.8 m).
Propagation: Cuttings.
Soil preferences: Well drained, slightly acidic.
Location: Sun to midshade.
Good points: Pink buds open to white flower balls 2 to 2 1/2 inches (5 to 6 cm) across that perfume the air around them. The leaves take on a dull, red fall color in good years.
Bad points: None.
Uses: Specimen; border; screen.
Cultivars: 'Aurora' has red buds and flowers that open pink and fade to white as they age.

Viburnum dentatum   Arrowwood

Comments: The straight shoots of this native upright shrub look as though they would make good arrows; perhaps this is how the common name originated.
Hardiness: Canadian zone 4; U.S. zone 4.

Availability: **M**.
Height: 8' (2.4 m). *Spread:* 6' (1.8 m).
Propagation: Cuttings in mist.
Soil preferences: Moist but well drained.
Location: Sun to mid-shade.
Good points: Flattened, scentless heads of creamy white flowers are borne in late spring. The berries are blue to black and attract birds. If grown in full sun, the dark green foliage turns red in fall.
Bad points: Very few; this is one of the least troubled viburnums.
Uses: Border; screen.

Viburnum dilatatum   Linden viburnum

Comments: The leaves are somewhat variable in shape, even on the same plant, but in general they are like a linden. The species tends to be an open shrub, but the new cultivars have a denser shape.
Hardiness: Canadian zone 5b; U.S. zone 5.
Availability: **F** in Canada; **A** in U.S. but this will probably improve as the cultivars become better known.
Height: 7' (2.1 m). *Spread:* 7' (2.1 m).
Propagation: Cuttings.
Soil preferences: Well drained.
Location: Sun to part shade.
Good points: Many small clusters of white flowers in spring give fall fruit that is among the best and brightest, lasting well into winter. It has good fall color most years.
Bad points: None.
Uses: Specimen; border; screen.
Cultivars: 'Catskill' is more compact at 5 feet (1.5 m), growing broader than tall with good fall color. 'Erie' is free-flowering so you get more, brighter fruit, and has an orange-red fall color. It too is compact, growing 6 feet (1.8 m) high and more across. 'Iroquois' has dark green leaves, creamy flowers and larger

fruit. 'Oneida' often reblooms during the summer and gives lots of fruit. These both grow about 10 feet (3 m) tall.

Viburnum lantana — Wayfaringtree

Comments: This is an old English common name. In fact, it is more shrub than tree. It forms a rounded bush and grows better on dryish soils than other viburnums.

Hardiness: Canadian zone 2b; U.S. zone 3.

Availability: **M**.

Height: 10' (3 m). *Spread:* 12' (3.5 m).

Propagation: Cuttings.

Soil preferences: Well drained to quite dry.

Location: Sun to part shade.

Good points: Flat heads of flowers contrast with dark green, leathery foliage. Fruit is multi-colored in the fall when leaves turn dark red.

Bad points: None.

Uses: Specimen; screen.

Cultivars: 'Mohican' has more compact growth, reaching around 8 feet (2.4 m), and the fruit persists longer.

Viburnum lentago — Nannyberry, sheepberry

Comments: I grow this for the interesting fruit, which changes from green to yellow, then pink, red and finally black, often all in the same cluster at once. The name comes from the smell of the fruit.

Hardiness: Canadian zone 2; U.S. zone 2.

Availability: **M**.

Height: 15' (4.5 m). *Spread:* 10' (3 m).

Propagation: Cuttings.

Soil preferences: Most.

Location: Sun or shade.

Good points: Glossy mid-green foliage turns brick-red most years. White flowers in mounded clusters are not fragrant; the fruit is its best feature.

Bad points: Mildew can be bad in shade; leaf beetles sometimes attack the foliage.

Uses: Specimen; screen.

Viburnum opulus — European bush-cranberry

Comments: The leaves are maple-like and more toothed than on the native high bush-cranberry *(V. trilobum)* but the clusters of red fruit in fall show it cannot be a maple.

Hardiness: Canadian zone 2b; U.S. zone 3.

Availability: **M**.

Height: 10' (3 m). *Spread:* 10' (3 m).

Propagation: Cuttings.

Soil preferences: Most.

Location: Sun.

Good points: Four-inch (10-cm), flat clusters of flowers with a ring of sterile flowers round the outside appear in spring. They are followed by bright red berries from midsummer through to fall, earlier than on high bush-cranberry.

Bad points: It attracts aphids, especially the cultivar 'Roseum'.

Uses: Screen; border.

Cultivars: 'Compactum' is a miniature version growing only half the height. 'Nanum' is a very small form growing only 2 feet (60 cm) tall that seldom flowers and makes a good small hedge. 'Roseum' (or 'Sterile'—the European snowball or Guelder rose) has round heads of flowers up to 3 inches (8 cm) in diameter; the flower head is composed of sterile flowers, which makes it very showy but no fruit is produced. Aphids can cause severe leaf distortion unless controlled.

Viburnum plicatum — Japanese snowball

Comments: There is a lot of confusion over the correct nomenclature for this species. The plant that is normally sold as *V. plicatum* is completely sterile and, by definition, a species must be able to reproduce. Whatever the correct name should be, this is a good plant that flowers freely.

Hardiness: Canadian zone 5b; U.S. zone 5.
Availability: **A**.
Height: 12' (3.5 m). *Spread:* 8' (2.4 m).
Propagation: Cuttings.
Soil preferences: Well drained.
Location: Sun.
Good points: Tennis-ball-sized globes of white flowers are carried on an upright bush in late spring. They turn geenish with age but last well.
Bad points: It flowers so well the weight of the blooms can bend the branches down.
Uses: Border; specimen.
Cultivars: 'Pink Sensation' has flowers that open pink and keep their color. 'Roseum' flowers open white and turn pink with age.

Viburnum plicatum var. *tomentosum*   Double-file viburnum

Comments: This forms a more spreading plant with almost horizontal branches in layers; the overall shape becomes a slightly flattened dome.

Hardiness: Canadian zone 6; U.S. zone 5.
Availability: **S** in Canada; **A** in U.S. (cultivars).
Height: 8' (2.4 m). *Spread:* 10' (3 m).
Propagation: Cuttings.
Soil preferences: Well drained.
Location: Sun to light shade.
Good points: The horizontal branches have numerous flat clusters of white flowers held above the upper surface that look like a host of lace doilies laid out to dry. The fruit and fruit stalks are equally showy, while the leaves are shiny dark green with conspicuous veins.
Bad points: Mildew can be a problem in humid summers.

Uses: Specimen shrub; border.
Cultivars: 'Lanarth' has larger flowers and a slightly more upright habit. 'Mariesii' has large flowers on longer stalks and good fall color. 'Shasta' is a recent introduction that is twice as wide as tall and probably has the largest flowers and brightest fruit. 'Summer Snowflake' is smaller than the other cultivars.

Viburnum trilobum   High bush-cranberry

Comments: The name bush-cranberry is a misnomer. The fruits are not really cranberries, as a taste will soon tell you, but they look similar.

Hardiness: Canadian zone 2; U.S. zone 2.
Availability: **M**.
Height: 12' (3.5 m). *Spread:* 10' (3 m).
Propagation: Cuttings.
Soil preferences: Well drained but moist.
Location: Sun to light shade.
Good points: A tall, rather open shrub with flat heads of white flowers and large, sterile outer flowers in late spring. The fruit turns yellow, then bright red and hangs on all winter unless the birds get really hungry.
Bad points: European viburnum beetle can play havoc with the foliage, eating it to tatters. It will also attack arrowwood *(V. dentatum)*, nannyberry *(V. lentago)* and European bush-cranberry *(V. opulus)*, but in my experience it is worst on this species.
Uses: Screen; border.
Cultivars: 'Compactum' is only half the height of the species and without any fall color. 'Alfredo' is an improved 'Compactum' with quite good fall color. 'Wentworth' has larger fruit that ripens later.

Weigela florida   **Weigela**

Comments: These are mostly midsized shrubs with white, pink or red flowers. The cultivars listed as hardy are at least one zone hardier than the zone listed below.

Hardiness: Canadian zone 5; U.S. zone 4.

Availability: **M.**

Height: 4-10' (1.2-3 m).

Spread: 4-6' (1.2-1.8 m).

Propagation: Cuttings.

Soil preferences: Well drained.

Location: Sun.

Good points: These free-flowering shrubs add a splash of color in late spring and early summer. The funnel-shaped flowers grow in small clusters.

Bad points: None. Renewal prune every two or three years after flowering.

Uses: Border; foundation.

Cultivars: See table below.

Yucca filamentosa   **Adam's needle**

Comments: This exotic-looking plant surprises many people with its hardiness. It does not grow well in heavy, wet soils. The closely related Spanish bayonet *(Y. glauca)* is similar but slightly hardier.

Hardiness: Canadian zone 4; U.S. zone 4.

Availability: **M.**

Height: 3' (.9 m) (flowers to 8'/2.4 m).

Spread: 4' (1.2 m).

Propagation: Division.

Soil preferences: Well drained.

Location: Full sun.

Good points: Rosette of leaves, tall spikes of long-lasting, waxy, creamy bells in midsummer.

Bad points: Sharp pointed leaves can be dangerous after dark.

Uses: Mixed border; specimen plant.

Cultivars: 'Golden Sword' has yellow-centered leaves.

Weigela variety	Flowers	Foliage	Size	Comments
'Bristol Ruby'	red	green	7 ft/2.1 m	
'Bristol Snowflake'	white	green	5 ft/1.5 m	Slow growing.
'Centennial'	red	green	8 ft/2.4 m	Hardy.
'Minuet'	bright pink	tinged purple	2 ft/60 cm	Hardy.
'Newport Red' ('Vanicek')	bright red	green	6 ft/1.8 m	May rebloom.
'Pink Princess'	pink	green	6 ft/1.8 m	Open habit.
'Red Prince'	bright red	green	6 ft/1.8 m	May rebloom.
'Rumba'	red with a yellow throat	purple-tinged	4 ft/1.2 m	Good rebloom.
'Variegata'	rose-pink	edged cream	4 ft/1.2 m	Open habit.

CONIFERS

Conifers are the major evergreen plants in most gardens, and they play an important role in the landscape. They come in a multitude of shapes and colors and add winter interest in addition to being focal points in the summer garden.

Abies concolor   **Silver fir, white fir**

Comments: An evergreen (or eversilver) tree with graceful, columnar growth that should be planted B & B or container-grown for best results.
Hardiness: Canadian zone 4; U.S. zone 4.
Availability: **M**.
Height: 60' (18 m). *Spread:* 40' (12 m).
Propagation: Stratified seed.
Soil preferences: Most, but not heavy clay.
Location: Sun.
Good points: A good specimen plant, it rarely loses its lower branches, remaining full to the ground; the flat needles, silver on both sides, enhance the effect. I consider it to be superior to the blue spruce.
Bad points: None.
Uses: Specimen; screen.

Chamaecyparis spp.   **False cypress**

Young forms have awl-shaped needles, while mature trees have leaves more like the white cedar *(Thuja occidentalis)*, making identification difficult. There are four main species, but hundreds of named forms, many of which are miniatures suitable for the rock garden. In general, this is not as widely grown as other conifers.

Chamaecyparis   **Nootka false cypress,**
 nootkatensis   **Alaska cedar, yellow cypress**

Comments: This grows into a stately tree and is becoming increasingly popular. The cultivar has survived -39° with no damage.
Hardiness: Canadian zone 6; U.S. zone 4.
Availability: **S**.
Height: 40' (12 m). *Spread:* 30' (9 m).
Propagation: Winter cuttings.
Soil preferences: Most.
Location: Sun.
Good points: A dark green, broadly conical tree with drooping branchlets.
Bad points: None.
Uses: Specimen.
Cultivars: 'Pendula', apart from being one zone hardier, has a more upright shape with the branches hanging vertically. It makes an attractive specimen plant and is becoming readily available.

Chamaecyparis   **Hinoki**
 obtusa   **false cypress**

Comments: Native to Japan, this is a large tree with a conical shape and horizontal branches. The species is rarely grown, but the many named forms (usually smaller) are readily available. Plant container-grown stock.
Hardiness: Canadian zone 5; U.S. zone 4.
Availability: **M**.
Height: 50' (15 m). *Spread:* 25' (7.5 m).
Propagation: Winter cuttings.
Soil preferences: Moist, well drained.
Location: Sun, but sheltered from wind.
Good points: It is slow growing, with dense foliage, and the many named forms give a wide range of sizes, colors and textures.
Bad points: This species tends to turn brown at low temperatures, losing some of its winter effect.
Uses: Specimen; foundation; rock garden; mixed border.
Cultivars: 'Aurea' is conical with golden foliage; 30 feet (9 m). 'Crippsii' is slow growing; makes a broad golden cone to 35 feet (10.5 m). 'Gracilis' is strong growing with pendulous

branches; it makes a mound 15 feet (4.5 m) high in time. 'Kosteri' is a slow growing dwarf form with bright green fans of foliage set on a slight tilt; it reaches about 30 inches (75 cm) after 10 years. 'Nana Gracilis' is a dwarf form with dark green fans of leaves that may reach 8 feet (2.4 m) eventually. 'Torulosa' has curious foliage that is almost coral-like, rather than growing in flat fans.

Chamaecyparis pisifera — Sawara false cypress

Comments: Here is another broadly conical tree that is seldom offered as the species. There is, however, a multitude of named forms, the most common of which are listed below.

Hardiness: Canadian zone 4b; U.S. zone 4.

Availability: **M** to **H**.

Height: 40' (12 m). *Spread:* 30' (9 m).

Propagation: Winter cuttings.

Soil preferences: Well drained, slightly acidic.

Location: Sun.

Good points: The wide range of shapes and sizes suits almost every situation. Foliage varies greatly among the cultivars.

Bad points: Plants may winter-burn in exposed locations.

Uses: Various, depending on form.

Cultivars: 'Boulevard' has soft blue foliage; it can grow to 10 feet (3 m) but winter-burns badly in cold, exposed locations. 'Filifera' has narrow thread-like foliage; slow growing and usually wider than tall, it is not as subject to winter damage. 'Filifera Aurea' is somewhat smaller and with yellow foliage. 'Filifera Aurea Nana' is much smaller and suitable for a large rock garden. 'Plumosa Aurea' has densely packed yellow foliage, soft to the touch. There are many other forms of 'Plumosa'. 'Snow' makes a very small plant with bluish foliage tipped white; it needs wind protection in winter. 'Squarrosa Intermedia' has dense grayish juvenile foliage forming a globe-shaped bush. 'Boulevard' and 'Snow' are forms of 'Squarrosa'.

Cryptomeria japonica — Japanese cedar

Comments: This evergreen for warmer climates is not as well known as it should be. Some cultivars are dwarf and suitable for the larger rock garden, but the species is a large conical tree.

Hardiness: Canadian zone 6; U.S. zone 5.

Availability: **S**.

Height: 50' (15 m). *Spread:* 25' (7.5 m).

Propagation: Seed or winter cuttings.

Soil preferences: Well drained.

Location: Sun.

Good points: Quite fast growing, attractive foliage, distinctive.

Bad points: None.

Uses: Specimen tree.

Cultivars: 'Compressa' is a very dwarf globe form, growing to 3 feet (.9 m) at maturity. 'Lobbii' is columnar, rather than conical, in shape and has a better green color in winter. 'Vilmoriniana' is another dwarf globe, similar to 'Compressa' but not quite as neat.

Ginkgo biloba — Maidenhair tree, ginkgo

Comments: A very ancient tree that was known from fossilized remains long before it was found still growing in China. Male and female flowers are on separate trees. It is most closely related to the conifers and so is included here. Prune, when needed, in spring.

Hardiness: Canadian zone 3; U.S. zone 3.

Availability: **M**.

Height: 50' (15 m) or more. *Spread:* 30' (9 m).

Propagation: Cuttings.

Soil preferences: Most.

Location: Sun.

Good points: Good pollution-tolerance makes this a good choice for city planting. A fairly upright habit makes it suitable for smallish gardens. It has very good yellow fall color and a distinctive leaf shape, rather like a maidenhair fern.

Bad points: It is slow to establish (three or four years), but then grows quite quickly. Fruit on female trees has a terrible odor as it rots. The nuts are edible (and prized by the Asian community), but the flesh can cause dermatitis. Wear rubber gloves if you want to collect the fruit.

Uses: Specimen or street tree.

Cultivars: 'Autumn Gold' was selected for its outstanding fall color. 'Princeton Sentry' has a narrow, columnar outline. Both of these (and most of the other named forms) are male clones.

Juniperus spp.   **Juniper**

A large group of evergreen shrubs and trees much used in the garden, junipers are tough and will survive with the minimum of care. As a result, they are widely planted, often in unsuitable locations. Remember, the cute little plant in a 2-gallon (8- L) container may have an ultimate spread of 15 feet (4.5 m).

After a few years there is a constant battle to keep the encroaching branches off a path, and a constant cursing while handling their prickly shoots. (For low-growing junipers, see the "Ground Covers" section of this chapter.)

Plant B & B or container-grown plants only. When pruning is needed (usually to control the size of spreading forms), cut back individual branches rather than shearing. Try to cut under a new branchlet to hide the stub.

Juniperus chinensis   **Chinese juniper**

Comments: Most forms of Chinese juniper are upright and there are many named forms. Even experts disagree on the correct affiliation of some cultivars, and plants listed here under hybrid juniper *(J. x media)* may be called Chinese juniper in some catalogs.

Hardiness: Canadian zone 4-5; U.S. zone 3-4.

Availability: **M.**

Height: Varies according to cultivar.

Propagation: Cuttings.

Soil preferences: Moist but well drained.

Location: Sun.

Good points: Available in a wide range of sizes and colors, there is a suitable plant for most locations.

Bad points: It is a host for cedar-apple rust and mites.

Uses: Specimen; foundation; screen.

Cultivars: The hardiness zones are given for Canada first, then for the United States. *See table opposite.*

Juniperus communis   **Common juniper**

Comments: This variable species contains both prostrate and upright forms.

Hardiness: Canadian zone 3-4; U.S. zone 3.

Availability: **A.**

Height: Varies according to cultivar.

Propagation: Cuttings.

Soil preferences: Most; grows well in dry soil.

Location: Sun.

Good points: It is salt-tolerant so it can be used for roadside plantings. The oil from the berries is used to flavor gin.

Bad points: This also is a host for cedar-apple rust and juniper blight causes branch dieback. The very prickly foliage makes it hard to handle. Upright forms can be damaged by snow if not wrapped.

Uses: Specimen; ground cover.

Chinese juniper variety	Height	Hardiness	Comments
'Blaauw'	5 ft (1.5 m)	C 4/US 3	Blue-green in summer, darker in winter.
'Fairview'	10 ft (3 m)	C 5/US 4	Upright and bright green.
'Mountbatten'	10 ft (3 m)	C 4/US 3	A gray-green narrow pyramid.
'San Jose'		C 4/US 3	A low spreader to 8 ft (2.4 m) wide.
'Spartan'	15 ft (4.5 m)	C 5/US 4	A mid-green, upright column.

Cultivars: 'Depressa Aurea' is somewhat vase-shaped, about 4 feet (1.2 m) high by 10 feet (3 m) wide; new growth is bright yellow, gradually darkening with time to green. 'Pencil Point' is a very narrow form up to 12 feet (3.5 m) tall in time; several others such as 'Compressa' and 'Sentinel' are similar in shape. 'Suecica' (Swedish juniper) is a columnar mid-green, not as narrow as 'Pencil Point'.

Juniperus x media — Hybrid juniper

Comments: According to some botanists, this hybrid is a cross between the Chinese and savin junipers. They look like Chinese, but have the distinctive smell of savin. Not all books and catalogs agree on how to list the cultivars.

Hardiness: Canadian zone 2-4; U.S. zone 2-3.
Availability: **M**.
Height: Varies according to the cultivar.
Propagation: Cuttings.
Soil preferences: Well drained.
Location: Sun.
Good points: Some of the most widely planted cultivars come from this cross. They are medium high or spreading in shape and fill many landscaping needs.
Bad points: They are prone to cedar-apple rust and mites.
Uses: Specimen; ground cover; foundation.
Cultivars: See table below.

Hybrid juniper variety	Height	Spread	Comments
'Gold Star'	3 ft (.9 m)	6 ft (1.8 m)	Golden new growth turns green with age.
'Hetzii'	15 ft (4.5 m)	15 ft (4.5 m)	Bluish-green, it sets many berries and has an arching habit.
'Mint Julep'	6 ft (1.8 m)	6 ft (1.8 m)	Mint-green shoots on an arching plant.
'Old Gold'	3 ft (.9 m)	4 ft (1.2 m)	Good yellow color year-round.
'Pfitzeriana'	10 ft (3 m)	10 ft (3 m)	Pale green with arching branches.
'Pfitzeriana Aurea'	8 ft (2.4 m)	10 ft (3 m)	A yellow form of 'Pfitzeriana'.
'Pfitzeriana Compacta'	3 ft (.9 m)	6 ft (1.8 m)	A miniature Pfitzer.
'Pfitzeriana Glauca'	3 ft (.9 m)	6 ft (1.8 m)	Like the last cultivar but with bluish foliage.
'Sea Green'	6 ft (1.8 m)	6 ft (1.8 m)	May be the same as 'Mint Julep'.

Juniperus scopulorum   **Rocky Mountain juniper**

Comments: The cultivars of this species are mostly upright shrubs to small trees, often with a silver to blue color.

Hardiness: Canadian zone 3; U.S. zone 3.

Availability: **M**.

Height: To 20' (6 m). *Spread:* Varies.

Propagation: Cuttings.

Soil preferences: Most.

Location: Sun.

Good points: They make excellent accent plants when used in moderation. The columnar forms add height to a mixed border without taking up much ground space.

Bad points: They are susceptible to a twig blight.

Uses: Specimen; mixed border; foundation.

Cultivars: 'Blue Heaven' is a broad columnar to pyramidal form with good blue foliage that can grow to 20 feet (6 m). 'Moonglow' is similar but broader, and has silvery-blue needles. 'Skyrocket' has a very narrow outline when grown properly. It should not get more than 2 feet (60 cm) across and 15 feet (4.5 m) tall. It is very popular, and to keep up with demand it is being propagated from side shoots. These do not give the proper, narrow outline and you end up with a pear shape rather than a rocket. 'Tollson's Weeping Blue' makes a small tree to about 15 feet (4.5 m) with arching branches from which hang slender branchlets like blue icicles. There is also a green form. 'Wichita Blue' is an upright form to 20 feet (6 m) and is one of the best blues.

Juniperus virginiana   **Red cedar**

Comments: These are evergreen trees and shrubs with many cultivated forms in a wide range of shapes and colors. The foliage has a cedar smell when bruised, and the wood is used for lining chests and closets. There is a wide range of heights and spreads in the many cultivars.

Hardiness: Canadian zone 2b-3b; U.S. zone 2.

Availability: **A** to **S** depending on the cultivar.

Height: 40' (12 m). *Spread:* 15' (4.5 m).

Propagation: Cuttings.

Soil preferences: Deep moist loam.

Location: Sun.

Good points: Red cedar will tolerate poor soils, transplants well B & B, and has interesting shredding bark on older plants.

Bad points: This is the chief host of cedar-apple rust and should not be planted near orchards. It suffers badly from bagworm (a caterpillar that can be controlled with *Bacillus thuringiensis*) in areas where these occur.

Uses: Hedge; screen; foundation and specimen plants.

Cultivars: There are about 25 named forms, but the following are the best and most readily available. 'Burkii'is broadly pyramidal to 25 feet (7.5 m), bluish in summer but with a purple tint in winter. 'Canaertii' forms a shorter, dark green pyramid to 20 feet (6 m). 'Grey Owl' is dwarf, about 3 feet (90 cm) tall and twice that across, with silvery-gray foliage. 'Hillii' is a slow-growing column to about 15 feet (4.5 m) at maturity, blue-green in summer, purple in winter. 'Manhatten Blue' is another pyramidal form with very blue needles that grows 20 feet (6 m) tall. 'Silver Spreader' is similar in shape to 'Grey Owl' but more silvery. 'Blue Arrow', 'Hillspire', 'Moonglow', 'Pendula' and 'Wintergreen' are also worth growing but harder to find.

Larix spp.   **Larch**

Larches are conifers that are distinctive because they lose their needles in fall after putting on a good display of autumn color. They are attacked occasionally by a specific caterpillar, larch casebearer. This hollows and kills the growing tips and makes small cigar-shaped cases with pieces of the needles. While it weakens the trees, it is seldom fatal. Control by spraying with lime sulphur in late winter following a mild infestation, or with methoxychlor or carbaryl as soon as the damage is noticed.

Larix decidua　　　　　**European larch**

Comments: This forms a graceful tree with small cones that can be used in dried flower arrangements.
Hardiness: Canadian zone 2b; U.S. zone 2.
Availability: **M**.
Height: 70' (21 m). *Spread:* 30' (9 m).
Propagation: Stratified seed.
Soil preferences: Moist, but well drained.
Location: Sun.
Good points: The new needles are a bright green when they emerge, becoming dark green in summer and dull yellow in fall.
Bad points: It is susceptible to larch casebearer; it sheds twigs in high winds, causing litter.
Uses: Specimen; windbreak; screen.
Cultivars: 'Pendula' is a form with weeping branchlets, although they tend to hang down on the species as well. It is easier to recognize this form from a distance than close up.

Larix kaempferi　　　　**Japanese larch**

Comments: Similar to the European larch, this species has a more open habit.
Hardiness: Canadian zone 2b; U.S. zone 2.
Availability: **A**.
Height: 70' (21 m). *Spread:* 30' (9 m).
Propagation: Stratified seed.
Soil preferences: Well drained, acidic.
Location: Sun.
Good points: This species is equally as attractive as the European larch in spring, but has a brighter fall color most years.

Bad points: Larch casebearer also attacks this species.
Uses: Specimen; screen.

Larix laricina　　**American larch, tamarack**

Comments: This native tree is a good choice for wet sites. It is very hardy and will grow where few other trees will survive.
Hardiness: Canadian zone 1; U.S. zone 1.
Availability: **A**.
Height: 60' (18 m). *Spread:* 25' (7.5 m).
Propagation: Stratified seed.
Soil preferences: Moist to wet.
Location: Sun to light shade.
Good points: The yellow fall color lights up the roadsides locally most years, after the broadleaf trees have had their moment of glory.
Bad points: Larch casebearer.
Uses: Specimen; naturalizing; windbreak.

Metasequoia　　　　　　**Dawn**
glyptostroboides　　　**redwood**

Comments: You probably won't even think about pronouncing the botanical name of this deciduous conifer. It was first described from fossils and then later discovered growing in China. Re-introduced to North America in 1944, there are already trees over 100 feet (30 m) tall.
Hardiness: Canadian zone 5; U.S. zone 4.
Availability: **M**.
Height: 120' (36 m). *Spread:* 25' (7.5 m).
Propagation: Cuttings.
Soil preferences: Deep, well drained.
Location: Sun.
Good points: This species grows rapidly into a narrow, pyramidal tree. Closely related to the giant redwood, it loses its foliage each fall.
Bad points: Do not plant in hollows (frost pockets) where early fall frosts can damage late growth.

Uses: Specimen tree; screen.

Cultivars: There are two, 'National' and 'Sheridan Spire', both with a more columnar shape, but they are rarely available.

Picea spp.   Spruce

These evergreen trees are economically very important as timber. Many of the cultivars are used in the garden: dwarf forms in the rock garden and taller ones in the border or as specimens. As with most of the evergreens, plant only B & B or container-grown stock. Do not plant in early spring or late fall, and give ample water for the first season. Prune, if needed, in spring.

Picea abies   Norway spruce

Comments: At a casual glance, I find it hard to tell Norway and white spruce apart. Both are good for windbreaks and shelterbelts, but use the cultivars for garden plants.

Hardiness: Canadian zone 3; U.S. zone 2.

Availability: **M**.

Height: 40' (12 m). *Spread:* 25' (7.5 m).

Propagation: Seed or cuttings in mist.

Soil preferences: Well drained, acidic.

Location: Sun.

Good points: The many shapes available in the named forms give this tree great versatility in the landscape.

Bad points: In addition to spruce budworm and canker, it may be attacked by adelgids—close relatives of aphids—that cause galls on the new growth.

Uses: Border; accent; foundation.

Cultivars: 'Little Gem' is very slow growing, eventually making a green mound 18 inches (45 cm) across with tiny needles. 'Nidiformis' (bird's nest spruce) has branchlets that tend to grow out but curve up at the tip, leaving a nest-like depression. It grows about three times as wide as tall and may get 2 feet

(60 cm) high. 'Ohlendorfii' forms a dense conical shape with a yellowish tint that can grow to 6 feet (1.8 m) tall. 'Pendula' is a catch-all name for weeping forms. If left flat, they will sprawl across a wide area; if staked upright, the branches will hang back to the ground. 'Pumila' is another small, flat-topped form that will grow to just over 3 feet (90 cm). 'Repens' has new growth that is somewhat drooping but straightens with age. The branches are in layers, forming a low mound that builds taller year by year.

Picea glauca   White spruce

Comments: Our native spruce is one of the mainstays of the pulp and paper industry. The species is useful in the extreme north where little else will grow or as a screen farther south.

Hardiness: Canadian zone 1; U.S. zone 1.

Availability: **M**.

Height: 50' (15 m). *Spread:* 20' (6 m).

Propagation: Seed.

Soil preferences: Moist.

Location: Sun.

Good points: Although the species is too large for most gardens, the three cultivars mentioned below are excellent garden plants.

Bad points: In addition to spruce budworm and canker (see *P. pungens*) and adelgids (see *P. abies*), mites can be a problem some summers, turning plants brown. The plants usually recover, but it's better to control the mites.

Uses: Specimen; border; foundation.

Cultivars: 'Conica' ('Albertiana Conica', dwarf Alberta spruce) is a natural dwarf found in 1904 in Alberta and now grown wherever spruce will survive; it is a dense, bright green cone growing to 10 feet (3 m) in time (about 30 years). Plants can be very lightly sheared in spring, once the new growth opens, to slow the growth still further. 'Densata' (Black Hills spruce) is another conical form but faster growing than 'Conica' and eventually 3 to 4 times as tall. 'Echiniformis' (hedgehog spruce) makes a dwarf globe with stiff shoots. It is slow growing but it can reach 20 feet (6 m) in about 40 years.

Picea omorika   **Serbian spruce**

Comments: This spruce grows into a slender, bright green column that makes a good accent in the garden.

Hardiness: Canadian zone 3; U.S. zone 3.

Availability: **M**.

Height: 50' (15 m). *Spread:* 10' (3 m).

Propagation: Seed.

Soil preferences: Well drained.

Location: Sun.

Good points: It grows equally well on acid and alkaline soils and is comparatively fast growing.

Bad points: It may wind-burn on exposed sites in winter.

Uses: Accent plant; specimen tree.

Cultivars: 'Nana' is a very dwarf, slow-growing form that can get to about 3 feet (.9 m) in time. 'Pendula' is like the species but with drooping branches and it grows only half as fast; an interesting tree.

Picea pungens   **Colorado spruce**

Comments: This species generally forms a slender tree, often with a distinct blue color. I have seen native stands in the foothills west of Denver that would make wonderful garden plants. The best blue forms are propagated by grafting and are slow growing, making them expensive. Quite good blues can come from a batch of seedlings, so if you can find a nursery growing them from seed you can save money, but check for a good color form when buying.

Hardiness: Canadian zone 2; U.S. zone 2.

Availability: **M**.

Height: 60' (18 m). *Spread:* 15' (4.5 m).

Propagation: Seed, grafting.

Soil preferences: Moist, but adaptable.

Location: Sun.

Good points: A good accent plant, but the blue forms must be placed with care to look right. The green forms can be used with greater abandon and their narrow outline means they don't take up a lot of space.

Bad points: Spruce budworm can attack new growth, causing brown tips on the branches (and eventual death after repeated attacks). A canker can cause branches to die from the bottom of the tree up. Look for sap weeping on the main trunk; this is also a symptom. Spray with Bordeaux mixture or any other copper-based fungicide.

Uses: Specimen tree; accent tree.

Cultivars: 'Glauca' is a collective name for blue seedlings. 'Glauca Globosa' is a compact blue form growing only 3 feet (.9 m) high and more wide. 'Hoopsii' is probably the best blue, pyramidal in shape and (relatively) fast growing. 'Koster' is the most popular selection and one of the first named blue forms. Branches are almost horizontal, but the shape can depend on the origin of the graft material. 'Montgomery' is a dwarfer, slow-growing form that makes a broad pyramid in time. 'Thompsen' is a silvery blue with very dense branches—worth searching for.

Pinus **spp.**   **Pines**

This is an important group of evergreen trees. They are mostly large, although a number of dwarf forms suitable for the rock garden are available from specialist growers.

Pines are classified by the number of needles in each cluster and the common ones are comparatively easy to identify, certainly when compared to spruce, for example. Always transplant B & B or container-grown stock. Pruning is seldom needed except for the removal of lower branches that die off due to age and shading.

Pinus aristata   **Bristlecone pine**

Comments: This is a very slow-growing pine, and one of the longest-living trees. Plants almost 5,000 years old have been documented. I have seen them growing at the treeline in Colorado: low, stunted, one-sided plants, with all the branches on the lee side of the tree and no bark on the windward side where it is abraded by the sand flung in strong winds. This is a 5-needle pine with white resin dots on each 1- to 1 1/2-inch-long (2.5- to 4-cm) needle.

Hardiness: Canadian zone 3; U.S. zone 3.
Availability: **M**.
Height: 15' (4.5 m). *Spread:* 10' (3 m).
Propagation: Seed.
Soil preferences: Well drained.
Location: Sun.
Good points: An interesting tree that can be used in a mixed border for accent or as a small specimen.
Bad points: It is quite slow growing, especially in poor soils. The resin dots on the needles are easy to mistake for scale.
Uses: Foundation; border.

Pinus banksiana   **Jack pine**

Comments: Jack pine is a good choice for the poorest soils. The cones need heat to open and release the seed; this is one of the first trees to germinate after a forest fire.

Hardiness: Canadian zone 1; U.S. zone 1.
Availability: **F**.
Height: 50' (15 m). *Spread:* 20' (6 m).
Propagation: Seed.

Soil preferences: Dry and acidic is best.
Location: Sun.
Good points: This is not a good specimen tree, but is useful for screens and shelterbelts on poor soils and in the coldest regions. It will also grow on slightly alkaline soils.
Bad points: It produces lots of resin which gets on skin and clothing at the slightest touch.
Uses: Screen; shelterbelt.

Pinus bungeana   **Lacebark pine**

Comments: This is a 3-needle pine that is easy to recognize by its very attractive bark.

Hardiness: Canadian zone 5b; U.S. zone 4.
Availability: **F**.
Height: 35' (10.5 m). *Spread:* 25' (7.5 m).
Propagation: Seed.
Soil preferences: Well drained.
Location: Sun.
Good points: The beautiful flaking brown bark comes off in patches to reveal green and gray inner bark. It is very striking and worth growing.
Bad points: The bark doesn't start to flake until the tree is about 10 years old.
Uses: Specimen tree.

Pinus cembra   **Swiss stone pine**

Comments: This is my personal favorite of all the pines. I like the way it keeps its lower branches and stays full to the ground. I know a 30-year-old tree that is still a green column, with no bare trunk showing.

Hardiness: Canadian zone 2; U.S. zone 4.
Availability: **M**.
Height: 35' (10.5 m). *Spread:* 20' (6 m).
Propagation: Stratified seed.
Soil preferences: Well drained.
Location: Sun.
Good points: This species transplants well. It is slow growing, so is useful for city gardens,

except those surrounded by high walls or buildings: this plant needs good air circulation to thrive.

Bad points: None.

Uses: Specimen tree.

Pinus contorta var. *latifolia* — Lodgepole pine

Comments: This very straight-growing 2-needle pine was used by Plains Indians to support their teepees. The species itself *(P. contorta)* is the shore pine of the west coast, while the variety grows in the mountains.

Hardiness: Canadian zone 1; U.S. zone 2.

Availability: **A**.

Height: 70' (21 m). *Spread:* 40' (12 m).

Propagation: Seed.

Soil preferences: Well drained to gravel.

Location: Sun.

Good points: This is a useful pine for an accent plant or for screening.

Bad points: None.

Uses: Shelterbelt; screen; specimen.

Pinus densiflora 'Umbraculifera' — Umbrella pine

Comments: This form of the Japanese red pine is the only one readily available. It forms a spreading plant with an almost flat top. Do not confuse this with *Sciadopitys*, also called umbrella-pine, which is described later.

Hardiness: Canadian zone 5b; U.S. zone 4.

Availability: **M**.

Height: 15' (4.5 m). *Spread:* 15' (4.5 m).

Propagation: Grafted onto seedlings.

Soil preferences: Acidic, well drained.

Location: Sun.

Good points: It has an interesting umbrella shape; the bark is a beautiful orange-red.

Bad points: None.

Uses: Specimen.

Pinus flexilis — Limber pine

Comments: This pine is a good choice for windy sites, as the branches bend readily without breaking. Needles are in groups of 5 and about 3 1/2 inches (9 cm) long.

Hardiness: Canadian zone 2b; U.S. zone 4.

Availability: **M**.

Height: 40' (12 m). *Spread:* 30' (9 m).

Propagation: Stratified seed.

Soil preferences: Well drained.

Location: Sun.

Good points: Limber pine is salt-tolerant, grows well in poor, sandy soils and suffers less from winter-burn than many other pines.

Bad points: None.

Uses: Specimen tree; soil reclamation.

Cultivars: 'Glauca' has blue-green needles. 'Vanderwolf's Pyramid' is more upright, with twisted needles.

Pinus mugo — Mountain pine

Comments: This highly variable species can get tall and wide. Don't be misled by the cute little thing in the garden center—it will grow. Look over a batch of plants and pick those with the shortest needles; they are usually the slowest growing.

Hardiness: Canadian zone 2b; U.S. zone 2.

Availability: **M**.

Height: 20' (6 m). *Spread:* 35' (10.5 m).

Propagation: Seed.

Soil preferences: Deep, well drained.

Location: Sun.

Good points: It can be kept from getting too large by pruning when the new growth (candles) start to open their needles. Cut them back by two-thirds.

Bad points: Every candle you cut back produces multiple shoots the following year. On a large shrub the task of pruning seems endless.

Uses: Foundation; border.

Cultivars: 'Gnom' is a slow-growing, dwarf selection. *P. mugo* var. *mugo* (Mugho pine) is slow growing and may only reach 8 feet (2.4 m). *P. mugo* var. *pumilo* is even more prostrate, but is variable when grown from seed.

Pinus nigra   Austrian pine, black pine

Comments: At one time the Austrian and black pines were classed as different subspecies of *Pinus nigra*, but botanists now consider them to be the same plant. The needles are in pairs, stiff, and 3 to 5 inches (8 to 13 cm) long.

Hardiness: Canadian zone 4; U.S. zone 4.

Availability: **M**.

Height: 50' (15 m). *Spread:* 30' (9 m).

Propagation: Seed.

Soil preferences: Deep, moist.

Location: Sun.

Good points: A tree with well-spaced, more or less horizontal branches, it withstands city conditions and is salt-tolerant.

Bad points: A disease called diplodia tip blight causes considerable injury in older plants. New growth is attacked and the current year's needles are killed. Given the number of different pines available, it might be wise to avoid planting this species if there are many other Austrian pines in your area.

Uses: Specimen tree; shelterbelt.

Pinus parviflora   Japanese white pine

Comments: This slow-growing, salt-tolerant pine has many dwarf forms suitable for the rock garden, none of which are widely available. The needles are 1 to 3 inches long (2.5 to 8 cm), curved, and in clusters of 5.

Hardiness: Canadian zone 5b; U.S. zone 4.

Availability: **H**.

Height: 40' (12 m). *Spread:* 40' (12 m).

Propagation: Stratified seed.

Soil preferences: Well drained.

Location: Sun.

Good points: This good small conifer has horizontal branches and a tidy habit; it makes a nice specimen plant in a lawn.

Bad points: None.

Uses: Specimen tree.

Cultivars: 'Glauca' is like the species but has blue-green needles.

Pinus ponderosa   Ponderosa pine, western yellow pine

Comments: This is the only common 3-needle pine other than lacebark pine. It can grow very tall in the wild (over 200 feet/60 m has been recorded) but the height given below is more likely in cultivated plants.

Hardiness: Canadian zone 2b; U.S. zone 3.

Availability: **F**.

Height: 60' (18 m). *Spread:* 30' (9 m).

Propagation: Seed.

Soil preferences: Well drained.

Location: Sun.

Good points: This is not as wide as many pines, so it is better suited to mid-sized properties.

Bad points: Harder to transplant than most pines.

Uses: Specimen tree.

Pinus resinosa   Red pine

Comments: This pine is easily identified by the long needles (5-6 inch/13-15 cm) in pairs, which break when bent. Needles stay on the tree for four years so it always looks full.

Hardiness: Canadian zone 2b; U.S. zone 2.

Availability: **F**.

Height: 60' (18 m). *Spread:* 40' (12 m).

Propagation: Seed.

Soil preferences: Most.

Location: Sun.

Good points: This pine grows well in poor, sandy or gravelly soils.

Bad points: It is soon damaged by salt, especially salty spray, so don't plant red pine where this might occur.

Uses: Specimen tree; screen.

Pinus strobus — White pine, eastern white pine

Comments: Bundles of 5 soft, blue-green needles up to 5 inches (13 cm) long make this tree easy to recognize.

Hardiness: Canadian zone 2b; U.S. zone 3.

Availability: **M**.

Height: 80' (24 m). *Spread:* 50' (15 m).

Propagation: Seed.

Soil preferences: Light and well drained.

Location: Sun.

Good points: Our native white pine transplants easily and will grow on a range of soils. It is a good choice for larger country properties where it makes a good windbreak.

Bad points: The needles are shed in their second year, so there is always a lot of litter in late summer. White pine blister rust can attack this species if currants are growing nearby. It is not a good choice for city conditions, particularly where roads are salted; trees near roads treated with salt turn brown on the roadside and eventually die.

Uses: Shelterbelt; screen.

Cultivars: There are several dozen, many of which are very dwarf forms for the rock garden. 'Nana' is a slow-growing dwarf that spreads wider than tall. 'Pendula' has branches that trail back down to the ground.

Pinus sylvestris — Scots pine

Comments: Scots pine can be recognized by its bark and by its stiff needles, flattened and twisted, up to 3 inches (8 cm) long, that grow in pairs. Trees that lose their leader when fairly young can achieve interesting shapes.

Hardiness: Canadian zone 2; U.S. zone 2.

Availability: **M**.

Height: 50' (15 m). *Spread:* 35' (10.5 m).

Propagation: Seed.

Soil preferences: Well drained.

Location: Sun.

Good points: An orange-buff inner bark is exposed on the top part of the tree, making it most attractive and easy to identify.

Bad points: Diplodia tip blight (see *P. nigra*) can also affect this species.

Uses: Specimen tree.

Cultivars: There are many cultivars varying in color and rate of growth, but the only one easy to find is 'Watereri', a slow-growing form with blue-green needles.

Pinus thunbergiana — Japanese black pine

Comments: This has two twisted needles up to 4 inches (10 cm) long. The tree has a rather spreading habit with an open form and makes a good specimen plant.

Hardiness: Canadian zone 4b; U.S. zone 4.

Availability: **F** in Canada; **A** in U.S.

Height: 50' (15 m). *Spread:* 30' (9 m).

Propagation: Seed.

Soil preferences: Well drained, sandy.

Location: Sun.

Good points: It is quite salt-tolerant and so is useful by roads or near the coast and has been used to stabilize sand banks and dunes.

Bad points: None.

Uses: Specimen; screen; erosion control.

Cultivars: Many, but few are readily available commercially.

Pseudotsuga menziesii var. glauca — Douglas fir

Comments: The common name celebrates David Douglas, who collected plants for the Royal Horticultural Society on the west coast from

1823-27 and who died after falling into a wild animal trap in Hawaii. The species name commemorates Archibald Menzies, who, as botanist on Captain Vancouver's ship the *Discovery*, had previously explored this area in 1792.

Two forms exist, the coastal (which is hardy to zone 7) and the interior, or Rocky Mountain, form, which is discussed here and is hardier and bluer.

Hardiness: Canadian zone 5; U.S. zone 4.
Availability: **M**.
Height: 100' (30 m). *Spread:* 25' (7.5 m).
Propagation: Seed.
Soil preferences: Well drained, not too alkaline.
Location: Sun.
Good points: A narrow tree, pyramidal when young, the Douglas fir becomes columnar with age. The foliage is blue-green and the smallish cones with a three-pronged bract protruding from each scale are good for cone wreaths.
Bad points: There are several pests and diseases that are troublesome in native stands, but individual trees are unlikely to be bothered outside its western native habitat.
Uses: Specimen tree.

Sciadopitys verticillata — Japanese umbrella-pine

Comments: The needles of umbrella-pine are of two different types; some are small and lie flat along the stem, while others are longer and radiate out in clusters like the ribs of an umbrella.
Hardiness: Canadian zone 6; U.S. zone 5.
Availability: **S** in Canada; **A** in U.S.
Height: 25' (7.5 m). *Spread:* 20' (6 m).
Propagation: Difficult; stratified seed.
Soil preferences: Moist, acidic.
Location: Sun.

Good points: Although it is slow growing at first, it makes a good, distinctive, pyramidal tree in time, like an inverted ice-cream cone.
Bad points: None.
Uses: Specimen tree.

Taxodium distichum — Bald cypress

Comments: You would expect to find this tree in Florida swamps, where the knees (part of the root system whose function is unclear) stick up above water. It is surprisingly hardy and will grow equally well on dry sites, but there it does not make knees.
Hardiness: Canadian zone 4; U.S. zone 4.
Availability: **S** in Canada; **A** in U.S.
Height: 70' (21 m). *Spread:* 40' (12 m).
Propagation: Softwood cuttings.
Soil preferences: Swampy to well drained.
Location: Sun.
Good points: This cone-bearing tree sheds its leaves in fall to show an attractive reddish bark. New growth is a bright green, darkening with age.
Bad points: Few.
Uses: Specimen tree; waterside.

Taxus spp. — Yew

These are evergreen shrubs (mostly) and trees used for accent, hedging and foundation planting. Wood of the English yew was used to make archery bows for medieval armies. The trees were always planted in the churchyard, which was enclosed, since the foliage is poisonous to cattle. This ensured a continual supply of bows but kept the herds safe. The fleshy (red) part of the fruit is not toxic, but the seeds themselves are highly poisonous.

Yews are susceptible to winter wind desiccation and salt damage and need winter protection at the limit of their range or where salt may drift. There are several native species, but they are rarely used in the landscape. Use B & B or container-grown stock, and plant in very well-drained soil. All yews can be easily trimmed into the desired shape, but buy the shape you need to save a lot of clipping.

Taxus baccata   English yew

Comments: This species can form large trees especially in its native Europe, but has limited use here as it is neither as hardy nor as heat-tolerant as the other species.
Hardiness: Canadian zone 6; U.S. zone 5.
Availability: **S**.
Height: 60' (18 m). *Spread:* 40' (12 m).
Propagation: Cuttings.
Soil preferences: Well drained.
Location: Sun to shade.
Good points: This species has dark green foliage and bright red berries in winter and is widely used for hedges and topiary work where conditions suit it.
Bad points: Black vine weevil attacks the roots.
Uses: Hedging; specimen; screen.
Cultivars: 'Repandens' is a dwarf form about 3 feet (1 m) tall and 9 feet (2.7 m) wide at maturity if pruned. It may be one zone hardier than the species. There are many other cultivars listed in books but few are available in North America.

Taxus cuspidata   Japanese yew

Comments: There are many cultivars other than those listed below; nurseries often sell them labeled simply as Spreading, Upright, Globe or Cone. This is the hardiest yew.
Hardiness: Canadian zone 4; U.S. zone 4.
Availability: **M**.
Height: 30' (9 m). *Spread:* Varies.
Propagation: Cuttings.
Soil preferences: Well drained.
Location: Sun to shade.

Good points: This species makes an excellent screen or hedge and the dense foliage can be clipped to keep it to the desired size.
Bad points: Winter desiccation can be severe in exposed locations.
Uses: Screen; hedge; border.
Cultivars: 'Aurescens' is a spreading golden form that needs full sun for best color; it grows 12 inches (30 cm) high by 6 feet (1.8 m) across. 'Capitata' forms a pyramid, growing to 30 feet (9 m) or more and takes clipping well (if you have a tall enough stepladder). 'Nana' is a dark green, spreading selection that grows about 4 feet (1.2 m) tall.

Taxus x media   Hybrid yew, Anglo-jap yew

Comments: A cross between the English and the Japanese species, this, in its many forms, is the most commonly planted yew. Some varieties have nearly all male flowers and very rarely set fruit. These are called male plants, while those with both male and female flowers, which set fruit, are called female.
Hardiness: Canadian zone 5; U.S. zone 4.
Availability: **M**.
Height / Spread: Varies according to the cultivar.
Propagation: Cuttings.
Soil preferences: Well drained.
Location: Sun to shade.
Good points: This is a versatile evergreen that will take clipping and can be used for topiary work. It has dark green needles and red winter fruits on female plants.
Bad points: It suffers badly from winter-burn in exposed locations.
Uses: Accent; hedge; border; foundation.
Cultivars: 'Brownii' is a broad form, taller than wide, that can be pruned to the desired height; it will reach about 8 feet (2.4 m) if left. It is a male clone so there are no berries, but it is one of the hardiest. 'Densiformis' is

similar to 'Brownii' but faster growing and it does not get as tall. 'Hicksii' has a columnar shape; it will reach 20 feet (6 m) and has berries. 'Hillii' forms a broad column with very dense needles that will reach 8 feet (2.4 m) tall. 'Wardii' is another fruiting form; it is quick-growing but it stays low and wide, growing to 6 feet by 15 feet (1.8 by 4.5 m).

Thuja occidentalis   **White cedar**

Comments: The plant known to gardeners in the east as cedar is listed as arborvitae in most books. I have yet to meet anyone who called it that.

 Dug up from the wild by the million, it is the hedging plant of choice for many regions. Selections, both from the wild and from nurseries, have given us an overabundance of named forms to choose from. The hardiness varies slightly from one form to another and the more tender ones are noted.

Hardiness: Canadian zone 2b; U.S. zone 2.

Availability: **M.**

Height: 40' (12 m). *Spread:* 15' (4.5 m).

Propagation: Seed for the species; cultivars from cuttings.

Soil preferences: Adaptable, but grows best on well-drained soils.

Location: Sun to light shade.

Good points: This versatile plant can be planted bare-root and survive, rare for a conifer. The named forms are best planted B & B. They are invaluable for providing winter shelter for birds and as a backdrop for flowering plants, especially perennial borders. Among the many forms there is plenty of choice in shape, color and eventual size. The shredding bark on mature plants is an added attraction.

Bad points: Cedars are subject to few problems, but leaf miners can turn new growth a pale brown. Cedars suffer from winter-burn fol-

lowing dry falls, so water thoroughly if rain is lacking in late fall. If grown close to roads that are salted, the spray will turn them brown. Finally, they are a favorite winter food of deer, and browsing can ruin a shapely specimen.

Uses: Foundation planting; hedge; specimen tree; shelterbelt.

Cultivars: With over a hundred named forms in existence, the following are the most widely available. *See table opposite.*

Thuja plicata   **Western red cedar**

Comments: Related to the white cedar, this western species is much used for house-building and for making garden structures such as arbors and decks. The species grows into a large tree but can be used for hedging and there are some selected forms that vary greatly in size.

Hardiness: Canadian zone 6; U.S. zone 5.

Availability: **A.**

Height: 50' (15 m). *Spread:* 25' (7.5 m).

Propagation: Stratified seed for the species; cuttings for the cultivars.

Soil preferences: Moist.

Location: Sun to light shade.

Good points: This conifer has a good conical shape with dense foliage. The wood is rot-resistant, hence its structural use.

Bad points: It grows too large for most city gardens.

Uses: Specimen; tall hedge.

Cultivars: 'Pygmea' is a dwarf form growing only about 2 feet (60 cm) tall. 'Stoneham Gold' has bright yellow new foliage turning green with age and it grows 6 feet (1.8 m) tall. 'Zebrina' is somewhat broader than the species, grows almost as tall and has foliage variegated with yellow.

White Cedar

Globe-shaped variety	Size	Comments
'Danica'	2 1/2 ft/75 cm	Bright green, becoming blue-green in winter.
'Golden Globe'	4 ft/120 cm	Slow growing with yellow foliage.
'Hetz Midget'	3 ft/90 cm	Very dense and grows about 1 inch (2.5 cm) per year.
'Little Champion'	2 1/2 ft/75 cm	Grows quickly at first but slows with age.
'Woodwardii'	4 ft/120 cm	Dark green and needs little trimming.

Broad pyramid variety	Height:spread	Comments
'Holmstrup'	8 ft/2.4 m:4 ft/1.2 m	Bright green and slow growing.
'Reingold'	6 ft/1.8 m:8 ft/2.4 m	Golden foliage turning coppery in winter.
'Smaragd'	7 ft/2.1 m:4 ft/1.2 m	Emerald-green and faster growing.
'Sunkist'	7 ft/2.1 m:3 1/2 ft/1.1 m	Fast growing, yellow cone.
'Techney'	15 ft/4.5 m:8 ft/2.4 m	Deep green with good winter color.

Upright plant variety	Height:spread	Comments
'Elegantissima'	15 ft/4.5 m:5 ft/1.5 m	Dark green tipped with yellow.
'Fastigiata'	15 ft/4.5 m:5 ft/1.5 m	Lighter green, turns bronzy in cold.
'Nigra'	25 ft/7.5 m:8 ft/2.4 m	Called the black cedar for its very dark foliage; not quite as hardy.
'Pyramidalis'	variable	A collective name for narrow plants dug from the wild.
'Wareana'	20 ft/6 m:6 ft/1.8 m	Bright green with very dense foliage.

Thujopsis dolobrata   **False arborvitae**

Comment: It makes a good dense tree that is very similar to the true arborvitae *(Thuja)*.
Hardiness: Canadian zone 6; U.S. zone 5.
Availability: **S**.
Height: 30' (9 m). *Spread:* 20' (6 m).
Propagation: Cuttings.
Soil preferences: Moist, acidic.

Location: Sun to light shade.
Good points: An evergreen with a dense habit and leaves that are whitish below, which adds interest in a breeze.
Bad points: It needs protection from winter winds.
Uses: Specimen evergreen.
Cultivars: 'Variegata' has leaves blotched with cream. 'Nana' only grows 3 feet (.9 m) tall.

Tsuga canadensis — Canadian hemlock

Comments: These native evergreen trees or shrubs grow well in light shade. The large number of cultivars range from small weeping forms to large trees.

Hardiness: Canadian zone 3; U.S. zone 3.

Availability: **M** to **H** depending on the cultivar.

Height: 50' (15 m). *Spread:* 25' (7.5 m).

Propagation: Stratified seed or cuttings for the species. Winter cuttings for the cultivars.

Soil preferences: Moist.

Location: Sun to light shade, sheltered.

Good points: All the hemlocks have soft green foliage that is most attractive. The weeping forms are the most often grown and add an interesting shape to the garden. They look especially good tumbling over a rock or beside a pond or stream.

Bad points: They can be liable to winter-burn on dry soils or windswept sites. Mites can also be a problem some years.

Uses: Specimen; screen; hedge.

Cultivars: 'Cole' and 'Gracilis' are two slow-growing weeping forms. 'Jeddeloh' is a nest-shaped dwarf that forms a compact globe. 'Pendula' ('Sargentii') is a large weeping form that can spread 12 feet (3.5 m) or more at maturity.

GROUND COVERS

There are many places where a ground-covering plant makes more sense than having to mow grass. The plants listed below vary greatly in height, but all will form a solid mat in time. Some weeding will be required at first unless you can use landscape fabric between the plants.

Arctostaphylos uva-ursi — Bearberry, kinnikinick

Comments: This is a good native evergreen ground cover where soil conditions are right. Transplant only container-grown plants.

Hardiness: Canadian zone 2; U.S. zone 3.

Availability: **M**.

Height: 1' (30 cm). *Spread:* 4' (1.2 m) or more.

Propagation: Seed or cuttings.

Soil preferences: Sandy, poor and acidic.

Location: Sun to part shade.

Good points: It has shiny dark green leaves, pinkish flowers and red berries (which attract bears). There is good fall color, the leaves turning a bronzy shade in fall and staying this color all winter. The foliage is salt-tolerant.

Bad points: It desiccates badly in winter if not covered in snow. Occasionally leaf galls may disfigure foliage.

Uses: Ground cover.

Cultivars: 'Vancouver Jade' has the best fall color, but may not be as hardy (zone 4?).

Calluna vulgaris — Heather

Comments: Heathers flower in summer and fall and grow best in cooler, maritime climates. I have seen marvellous plantings on both the east and west coast, but heathers can also be grown well inland.

Hardiness: Canadian zone 5-6; U.S. zone 4-5.

Availability: **S**.

Height: 1' (30 cm). *Spread:* 2' (60 cm).

Propagation: Seed; cultivars by cuttings.

Soil preferences: Acidic and humusy; well drained.

Location: Sun to light shade for part of the day.

Good points: As long as their soil requirements are met they can be grown away from the coast, but growth is slower and flowering not as prolific.

Bad points: Heathers do not thrive in hot, humid conditions.

Uses: Ground cover; rock garden.

Cultivars: There are literally hundreds of named forms if you search, but few of them are widely available.

Cornus canadensis   **Bunchberry**

Comments: This is a native woodland ground cover that grows best in cool conditions. Wonderful carpets of bunchberry may be found growing under trees on the north shore of Lake Superior.

Hardiness: Canadian zone 2; U.S. zone 2.

Availability: **F**.

Height: 6" (15 cm). *Spread:* 2' (60 cm).

Propagation: Seed (difficult).

Soil preferences: Acidic, woodsy.

Location: Shade.

Good points: The flowers are white and quite showy, with four large petals (really modified leaves called bracts). The red berries are held just above the cluster of leaves and look as though they were on a plate, hence the common name.

Bad points: It is difficult to transplant and establish. Use container-grown plants only.

Uses: Ground cover in shade.

Cotoneaster dammeri   **Bearberry cotoneaster**

Comments: This excellent ground cover for banks and slopes soon gives an almost complete cover. It is generally evergreen, but may lose its foliage in cold regions. We don't have many bears, but partridges dig through the snow to find the berries in winter. Plant container-grown specimens.

Hardiness: Canadian zone 4; U.S. zone 4.

Availability: **M**.

Height: 1-2' (30-60 cm). *Spread:* 6' (1.8 m).

Propagation: Cuttings.

Soil preferences: Well drained.

Location: Sun to light shade.

Good points: Its white flowers in late spring are attractive, but not as showy as the bright red fruit. Glossy green foliage all summer turns a bronzy color in fall.

Bad points: It may suffer winter dieback above the snowline at the limits of hardiness. Pruning off dead growth is difficult and time-consuming.

Uses: Ground cover.

Cultivars: 'Coral Beauty' has coral-colored berries, rather than red, and is slightly taller. 'Royal Beauty' is probably the same variety. 'Skogholm' is more vigorous and will quickly cover an area. There seem to be two forms, one of which is not free-fruiting. Try to buy this plant in the fall when you can see the fruit. It is worth visiting several nurseries to get the good form.

Cotoneaster horizontalis   **Rockspray**

Comments: A ground-hugging plant, it is suitable for large rock gardens or atop a wall or retaining bank, where it will grow downwards and follow the contours. It is generally deciduous but may keep its leaves in warmer parts.

Hardiness: Canadian zone 5; U.S. zone 4.

Availability: **M**.

Height: 1' (30 cm). *Spread:* 5' (1.5 m).

Propagation: Stratified seed or summer cuttings.

Soil preferences: Not heavy.

Location: Sun.

Good points: Herring-bone branch structure gives winter interest. Pink summer flowers produce bright red fruit that clothes the branches and is eye-catching. Interesting habit of growth.

Bad points: None serious.

Uses: Rock garden; ground cover.

Cultivars: 'Purpusilla' is a very prostrate miniature form. It may be listed as a species *(C. perpusillus)* in some sources.

Cotoneaster nanshen   **Creeping cotoneaster**

Comments: This has had a botanical name change and may still be labelled *Cotoneaster adpressus* var. *praecox* in your local nursery. It is a low, creeping, usually evergreen shrub that roots down readily and is good for holding soil. Buy container-grown plants.

Hardiness: Canadian zone 3; U.S. zone 3.

Availability: **M**.

Height: 18" (45 cm). *Spread:* 4' (1.2 m).

Propagation: Layering.

Soil preferences: Well drained.

Location: Sun.

Good points: It has white flowers and glossy red fruit that persists into winter.

Bad points: Few.

Uses: Ground cover; erosion control.

Cultivars: 'Boer' has larger fruit that turns red earlier.

Epigaea repens   **Trailing arbutus**

Comments: This challenging native plant resents disturbance, but given the right conditions it is a delightful plant. Only plant container-grown stock.

Hardiness: Canadian zone 2; U.S. zone 3.

Availability: **H**.

Height: 6" (15 cm). *Spread:* 2' (60 cm).

Propagation: Difficult.

Soil preferences: Well drained, acidic.

Location: Light shade.

Good points: In early spring, the fragrant white flowers contrast with the leathery, evergreen leaves.

Bad points: It is difficult both to transplant and establish.

Uses: Woodland ground cover.

Erica spp.   **Heath**

Comments: Heaths are mostly winter- and spring-flowering but otherwise need similar conditions to heathers *(Calluna)*. They also thrive in the cooler maritime climates.

Hardiness: Canadian zone 5-6; U.S. zone 4-5.

Availability: **S**.

Height: 12" (30 cm). *Spread:* 20" (50 cm).

Propagation: Seed or cuttings.

Soil preferences: Acidic, humusy.

Location: Dappled shade; will take full sun in cooler regions.

Good points: Several heaths set their flower buds in the fall and burst into bloom in spring. With reliable snow cover they will survive at least -20°F (-28°C) and bloom well once the snow melts. Plant pot-grown plants. There are several different species of *Erica* that bloom at different seasons.

Bad points: Few, given the right conditions.

Uses: Ground cover; rock gardens.

Cultivars: 'Springwood White' and 'Springwood Pink' are the most common. Both form low mats covered with springtime flowers.

Euonymus fortunei   **Wintercreeper**

Comments: In mild climates, this evergreen ground cover can be trained up a wall or used to cover a stump.

Hardiness: Canadian zone 5 or 5b; U.S. zone 4.

Availability: **M**.
Height: 3' (90 cm). *Spread:* 3' (90 cm).
Propagation: Cuttings.
Soil preferences: Most but not wet.
Location: Sun.
Good points: The wide range of color and leaf patterns in the cultivars give a variety of choices. Some of the brighter forms should be used in moderation as they can be quite garish.
Bad points: Euonymus scale.
Uses: Ground cover; wall cover; front of a mixed border.
Cultivars: 'Canadale Gold' has light green leaves edged in yellow. 'Coloratus' is low-growing; dark green leaves turn purple in the cold. 'Emerald 'n Gold' has dark green leaves edged with gold. 'Emerald Gaiety' is more upright; the green leaves edged in cream become pinkish in the fall. 'Gold Tip' has new leaves that are variegated with yellow, which become green with age. 'Sarcoxi' is upright, heat-tolerant and dark green. 'Sunspot' has green leaves with yellow centers. 'Vegetus' is the hardiest and makes a small shrub; it is known as the bigleaf wintercreeper.

Forsythia viridissima Greenstem forsythia

Comments: The species is rarely grown, just the cultivar. Two other hybrids suitable for use as ground covers are listed in the hybrid forsythias in the "Shrubs" section of this chapter.
Hardiness: Canadian zone 5b; U.S. zone 4.
Availability: **A**.
Height: 6' (1.8 m). *Spread:* 4' (1.2 m).
Propagation: Cuttings.
Soil preferences: Well drained.
Location: Sun.
Good points: There are abundant bright yellow flowers in early spring.

Bad points: It needs careful pruning to keep the shape without allowing it to become so open weeds can become established.
Uses: Ground cover (cultivar).
Cultivars: 'Bronxensis' is a low-growing form, reaching 1 by 3 feet (30 by 90 cm), that flowers well.

Gaultheria procumbens Wintergreen

Comments: This native woodland plant has a distinctive odor when the leaves are crushed. Wintergreen oil is extracted from both the leaves and fruits. It is a good ground cover under rhododendrons. Plant container-grown stock.
Hardiness: Canadian zone 4; U.S. zone 4.
Availability: **M**.
Height: 6" (15 cm). *Spread:* 3' (90 cm).
Propagation: Seed.
Soil preferences: Acid humus.
Location: Shade.
Good points: This makes an excellent ground cover for shade where the soil acidity is right; small, white, lily-of-the-valley-like flowers in spring are followed by red fruit.
Bad points: Difficult to establish.
Uses: Ground cover.

Genista pilosa Silky woadwaxen

Comments: This is quite similar to the common woadwaxen *(G. tinctoria)*, but it has hairs on the underside of the leaves. Lydia woadwaxen *(G. lydia)* is also similar, but it has more needle-like leaves pressed close to the stems, and it is hardier.
Hardiness: Canadian zone 5; U.S. zone 4.
Availability: **M**.
Height: 1' (30 cm). *Spread:* 3' (90 cm).
Propagation: Cuttings.
Soil preferences: Well drained.
Location: Sun.

Good points: This makes a low, spreading plant with golden flowers that bloom a little later than the common woadwaxen.

Bad points: None.

Uses: Ground cover.

Cultivars: 'Vancouver Gold', an introduction from the University of British Columbia, forms a yellow carpet.

Genista   Common woadwaxen,
tinctoria   Dyer's greenweed

Comments: These make low shrubs with small, neat foliage that are attractive when not in flower, and an attention-grabber when they are. They were once used for a green dye.

Hardiness: Canadian zone 3; U.S. zone 3.

Availability: **F**.

Height: 3' (90 cm). *Spread:* 3' (90 cm).

Propagation: Cuttings.

Soil preferences: Sandy, well drained.

Location: Sun.

Good points: These are good plants for dry, sandy locations in full sun; in spring they smother themselves with golden-yellow blooms.

Bad points: None.

Uses: Ground cover for hot spots.

Cultivars: 'Plena' only grows about 12 inches (30 cm) high with double flowers like tiny yellow pompons covering the stems; a great plant. 'Royal Gold' is shorter than the species (2 feet/60 cm) with a more upright habit.

Hedera helix   English ivy

Comments: There is a plant society dedicated to the culture of English ivy and a host of cultivars. Most of these are grown indoors; only a few are regularly grown in the garden.

Hardiness: Canadian zone 5b (most); U.S. zone 4.

Availability: **A**.

Height: 1-2' (30-60 cm). *Spread:* Infinite.

Propagation: Cuttings.

Soil preferences: Most.

Location: Sun to heavy shade.

Good points: In many parts of North America this is an excellent ground cover, even in dense shade. It can also climb trees and clothe walls.

Bad points: Given very good growing conditions ivy can become rampant—it may strangle trees and often damages brickwork. Mites can cause problems in summer. Spiders and sparrows nest in ivy on walls. The fruit is poisonous, but it only forms on mature plants.

Uses: Ground cover; climbing vine.

Cultivars: 'Baltica' is a selection from Latvia that is a zone hardier. 'Thorndale' has large leaves with the veins marked in white.

Hypericum spp.   St. John's wort

The St. John's worts have never grown well for me, and in consequence they are not one of my favorite shrubs. I have seen good plants in other gardens and am content to admire them from afar. In general, they are plants for sandy soils and full sun, but they do not like hot, humid summers and do best in cooler coastal regions. Plant container-grown or B & B stock.

Hypericum   Aaronsbeard
calycinum   St. John's wort

Comments: An evergreen in the south, this plant is deciduous for us.

Hardiness: Canadian zone 5b; U.S. zone 5.

Availability: **F** in Canada; **A** in U.S.

Height: 1' (30 cm). *Spread:* 1 1/2' (45 cm).

Propagation: Cuttings.

Soil preferences: Light and well drained.

Location: Sun.

Good points: The bright yellow flowers appear in mid- to late summer when few other shrubs are in bloom.

Bad points: Few if grown where it does well.

Uses: Ground cover; front of the border.

Hypericum 'Hidcote' — Hidcote St. John's wort

Comments: Another ground-cover plant, 'Hidcote' has the largest flowers of all this group. A hybrid of somewhat uncertain parentage, it is named for the famous English garden where it originated.

Hardiness: Canadian zone 6b; U.S. zone 6.

Availability: **S** in Canada; **A** in U.S.

Height: 3' (90 cm). *Spread:* 3' (90 cm).

Propagation: Cuttings.

Soil preferences: Light and well drained.

Location: Sun.

Good points: This plant will take light shade and still flower from midsummer to frost. It will grow back from the roots if the tops are winter-killed at the limits of its range.

Bad points: None.

Uses: Ground cover; border.

Hypericum kalmianum — Kalm St. John's wort

Comments: A native species found growing along streamsides, it is better adapted to moist soils than the other St. John's worts.

Hardiness: Canadian zone 3; U.S. zone 3.

Availability: **M**.

Height: 2' (60 cm). *Spread:* 2' (60 cm).

Propagation: Cuttings.

Soil preferences: Moist, but will take dry.

Location: Sun.

Good points: It has blue-green foliage and plentiful, but smaller, flowers. This is the most adaptable of all the St. John's worts and the best choice for areas with humid summers.

Bad points: None.

Uses: Ground cover; border.

Juniperus spp. — Juniper

These evergreen plants are much used for foundation planting, but several species also make good ground covers. In addition to the species described below, there are a number of other junipers that make excellent ground covers, but as they are cultivars of more upright species, they are covered under "Conifers" earlier in this chapter.

Juniperus horizontalis — Creeping juniper

Comments: As the name suggests, these are predominantly low-growing forms. They have green to blue foliage that often takes on a purple tinge in fall. The fall coloring is brighter on fertile soils than on poor.

Hardiness: Canadian zone 2; U.S. zone 2.

Availability: **M**.

Height: 1-2' (30-60 cm). *Spread:* 6-10' (1.8-3 m).

Propagation: Cuttings.

Soil preferences: Most.

Location: Sun.

Good points: This native plant, found wild along the east coast, is very salt-tolerant. Most cultivars form a dense cover that will smother weeds.

Bad points: It needs more space than most people allow.

Uses: Ground cover; foundation.

Cultivars: See table on following page.

Juniperus procumbens — Japgarden juniper

Comments: This low-growing species has become popular in recent years.

Hardiness: Canadian zone 4; U.S. zone 4.

Availability: **M**.

Height: 2' (60 cm). *Spread:* 2-10' (up to 3 m).

Propagation: Cuttings.

Soil preferences: Most.

Location: Sun.

Creeping juniper variety	Spread	Comments
'Bar Harbour'	6 ft (1.8 m)	Bright blue turning purplish in fall.
'Blue Chip'	10 ft (3 m)	Very dwarf with silver-blue foliage.
'Douglasii'	8 ft (2.4 m)	More open growth allows weeds to grow; common name is waukegan juniper.
'Hughes'	9 ft (2.7 m)	Silver-green with dense foliage.
'Plumosa'	10 ft (3 m)	The arching growth makes this taller; it is known as the Andorra juniper.
'Plumosa Compacta'	10 ft (3 m)	Only grows half as tall as 'Plumosa' at 12 inches (30 cm); both turn purple in cold.
'Prince of Wales	8 ft (2.4 m)	Very prostrate and a bluish-green tinged with purple in winter.
'Wiltonii'	6 ft (1.8 m)	The best blue, it makes a living carpet; also called 'Blue Rug' and 'Wilton Carpet'.
'Yukon Belle'	6 ft (1.8 m)	Silver-blue with soft foliage; very hardy.

Good points: It makes a good ground cover that forms a dense, weed-smothering carpet and follows the slope.

Bad points: It can be infected with cedar-apple rust.

Uses: Ground cover; border edging.

Cultivars: 'Nana' is the form usually available; it has layers of overlapping mid-green branchlets.

Juniperus sabina Savin juniper

Comments: The various cultivars make low to mounded shrubs that are widely grown.

Hardiness: Canadian zone 4; U.S. zone 3.

Availability: **M**.

Height: 2' (60 cm). *Spread:* 10-15' (3-4.5 m).

Propagation: Cuttings or layering.

Soil preferences: Well drained.

Location: Sun.

Good points: A good choice for poor soils, exposed locations, and areas where pollution might be a problem, such as city gardens.

Bad points: They are prone to juniper blight. The distinctive resinous smell of the foliage is not everyone's cup of tea.

Uses: Ground cover; foundation.

Cultivars: See table opposite.

Juniperus squamata Singleseed juniper

Comments: This is one of the more prickly junipers. The cultivar 'Meyeri', once very popular, is now being replaced by less rampant forms.

Hardiness: Canadian zone 5; U.S. zone 4.

Availability: **A**.

Height: 2' (60 cm). *Spread:* 10' (3 m).

Propagation: Cuttings.

Soil preferences: Well drained to sandy.

Savin juniper variety	Height	Spread	Comments
'Arcadia'	18 in (45 cm)	4 ft (1.2 m)	Slightly arching, bright green.
'Blue Danube'	4 ft (1.2 m)	8 ft (2.4 m)	Outside branches root easily; a good ground cover.
'Broadmoor'	3 ft (90 cm)	10 ft (3 m)	Low growing, it mounds with age.
'Buffalo'	12 in (30 cm)	8 ft (2.4 m)	Bright green, slow growing.
'Calgary Carpet'	12 in (30 cm)	6 ft (1.8 m)	Lime-green new growth in feathery trusses.
'Skandia'	18 in (45 cm)	10 ft (3 m)	Like 'Arcadia' with blue-green foliage.
'Tamariscifolia' (tamarix juniper)	18 in (45 cm)	15 ft (4.5 m)	Mid-green with upright branchlets; widely planted.

Location: Sun.
Good points: These are some of the best blue ground covers.
Bad points: They are susceptible to cedar-apple rust.
Uses: Ground cover.
Cultivars: 'Blue Carpet', a low, flat plant with bluish foliage, may get to 5 feet (1.5 m) across in time. Don't confuse this with 'Blue Rug' (creeping juniper). 'Blue Star' is a very compact, slow-growing form with dense, congested foliage; one of the best blues.

Lonicera xylosteum   Fly honeysuckle

Comments: This is mostly grown as the two dwarf cultivars listed.
Hardiness: Canadian zone 4; U.S. zone 3b.
Availability: **M**.
Height: 10' (3 m). *Spread:* 10' (3 m).
Propagation: Seed or cuttings.
Soil preferences: Most.
Location: Sun.
Good points: The species has creamy flowers and red fruits. The cultivars are more useful but not as showy.

Bad points: Aphids.
Uses: Hedge; ground cover.
Cultivars: 'Emerald Mound' ('Nana') has bluish foliage and grows to only 3 feet (90 cm) tall but twice as wide. 'Miniglobe' is even more compact and is hardier (zone 2 Canadian and U.S.).

Microbiota decussata   Russian arborvitae

Comments: A dwarf, spreading evergreen that is becoming more readily available.
Hardiness: Canadian zone 3; U.S. zone 3.
Availability: **A**.
Height: 1' (30 cm). *Spread:* 10' (3 m).
Propagation: Cuttings.
Soil preferences: Well drained.
Location: Sun to light shade.
Good points: It is bright green in summer, turning a purplish-brown shade in cold weather and does best in cooler climates.
Bad points: This is too large at maturity for small gardens and needs frequent pruning.
Uses: Ground cover.

Pachysandra terminalis   Pachysandra, Japanese spurge

Comments: This is one of the best ground covers for shade.

Hardiness: Canadian zone 3; U.S. zone 3.

Availability: **M**.

Height: 1' (30 cm). *Spread:* 3' (90 cm).

Propagation: Semi-ripe cuttings.

Soil preferences: Organic and acidic, but it is adaptable.

Location: Light to deep shade.

Good points: White flowers are borne on short spikes just above the leaves in spring. The dark evergreen foliage makes a dense, weed-free cover in time.

Bad points: This plant is slow growing, so it may need weeding for the first year or two. It spreads by underground runners and can appear where you don't want it. A leaf blight can blacken stems and foliage and eventually kill plants. Spray with a copper-based fungicide or ferbam.

Uses: Ground cover.

Cultivars: 'Green Carpet' is a more compact form with glossy, dark green leaves. 'Variegata' has leaves marked with white, but the plant is even less vigorous.

Paxistima canbyi   Pachistima

Comments: Also known as ratstripper for some reason, this is a good ground cover for full sun. Container-grown plants grow away fastest.

Hardiness: Canadian zone 2b; U.S. zone 3.

Availability: **M**.

Height: 1' (30 cm). *Spread:* 3' (90 cm).

Propagation: Division or cuttings.

Soil preferences: Well drained.

Location: Sun to light shade.

Good points: It quickly makes a dense mat that crowds out weeds. Evergreen leaves turn a bronzy shade in the cold.

Bad points: Few; it may need cutting back hard every few years.

Uses: Ground cover.

Rhus aromatica   Fragrant sumac

Comments: Native from Ontario southwards, this is a good plant for banks and slopes as the branches root easily.

Hardiness: Canadian zone 3; U.S. zone 3.

Availability: **M**.

Height: 4' (1.2 m). *Spread:* 8' (2.4 m).

Propagation: Cuttings or layering.

Soil preferences: Most.

Location: Sun to mid-shade.

Good points: Small flowers appear in early spring before the leaves, which are fragrant when crushed and have good fall color; there are red berries on female plants.

Bad points: None.

Uses: Ground cover.

Cultivars: 'Gro-Low' is a compact form growing up to 2 feet (60 cm) tall. It is the best form to use as a ground cover, but plant several to be sure of getting fruit.

Stephanandra incisa 'Crispa'   Cutleaved stephanandra

Comments: The cultivar is listed here because it is easier to find than the species, which is taller (about 5 feet/1.5 m) and can be used for hedging, screens or in the border.

Hardiness: Canadian zone 5; U.S. zone 4.

Availability: **M**.

Height: 3' (90 cm). *Spread:* 3' (90 cm).

Propagation: Cuttings.

Soil preferences: Moist, acidic.

Location: Sun.

Good points: This is a good ground-cover plant with dissected leaves that are a light green all summer and turn reddish in fall. There are small heads of white flowers in early summer, but they are nothing special and the plant would still be worth growing without them.

Bad points: None.

Uses: Ground cover.

Vinca minor   **Periwinkle**

Comments: Don't confuse this with the annual periwinkle, a plant for hot sun. This is a shade-loving ground cover. Plant pot-grown plants about 12 inches (30 cm) apart to cover an area reasonably quickly.

Hardiness: Canadian zone 3; U.S. zone 3.

Availability: **M**.

Height: 6" (15 cm). *Spread:* 2-3' (60-90 cm).

Propagation: Cuttings.

Soil preferences: Well drained.

Location: Shade.

Good points: Periwinkle has glossy, dark, evergreen leaves and blue flowers in spring, and it forms a dense mat in time. Try planting daffodils, especially the small-flowered types like 'Thalia' or 'Tete-a-Tete', through it for a lovely spring picture.

Bad points: Stem dieback can cause problems in dense plantings; this is more common in areas with high summer humidity. It can become aggressive, especially in warmer regions and on rich soils.

Uses: Ground cover for shade.

Cultivars: There are many with flowers of white, pink or mauve, or with variegated leaves, but they are hard to find, slower growing and not as likely to seed.

CLIMBING VINES

Climbing plants can play a large role in the garden. They give us the opportunity to make use of normally ignored surfaces—walls, fences and arbors—and increase the range of plants we can grow.

Actinidia spp.   **Hardy kiwi vine**

These are rampant vines that need severe pruning to keep them in check. They are useful where you need a quick cover and they produce edible fruit. The fruit differs from the kiwi fruit in the supermarkets, which is from a tender species; this fruit is smaller and doesn't need peeling. All kiwis have separate male and female plants and you need both to get fruit, with the exception of *A. arguta* 'Issai'.

Actinidia arguta   **Tara vine**

Comments: This vigorous vine will climb into trees. It needs support so cannot be used on bare walls.

Hardiness: Canadian zone 4; U.S. zone 4.

Availability: **A**.

Height: 30' (9 m).

Propagation: Cuttings.

Soil preferences: Most, but slow growing in sand.

Location: Sun.

Good points: The dark green lustrous leaves turn yellowish, then hang on to late in the fall. It reportedly has tasty fruit, rich in vitamin C, potassium and fiber. A pair of mature vines can produce up to 10 gallons (40 L) of fruit per year.

Bad points: None.

Uses: Fence; trellis; arbor.

Cultivars: 'Issai' is a self-fertile form so you only need one for fruit production; it is hard to find at the time of writing, but this will probably change once there is a demand.

Actinidia kolomikta — Kolomikta vine

Comments: This vine is not as fast growing as the tara vine, but it has more attractive foliage. The edible fruit is small, sweet and freely produced.

Hardiness: Canadian zone 4; U.S. zone 4.

Availability: **A**.

Height: 20' (6 m).

Propagation: Cuttings.

Soil preferences: Most.

Location: Sun—for good foliage color.

Good points: The attractive leaves are irregularly blotched with pink and white, but they can quickly change to plain green if they are shaded as the plant grows. Kolomikta vine is becoming more popular, so the availability should improve.

Bad points: You need room for two vines to get fruit.

Uses: Fence; trellis; arbor.

Ampelopsis brevipedunculata — Porcelain vine

Comments: This is another of horticulture's underused gems. It is a deciduous vine related to Virginia creeper *(Parthenocissus)*, but is far more attractive.

Hardiness: Canadian zone 4; U.S. zone 4.

Availability: **S** in Canada; **A** in U.S.

Height: 25' (7.5 m).

Propagation: Cuttings.

Soil preferences: Any but wet.

Location: Sun.

Good points: It has bright green leaves and shiny berries that look like porcelain beads. They start green, turn yellow, then lilac, and finally blue. All the colors can be present at the same time in each cluster.

Bad points: Japanese beetles love it.

Uses: Screening fence; on stumps and rock piles; on a trellis or pergola.

Cultivars: 'Elegans' is not as vigorous and has smaller leaves variegated with white.

Aristolochia macrophylla — Dutchman's pipe

Comments: This is another plant that has undergone a name change amd may be listed under its old name, *A. durior*. It is a vigorous deciduous vine, native to the central U.S.

Hardiness: Canadian zone 5; U.S. zone 4.

Availability: **M**.

Height: 25' (7.5 m).

Propagation: Seed or cuttings.

Soil preferences: Moist, well drained.

Location: Sun.

Good points: Often used to screen porches, the large leaves and rapid growth give fast cover. Flowers are greenish and look like Meerschaum pipes—hence the common name.

Bad points: None.

Uses: Screen (with support).

Campsis radicans — Trumpet vine

Comments: In milder climates, this native climbing vine is a real weed, strangling trees and seeding freely. It is only hardy in sheltered gardens in colder areas and thus we think highly of it.

Hardiness: Canadian zone 5; U.S. zone 4.

Availability: **M**.

Height: 40' (12 m).

Propagation: Seed, cuttings or root cuttings.

Soil preferences: Any.

Location: Sun.

Good points: Orange-red, trumpet-shaped flowers bloom for most of the summer.

Bad points: It is so vigorous and heavy that it needs very strong supports.

Uses: Arbor; trellis; covering a tree stump.

Celastrus scandens   **Bittersweet**

Comments: This rampant native climbing vine has male and female flowers on different plants. Both are needed to produce fruit (the only reason to grow it), so ask for both sexes at the nursery, or plant several and hope you get both.

Hardiness: Canadian zone 3; U.S. zone 3.
Availability: **M**.
Height: 20' (6 m). *Spread:* up to 20' (6 m).
Propagation: Stratifed seed; softwood cuttings in late summer are best as you then know the sex of the parent plant.
Soil preferences: Poor; rich soil causes excessive growth.
Location: Sun to light shade (grows naturally in woods).
Good points: Yellow and orange fruit clusters are used for winter decoration and dried arrangements. Good fall color.
Bad points: It is very aggressive and can kill trees by strangling them.
Uses: Screen for old fences, dead trees or walls.

Clematis spp.   **Clematis**

Clematis is the queen of climbers. The more clematis I grow, the more ways I find to use them. There are many types other than the large-flowered hybrids commonly grown. By careful selection, you could have clematis in flower from just after spring thaw to freeze-up. Although the hardiness of the different species varies greatly, even the coldest areas can grow at least one.

Clematis climb by twisting their leaf stalks in a spiral, so provide support that is small enough to allow them to do this. At Minnesota Landscape Arboretum, they use a wooden frame with chicken wire stapled onto it. Use the 2-inch (5-cm) mesh, rather than the more commonly available 1-inch (2.5-cm) wire.

Large-flowered clematis are hybrids of various species and the parents determine the hybrid's hardiness and the way it produces flowers. This in turn governs the method of pruning. Most books divide the pruning into three main groups. If you are growing several different plants, hang a label nearby with the method of pruning for each; this saves you having to recheck each year.

The first group—Group A—flowers on wood made the previous season and is pruned soon after flowering. I grew one of these, and while the plant survived it never bloomed. It took me some time to realize that although the plant was root-hardy, the old growth (including flower buds) was killed each winter.

Group B flowers early in spring on the previous year's wood, then again in summer on the current growth. The flowers are often double first, then single on the new growth. Prune out weak growth in early spring, then cut back the remaining shoots to a pair of strong buds. Obviously, you need to wait until growth has just started to see these.

The third group, C, flowers on the growth produced in the current season. Cut them back almost to the ground once you can see new growth in spring. Many of the large-flowered hybrids are in this group.

Clematis need hot tops and cool bottoms. Plant them where they will grow in full sun but have shaded roots. Plant annuals or small shrubs to shade the roots, or cover the soil around the stems and roots with flat stones.

If you are planting against a wall, dig the hole at least a foot (30 cm) away and plant on a slight angle towards the wall. Knock the plant out of its pot and loosen the roots if they were curled round the pot base. Plant the clematis about 2 inches (5 cm) deeper than it was growing in the pot. This will allow dormant buds below ground to renew the plant should anything happen to the stem.

In general, clematis like a well-drained, but moisture-retentive soil, slightly acidic to slightly alkaline, with a pH of 6.5 to 8. They will not grow well in very wet soils, but one in my garden is doing very well in almost pure sand that was enriched with compost and old manure. It also gets plenty of moisture from a downspout.

The only serious disease to affect clematis, wilt, causes shoots to droop suddenly for no apparent reason. Cut out affected shoots and water the plant with benomyl. Apart from the inevitable aphids, the worst pest is earwigs, which eat holes in the petals.

The species clematis can be propagated by seed, while the hybrids are increased by stem cuttings. They are not easy to root and even harder to grow into a plant large enough to set out.

Clematis alpina   Alpine clematis

Comments: One of the first to flower in early spring, a real treat after winter. The flowers are small nodding bells in white, blue or pink.

Hardiness: Canadian zone 4; U.S. zone 4.
Availability: **S** (but getting easier to find).
Height: 10' (3 m).
Pruning Group: A.
Cultivars: 'Francis Rivis' has large, deep blue flowers. 'Pamela Jackman' is a paler blue. 'Pink Flamingo' has white bells flushed with pink at the base. 'Willy' is pale pink with a darker petal base. All are early flowering and grow the same height as the species.

Clematis hybrids Large-flowered clematis

Comments: These are the plants that come to mind when you hear the word clematis. The big, flamboyant flowers look spectacular, if the plants are growing well. They can also be frustrating by refusing to bloom when all your neighbors have wonderful displays of flowers.

Hardiness: Canadian zone 3b; U.S. zone 3.
Availability: **M.**
Cultivars: See table below.

Cut back to strong buds (pruning group B).

Variety	Color	Flowering time	Height	Comments
'Belle of Woking'	silvery-mauve	May-June	8 ft/2.4 m	Double flowers.
'Crimson King'	bright red	June-Sept.	12 ft/3.5 m	Petals reflex with age.
'Dr. Ruppel'	bright pink	May-June	8 ft/2.4 m	Semi-double.
'Duchess of Edinburgh'	white	June-Sept.	8 ft/2.4 m	Showy yellow stamens.
'Elsa Spath'	lavender	June-Sept.	8 ft/2.4 m	Reddish stamens.
'General Sikorski'	mid-blue	June-Sept.	7 ft/2.1 m	Golden stamens.
'Henryi'	white	June-Sept.	12 ft/3.5 m	Good for cutting.
'Mrs N. Thompson'	violet	May and Sept.	8 ft/2.4 m	Scarlet stripe on each sepal.
'Nelly Moser'	pale pink	June-Sept.	8 ft/2.4 m	Striped carmine.
'The President'	purple-blue	June-Sept.	8 ft/2.4 m	Pointed sepals.
'Vyvyan Pennell'	violet-blue	May and Sept.	8 ft/2.4 m	Double flowers, then single ones.

Cut almost to ground (pruning group C).

Variety	Color	Flowering time	Height	Comments
'Comtesse de Bouchard' ✓	bright pink	June-Sept.	9 ft/2.7 m	Free-flowering.
'Gypsy Queen'	purple	July-Oct.	12 ft/3.5 m	Vigorous plant.
'Hagley Hybrid' ('Pink Chiffon')	pink	June-Sept.	8 ft/2.4 m	Pointed sepals.
'Huldine'	white	June-Oct.	15 ft/4.5 m	Mauve reverse.
x *jackmanii* ✓	purple	June to Sept.	18 ft/5.4 m	Old but popular.
'Lady Betty Balfour'	purple, becoming paler with age	Sept.-Oct.	15 ft/4.5 m	White stamens.
'Red Cardinal'	bright red	July-Sept.	8 ft/2.4 m	Recurved sepals.
'Ville de Lyon'	carmine red	July-Oct.	12 ft/3.5 m	Golden stamens.

Prune by method B for early flowering or method C for later flowering.

Variety	Color	Height	Comments
'Ernest Markham' ✓	red	12 ft/3.5 m	Rounded sepals and golden stamens.
'Marie Boisselot ('Mme le Coultre')	white	15 ft/4.5 m	Two rings of sepals.
'Niobe'	deep red	8 ft/2.4 m	Pointed sepals and golden stamens.
'Ramona'	lavender	14 ft/4.2 m	Free-flowering with dark stamens.
'Will Goodwin'	lavender	12 ft/3.5 m	Frilled edges to sepals.

Clematis macropetala   **Bigpetal clematis**

Comments: Early flowering, but later than the alpine group. This clematis has a double row of petals which gives a fuller appearance. It may rebloom in midsummer with single flowers.

Hardiness: Canadian zone 2-3; U.S. zone 2.

Availability: **S**.

Height: 12-15' (3.5-4.5 m).

Pruning Group: A—but not every year.

Cultivars: 'Blue Bird' is deep blue with long twisted petals and some rebloom. 'Rosie O'Grady' is pink with pointed petals and repeat bloom. 'Maidwell Hall' is lighter blue.

'Markham's Pink' has lavender-pink petals with paler margins. 'Snowbird' is white and later flowering, so it extends the season.

Clematis montana   **Mountain clematis**

Comments: One of the most vigorous types of clematis, it flowers from early spring to summer. I have seen it growing 30 feet (9 m) up a pine in full sun. The 3-inch (8-cm) flowers are fragrant, and it would look lovely around a bedroom window. It is root-hardy to zone 4, but at those temperatures the tops are killed and no flowers are produced.

Hardiness: Canadian zone 6b; U.S. zone 5.

Availability: **F**.
Height: 40' (12 m).
Pruning Group: A.
Cultivars: See table below.

Clematis tangutica   Russian virgin's bower

Comments: Bright yellow, one inch (2.5 cm), pendulous bells bloom from July to late fall on a very vigorous plant. Ours grows over an archway leading into the herb garden and we have to chop it back several times each summer so we can close the gate. The silky seed heads are a bonus and last well into the winter. They look cute with a hat of snow.
Hardiness: Canadian zone 1b; U.S. zone 1.
Availability: **M**.
Height: 20' (6 m) or more.
Pruning Group: C.

Clematis texensis   Scarlet clematis

Comments: This long-flowering clematis has small blooms, a little larger than those of *C. tangutica*, freely produced. They look like little bells at first, then open into a four-petaled star. The tough, leathery petals withstand heavy rain and early frosts. Mine sprawls through an old apple tree and flowers from late June to hard frost.

Hardiness: Canadian zone 4; U.S. zone 4.
Availability: **F**.
Height: 30' (9 m).
Pruning Group: C.
Cultivars: 'Duchess of Albany' is deep pink with a darker stripe on each petal. 'Gravetye Beauty' is crimson, with wider-opening flowers. 'Sir Trevor Lawrence' is deep carmine.

Clematis viticella   Virgin's bower

Comments: Small, purple, saucer-like flowers bloom from July to October. The named forms extend the color range and include some with double flowers.
Hardiness: Canadian zone 3; U.S. zone 2.
Availability: **F**.
Height: 20' (6 m).
Pruning Group: C.
Cultivars: 'Abundance' is wine red with darker veins. 'Betty Corning' is listed as lavender-blue, but the plants I have seen have been closer to lilac, dark inside and silvery outside. Flowers stay bell-like, not saucer-like. 'Mary Rose' has double blooms of dark amethyst; it is a very old variety mentioned in 1629 writings. 'Polish Spirit' is bright purple with open flowers.

Mountain clematis variety		Color	Bloom size	Bloom time	Comments
'Elizabeth'	pale pink	3 1/2 in/9 cm	May	Very fragrant.	
'Grandiflora'	white	4 in/10 cm	May	Unscented.	
'Pink Perfection'	deep pink	3 1/2 in/9 cm	May	Vanilla-scented.	
var. *rubens*	mauve	2 in/5 cm	May-June	New leaves purple-tinged.	
'Tetrarose'	mauve-pink	3 in/8 cm	May-June	Slight fragrance.	
var. *wilsonii*	white	3 1/2 in/9 cm	late June	Chocolate-scented.	

Hedera helix   **English ivy**

A dual-purpose plant, but used more often as a ground cover and described in that section of the listings.

Hydrangea spp.   **Hydrangea**

Most of the hydrangeas are shrubs and will be found in that section of the listings, but this species is a climber.

Hydrangea anomala   **Climbing**
 ssp. *petiolaris*   **hydrangea**

Comments: At the limits of its hardiness, this grows best on an east-facing wall. On a south wall, it warms up in winter sun and is often killed. In warmer climates, a south or west wall is suitable. Don't plant close to a wall where the soil is dry—set new plants at least 12 inches (30 cm) away from the wall and water frequently until established. Pruning is seldom needed.

Hardiness: Canadian zone 5(b); U.S. zone 4.
Availability: **M**.
Height: 25' (7.5 m).
Propagation: Seed.
Soil preferences: Rich, well drained.
Location: Sun to light shade.
Good points: White flowers in large flat clusters in summer are outstanding. Flaking bark on old stems adds winter interest.
Bad points: None, although it can be slow to establish.
Uses: Covering for walls; arbors; tree stumps.

Lonicera spp.   **Honeysuckle**

The majority of honeysuckle species are shrubs and may be found in that section of the listings, but the following are readily available deciduous vines.

Lonicera   **'Dropmore Scarlet'**
 x *brownii*   **Scarlet trumpet honeysuckle**

Comments: While there are other cultivars of this cross, this is the only one currently available. Raised at Dropmore, Manitoba, it is obviously hardy.

Hardiness: Canadian zone 3; U.S. zone 2b.
Availability: **M**.
Height: 15' (4.5 m).
Propagation: Cuttings.
Soil preferences: Most.
Location: Sun.
Good points: Red tubular flowers appear from midsummer to frost.
Bad points: Aphids.
Uses: Fence; wall.

Lonicera   **Goldflame**
 x *heckrottii*   **honeysuckle**

Comments: This popular twining vine is a hybrid of uncertain parentage that has been around for more than a hundred years.

Hardiness: Canadian zone 4; U.S. zone 4.
Availability: **M**.
Height: 15' (4.5 m).
Propagation: Cuttings.
Soil preferences: Most.
Location: Sun.
Good points: The red buds open to show a yellow interior and the flowers are slightly fragrant. It grows well on chain-link fences and flowers for most of the summer with large clusters of blooms.
Bad points: Aphids.
Uses: Screening.

Lonicera japonica   **Japanese honeysuckle**

Comments: The species has become an invasive weed in many places, but the variegated cultivar has a place in the garden and 'Halliana' is grown for its perfume.

Hardiness: Canadian zone 6; U.S. zone 5.
Availability: **M** or **F**.
Height: 20' (6 m).
Propagation: Cuttings.
Soil preferences: Most.
Location: Sun.
Good points: Free-flowering and very fragrant.
Bad points: Invasive.
Uses: Vine for walls and fences; ground cover for banks.
Cultivars: 'Aureo-maculata' has leaves that are veined in yellow; it is much slower-growing and not free-flowering. 'Halliana' blossoms are white, turning pale yellow; honeysuckle perfume is based on this cultivar, which is readily available.

Parthenocissus **spp.**

These vines climb with twining tendrils that have sticky tips. They can even stick to aluminum siding once started.

Parthenocissus quinquefolia   **Virginia creeper**

Comments: The leaf has five lobes (hence the species name) and is a dull green turning red to brick-red in fall. It can be used as a ground cover but it will climb anything in its path. Keep moving!
Hardiness: Canadian zone 2b; U.S. zone 3.
Availability: **M**.
Height: 30-50' (9-15 m).
Propagation: Cuttings.
Soil preferences: Most.
Location: Sun to shade.
Good points: This is salt- and pollution-tolerant, so it does well in cities. It can be used to cover trees, walls and fences and will grow 10 feet (3 m) a year once established.
Bad points: A species of flea beetle eats holes in the leaves, leaving them very tattered.

Uses: Climbing vine; ground cover.
Cultivars: 'Engelmannii' has smaller leaves and is slightly slower growing.

Parthenocissus tricuspidata   **Boston ivy**

Comments: The leaf has three lobes and is glossy green, turning orange in fall. One of the best climbing vines, it clothes many an old house.
Hardiness: Canadian zone 5b; U.S. zone 4.
Availability: **M**.
Height: 30-50' (9-15 m).
Propagation: Cuttings.
Soil preferences: Most.
Location: Sun to shade.
Good points: This vine is more refined (that is, less rampant) than Virgina creeper. The black fruit stays on after leaf fall.
Bad points: It quickly covers windows and provides a good home for spiders and sparrows.
Uses: Climbing vine.
Cultivars: 'Veitchii', the type most commonly sold, has smaller leaves.

Polygonum aubertii   **Silverlace vine**

Comments: This deciduous vine has recently had a name change to *Fallopia baldschuanica*, but it will probably take several years for the new name to come into general use. Do not confuse this with *P. cuspidatum* (Japanese, Chinese or Mexican bamboo), a real thug that no right-minded person would plant—twice anyway.
Hardiness: Canadian zone 5; U.S. zone 4.
Availability: **A**.
Height: 30' (9 m).
Propagation: Seed or cuttings.
Soil preferences: Most, including dry.
Location: Sun to shade.
Good points: It has fairly rampant growth and is covered with trusses of white flowers in the latter half of summer.

Bad points: It climbs by twisting but may need tying up to get it started. It can be somewhat invasive.

Uses: Covering for fences, tree stumps etc.

Wisteria floribunda   Japanese wisteria

Comments: Driving in New York State, I saw a large tree covered in bluish flowers beside the freeway. It took me a while to realize that I had really seen a wisteria climbing a pine. Wisteria is spectacular but can take a while to become established: plant container-grown stock and be patient. Chinese wisteria *(W. sinensis)* is similar but a zone more tender.

Hardiness: Canadian zone 5b; U.S. zone 4.

Availability: **A**.

Height: 60' (18 m) or more.

Propagation: Seed; root cuttings.

Soil preferences: Deep, well drained.

Location: Sun.

Good points: Long tresses of violet to blue or white flowers bloom in spring. Once growing well it is a rampant vine that needs strong support for its heavy mass of twisted stems, but the flowers make it all worthwhile.

Bad points: Plants may take several years to come into flower. Once the plant is mature, flowering can be encouraged by shortening new growth back to about 6 inches (15 cm) in late summer to encourage flower bud formation. In winter, prune again, shortening shoots back to 2 or 3 buds.

Uses: Climbing vine.

Cultivars: 'Lawrence' has pale blue flowers and is the hardiest form. It blooms (most years) in the northern part of the zone. 'Rosea' has pale, rose-colored, fragrant flowers in 16-inch (40-cm) clusters.

Plants for Special Locations

The final column indicates the location of descriptions: T—deciduous trees; S—shrubs; C—conifers; G—ground covers; V—climbing vines.

Plants for moist and wet soils

Alnus glutinosa	Common alder	T
Aronia melanocarpa	Black chokeberry	S
Betula alleghaniensis	Yellow birch	T
Betula nigra	River birch	T
Calycanthus floridus	Carolina allspice	S
Celtis occidentalis	Hackberry	T
Cephalanthus occidentalis	Buttonbush	S
Chionanthus virginicus	Fringetree	T
Clethra alnifolia	Summersweet	S
Cornus stolonifera	Red osier dogwood	S
Dirca palustris	Leatherwood	S
Fraxinus excelsior	European ash	T
Fraxinus nigra	Black ash	T
Hamamelis vernalis	Vernal witch hazel	S
Hamamelis virginiana	Common witch hazel	S
Hypericum kalmianum	Kalm St. John's wort	G
Ilex verticillata	Winterberry	S
Itea virginica	Sweetspire	S
Kalmia latifolia	Mountain laurel	S
Larix laricina	American larch	C
Lindera benzoin	Spicebush	S
Nyssa sylvatica	Tupelo	T
Picea glauca	White spruce	C
Ptelea trifoliata	Hoptree	T
Quercus bicolor	Swamp white oak	T
Quercus palustris	Pin oak	
Salix spp.	Willow	T
Sciadopitys verticillata	Japanese umbrella-pine	C
Stephanandra incisa	Cutleaved stephanandra	G
Taxodium distichum	Bald cypress	C
Thujopsis dolobrata	False arborvitae	C
Tsuga canadensis	Canadian hemlock	C

Plants for dry soils

Ailanthus altissima	Tree of heaven	T
Amorpha fruticosa	False indigo	S
Arctostaphylos uva-ursi	Bearberry	G
Celtis occidentalis	Hackberry	T
Colutea arborescens	Bladder senna	S
Cornus racemosa	Gray dogwood	S
Corylus spp.	Filbert	S
Cytisus spp.	Broom	S
Daphne cneorum	Rose daphne	S
Daphne mezereum	February daphne	S
Elaeagnus commutata	Silverberry	S
Elaeagnus umbellatus	Autumn olive	S

Plants for dry soils (continued)

Genista spp.	Woadwaxen	G
Hypericum spp.	St. John's wort	G
Juniperus communis	Common juniper	C
Juniperus sabina	Savin juniper	G
Myrica pennsylvanica	Bayberry	S
Pinus banksiana	Jack pine	C
Pinus contorta var. *latifolia*	Lodgepole pine	C
Pinus resinosa	Red pine	C
Pinus thunbergiana	Japanese black pine	C
Potentilla fruticosa	Cinquefoil	S
Prinsepia sinensis	Cherry prinsepia	S
Pyracantha spp.	Firethorn	S
Sheperdia argentia	Buffalo berry	S
Tamarix ramosissima	Tamarix	S
Yucca filamentosa	Adam's needle	S
Yucca glauca	Spanish bayonet	S

Plants for acidic soils

Arctostaphylos uva-ursi	Bearberry	G
Berberis julianae	Wintergreen barberry	S
Calluna vulgaris	Heather	G
Chamaecyparis pisifera	Sawara false cypress	C
Cladrastis lutea	Yellowwood	T
Clethra alnifolia	Summersweet	S
Cornus alternifolia	Pagoda dogwood	T
Cornus canadensis	Bunchberry	G
Cytisus spp.	Broom	S
Deutzia spp.	Deutzia	S
Dirca palustris	Leatherwood	S
Enkianthus campanulatus	Redvein enkianthus	S
Epigaea repens	Trailing arbutus	G
Erica spp.	Heath	G
Fothergilla spp.	Fothergilla	S
Gaultheria procumbens	Wintergreen	G
Halesia caroliniana	Silverbells	T
Hamamelis mollis	Chinese witch hazel	S
Hydrangea macrophylla	Florist's hydrangea	S
Kalmia latifolia	Mountain laurel	S
Larix kaempferi	Japanese larch	C
Leucothoe fontanesia	Fetterbush	S
Liquidambar styraciflua	Sweetgum	T
Magnolia spp.	Magnolia	S
Nyssa sylvatica	Tupelo	T

Picea omorika	Serbian spruce	C
Pieris japonica	Japanese pieris	S
Pinus banksiana	Jack pine	C
Pinus densiflora	Umbrella pine	C
Quercus coccinea	Scarlet oak	T
Quercus palustris	Pin oak	T
Quercus rubra	Red oak	T
Rhododendron spp.	Rhododendron, azalea	S
Sciadopitys verticillata	Japanese umbrella-pine	C
Stephanandra incisa	Cutleaved stephanandra	G
Styrax japonicus	Snowbell	T
Thujopsis dolobrata	False arborvitae	C

Salt-tolerant plants

Acer platanoides	Norway maple	T
Ailanthus altissima	Tree of heaven	T
Arctostaphylos uva-ursi	Bearberry	G
Caragana spp.	Peashrub	S
Carya ovata	Shagbark hickory	T
Cladrastis lutea	Yellowwood	T
Clethra alnifolia	Summersweet	S
Cytisus spp.	Broom	S
Elaeagnus angustifolius	Russian olive	S
Euonymus alatus	Winged euonymus	S
Fraxinus americana	White ash	T
Hippophae rhamnoides	Sea buckthorn	S
Juniperus communis	Common juniper	C
Juniperus horizontalis	Creeping juniper	G
Juniperus virginiana	Red cedar	C
Lonicera spp.	Honeysuckle	S, V
Morus alba (possibly)	White mulberry	T
Myrica pennsylvanica	Bayberry	S
Parthenocissus quinquefolia	Virginia creeper	V
Picea pungens	Colorado spruce	C
Pinus banksiana	Jack pine	C
Pinus flexilis	Limber pine	C
Pinus mugo	Mountain pine	C
Pinus nigra	Austrian pine	C
Pinus parviflora	Japanese white pine	C
Pinus thunbergiana	Japanese black pine	C
Populus deltoides	Cottonwood	T
Prunus virginiana	Chokecherry	T
Quercus rubra	Red oak	T

Salt-tolerant plants (continued)

Rhus typhina	Staghorn sumac	S
Robinia pseudoacacia	Black locust	T
Syringa spp.	Lilac	S
Tamarix ramosissima	Tamarix	S

Salt-intolerant plants

Acer negundo	Manitoba maple	T
Amelanchier spp.	Serviceberry	T, S
Betula papyrifera	Paper birch	T
Catalpa speciosa	Northern catalpa	T
Chaenomeles spp.	Flowering quince	S
Cornus stolonifera	Red osier dogwood	S
Crataegus spp.	Hawthorn	T
Fagus spp.	Beech	T
Fraxinus pennsylvanica	Green ash	T
Juglans spp.	Walnut	T
Kolkwitzia amabilis	Beautybush	S
Malus spp.	Crab apple	T
Ostrya virginiana	Hophornbeam	T
Philadelphus spp.	Mock orange	S
Picea glauca	White spruce	C
Pinus resinosa	Red pine	C
Pinus strobus	White pine	C
Pinus sylvestris	Scots pine	C
Spiraea x *bumalda*	Bumalda spirea	S
Taxus spp.	Yew	C
Thuja occidentalis	White cedar	C
Tilia spp.	Linden	T
Tsuga canadensis	Canadian hemlock	C
Viburnum opulus	European bush-cranberry	S

Plants for full (all-day) shade

Acer pensylvanicum	Striped maple	T
Carpinus carolinianus	American hornbeam	T
Cornus alba	Tatarian dogwood	S
Cornus canadensis	Bunchberry	G
Gaultheria procumbens	Wintergreen	G
Hedera helix	English ivy	G
Kalmia latifolia	Mountain laurel	S
Kerria japonica	Japanese kerria	S
Leucothoe fontanesia	Fetterbush	S
Ostrya virginiana	Hophornbeam	T
Pachysandra terminalis	Pachysandra	G

Ptelia trifoliata	Hoptree	T
Ribes alpinum	Alpine currant	S
Staphylea trifolia	Bladdernut	S
Symphoricarpos albus	Snowberry	S
Taxus spp.	Yew	C
Viburnum lentago	Nannyberry	S
Vinca minor	Periwinkle	G

Plants for dappled (part) shade

Acer palmatum	Japanese maple	S
Alnus glutinosa	Common alder	T
Arctostaphylos uva-ursi	Bearberry	G
Aronia spp.	Chokeberry	S
Buxus hybrids	Boxwood	S
Calluna vulgaris	Heather	G
Calycanthus floridus	Carolina allspice	S
Catalpa speciosa	Northern catalpa	T
Celastrus scandens	Bittersweet	V
Clethra alnifolia	Summersweet	S
Cornus alternifolia	Pagoda dogwood	T
Cornus stolonifera	Red osier dogwood	S
Cotoneaster dammeri	Bearberry cotoneaster	G
Epigaea repens	Trailing arbutus	G
Erica spp.	Heath	G
Hamamelis vernalis	Vernal witch hazel	S
Hamamelis virginiana	Common witch hazel	S
Hippophae rhamnoides	Sea buckthorn	S
Hydrangea anomala ssp. *petiolaris*	Climbing hydrangea	V
Hydrangea arborescens	Smooth hydrangea	S
Hydrangea quercifolia	Oakleaved hydrangea	S
Hypericum 'Hidcote'	Hidcote St. John's wort	G
Ilex verticillata	Winterberry	S
Itea virginica	Sweetspire	S
Laburnum x *watereri*	Goldenchain tree	T
Lindera benzoin	Spicebush	S
Magnolia x *soulangeana*	Saucer magnolia	S
Magnolia stellata	Star magnolia	S
Mahonia aquifolium	Oregon grape	S
Microbiota decussata	Russian arborvitae	G
Myrica pennsylvanica	Bayberry	S
Pieris japonica	Japanese pieris	S
Polygonum aubertii	Silverlace vine	V
Rhamnus frangula	Alder buckthorn	S
Rhododendron spp.	Rhododendron, azalea	S

Plants for dappled shade (continued)

Rhus aromatica	Fragrant sumac	G
Sorbaria sorbifolia	False spirea	S
Styrax japonicus	Snowbell	T
Thujopsis dolobrata	False arborvitae	C
Tsuga canadensis	Canadian hemlock	C
Viburnum carlesii	Korean spice viburnum	S
Viburnum dentatum	Arrowwood	S
Viburnum lantana	Wayfaringtree	S

Plants for formal (clipped) hedges

Aronia spp.	Chokeberry	S
Berberis spp.	Barberry	S
Buxus spp.	Boxwood	S
Caragana arborescens	Siberian peashrub	S
Caragana frutex	Russian peashrub	S
Carpinus spp.	Hornbeam	T
Cornus stolonifera	Red osier dogwood	S
Cotoneaster lucidus	Hedge cotoneaster	S
Crataegus crus-galli	Cockspur hawthorn	T
Euonymus alatus	Winged euonymus	S
Euonymus nanus	Dwarf euonymus	S
Fagus spp.	Beech	T
Fothergilla spp	Fothergilla	S
Hamamelis virginiana	Common witch hazel	S
Hippophae rhamnoides	Sea buckthorn	S
Ilex x *meserveae*	Blue holly	S
Juniperus virginiana	Western red cedar	C
Ligustrum amurensis	Amur privet	S
Ligustrum x *vicaryi*	Golden privet	S
Ligustrum vulgare	Common privet	S
Lonicera caerulea	Bearberry honeysuckle	S
Lonicera korolkowii	Blueleaf honeysuckle	S
Lonicera tatarica	Tatarian honeysuckle	S
Lonicera xylosteum	Fly honeysuckle	G
Lonicera x *xylostoides*	Clavey's dwarf honeysuckle	S
Physocarpus opulifolius	Ninebark	S
Prinsepia sinensis	Cherry prinsepia	S
Prunus x *cistena*	Purple-leaved sand cherry	S
Prunus tomentosa	Nanking cherry	S
Pyracantha spp.	Firethorn	S
Rhamnus frangula	Alder buckthorn	S
Salix purpurea	Arctic willow	S
Shepherdia argentia	Buffalo berry	S

Syringa meyeri	Dwarf Korean lilac	S
Syringa x *prestoniae*	Preston lilac	S
Syringa villosa	Late lilac	S
Syringa vulgaris	Common lilac	S
Taxus spp.	Yew	C
Thuja occidentalis	White cedar	C
Thuja plicata	Western red cedar	C
Tsuga spp.	Hemlock	C
Viburnum opulus	European bush-cranberry	S

Plants for informal (unclipped) hedges

Berberis julianae	Wintergreen barberry	S
Chaenomeles spp.	Flowering quince	S
Cornus alba	Tatarian dogwood	S
Deutzia gracilis	Slender deutzia	S
Forsythia ovata	Early forsythia	S
Forsythia suspensa	Weeping forsythia	S
Hydrangea arborescens	Smooth hydrangea	S
Lonicera x *xylostoides*	Clavey's dwarf honeysuckle	S
Philadelphus spp.	Mock orange	S
Physocarpus opulifolius	Ninebark	S
Potentilla fruticosa	Cinquefoil	S
Rosa 'Champlain'	Champlain rose	S
Rosa x *harisonii*	Harison's yellow rose	S
Spiraea x *bumalda*	Bumalda spirea	S
Spiraea nipponica	Nippon spirea	S
Syringa x *persica*	Persian lilac	S

Trees with colored foliage (often only in the cultivars)

Abies concolor	Silver fir (silver)	C
Acer platanoides	Norway maple (purple; green & white)	T
Cercis canadensis	Redbud (red-purple)	T
Fagus sylvatica	European beech (purple; multicolored)	T
Gleditsia triacanthos	Honeylocust (yellow)	T
Juniperus virginiana	Red cedar (bluish)	C
Picea pungens	Colorado spruce (silver-blue)	C
Prunus cerasifera	Cherry plum (purple)	T

Trees with colored foliage (continued)

Prunus virginiana	Chokecherry (purple)	T
Pyrus salicifolia	Willow-leaved pear (silver)	T
Robinia pseudoacacia	Black locust (yellow)	T

Shrubs with colored foliage (often only in the cultivars)

Acer palmatum	Japanese maple (red to purple)	S
Ampelopsis brevipedunculata	Porcelain vine (green and white)	V
Berberis thunbergii	Japanese barberry (red to purple; yellow)	S
Buddleja alternifolia	Fountain buddleia (silver)	S
Cornus alba	Tatarian dogwood (cream- or yellow-edged)	S
Corylus avellana	European filbert (yellow)	S
Cotinus coggygria	Smokebush (purple)	S
Daphne x *burkwoodii*	Burkwood daphne (white-edged)	S
Euonymus fortunei	Wintercreeper (white, cream or yellow markings)	G
Hedera helix	English ivy (white-veined)	G
Hippophae rhamnoides	Sea buckthorn (gray)	S
Juniperus chinensis	Chinese juniper (blue-green; gray)	C
Juniperus communis	Common juniper (yellow)	C
Juniperus horizontalis	Creeping juniper (silver-blue; blue)	G
Juniperus x *media*	Hybrid juniper (yellow)	C
Juniperus scopulorum	Rocky Mountain juniper (blue)	C
Juniperus squamata	Singleseed juniper (blue)	G
Juniperus virginiana	Red cedar (silver; blue)	C

Kerria japonica	Japanese kerria (white-edged)	S
Leucothoe fontanesia	Fetterbush (multicolored in spring)	S
Ligustrum x *vicaryi*	Golden privet (yellow)	S
Lonicera japonica	Japanese honeysuckle (yellow-veined)	V
Pachysandra terminalis	Pachysandra (green and white)	G
Physocarpus opulifolius	Ninebark (yellow)	S
Picea abies	Norway spruce (yellowish)	C
Pieris japonica	Japanese pieris (multicolored)	S
Prunus x *cistena*	Purple-leaved sand cherry (purple)	S
Sambucus spp.	Elder (gold; cream-edged)	S
Spireae x *bumalda*	Bumalda spirea (red to yellow; lime)	S
Spiraea japonica	Japanese spirea (yellow)	S
Syringa reticulata	Japanese tree lilac (yellow-edged)	S
Taxus cuspidata	Japanese yew (yellow)	C
Thuja occidentalis	White cedar (golden)	C
Thuja plicata	Western red cedar (yellow)	C
Thujopsis dolobrata	False arborvitae (cream blotched)	C
Weigela florida	Weigela (purple-tinged; cream-edged)	S
Yucca filamentosa	Adam's needle (yellow center)	S

Plants for fall color

Acer griseum	Paperbark maple	T
Acer palmatum	Japanese maple	S
Acer rubrum	Red maple	T
Acer saccharum	Sugar maple	T
Acer tataricum ssp. *ginnala*	Amur maple	S
Actinidia arguta	Tara vine	V
Amelanchier spp.	Serviceberry	T, S

Plants for fall color (continued)

Arctostaphylos uva-ursi	Bearberry	G
Aronia spp.	Chokeberry	S
Berberis x mentorensis	Mentor barberry	S
Calycanthus floridus	Carolina allspice	S
Carpinus carolinianus	American hornbeam	T
Carya ovata	Shagbark hickory	T
Celastrus scandens	Bittersweet	V
Cercidiphyllum japonicum	Katsura tree	T
Cercis canadensis	Redbud	T
Chionanthus virginicus	Fringetree	T
Clethra alnifolia	Summersweet	S
Cornus kousa	Kousa dogwood	T
Cornus stolonifera	Red osier dogwood	S
Cotinus coggygria	Smokebush	S
Crataegus crus-galli	Cockspur hawthorn	T
Crataegus phaenopyrum	Washington hawthorn	T
Dirca palustris	Leatherwood	S
Enkianthus campanulatus	Redvein enkianthus	S
Euonymus alatus	Winged euonymus	S
Euonymus europaeus	Spindle tree	T
Euonymus nanus	Dwarf euonymus	S
Fagus spp.	Beech	T
Fothergilla spp.	Fothergilla	S
Fraxinus americana	White ash	T
Fraxinus nigra	Black ash	T
Fraxinus pennsylvanica	Green ash	T
Ginkgo biloba	Maidenhair tree	C
Gleditsia triacanthos	Honeylocust	T
Halesia caroliniana	Silverbells	T
Hamamelis spp.	Witch hazel	S
Hydrangea quercifolia	Oakleaved hydrangea	S
Itea virginica	Sweetspire	S
Juniperus horizontalis	Creeping juniper	G
Koelreuteria paniculata	Varnish tree	T
Larix spp.	Larch	C
Lindera benzoin	Spicebush	S
Liquidambar styraciflua	Sweetgum	T
Liriodendron tulipifera	Tulip tree	T
Magnolia stellata	Star magnolia	S
Mahonia aquifolium	Oregon grape	S
Nyssa sylvatica	Tupelo	T

Ostrya virginiana	Hophornbeam	T
Parrotia persica	Persian parrotia	T
Parthenocissus quinquefolia	Virginia creeper	V
Parthenocissus tricuspidata	Boston ivy	V
Populus tremuloides	Quaking aspen	T
Prunus sargentii	Sargent's cherry	T
Prunus serrulata	Japanese flowering cherry	T
Pyrus calleryana	Callery pear	T
Pyrus ussuriensis	Ussurian pear	T
Quercus coccinea	Scarlet oak	T
Quercus palustris	Pin oak	T
Quercus rubra	Red oak	T
Rhododendron 'PJM'	PJM rhododendron	S
Rhus aromatica	Fragrant sumac	G
Rhus typhina	Staghorn sumac	S
Ribes aureum	Golden currant	S
Securinega suffruticosa	Spoil axe	S
Sorbus alnifolia	Korean mountain ash	T
Sorbus x thuringiaca	Oakleaved mountain ash	T
Spiraea x bumalda	Bumalda spirea	S
Styrax japonicus	Snowbell	T
Symphoricarpos orbiculatus	Coralberry	S
Syringa patula	Korean lilac	S
Viburnum x carlcephalum	Fragrant snowball	S
Viburnum dentatum	Arrowwood	S
Viburnum dilatatum	Linden viburnum	S
Viburnum lentago	Nannyberry	S
Zelkova serrata	Japanese zelkova	T

Plants with conspicuous fall fruit

Acer tataricum ssp. ginnala	Amur maple	S
Ampelopsis brevipedunculata	Porcelain vine	V
Arctostaphylos uva-ursi	Bearberry	G
Aronia spp.	Chokeberry	S
Berberis thunbergii	Japanese barberry	S
Catalpa speciosa	Northern catalpa	T
Celastrus scandens	Bittersweet	V
Chaenomeles spp.	Flowering quince	S
Colutea arborescens	Bladder senna	S

Plants with conspicuous fall fruit (continued)

Cornus spp.	Dogwood, most	T, S, G
Cotoneaster spp.	Cotoneaster	S, G
Crataegus spp.	Hawthorn	T
Elaeagnus angustifolius	Russian olive	S
Elaeagnus commutata	Silverberry	S
Elaeagnus umbellatus	Autumn olive	S
Euonymus alatus	Winged euonymus	S
Euonymus europaeus	Spindle tree	T
Gymnocladus dioicus	Kentucky coffeetree	T
Halesia caroliniana	Silverbells	T
Hamamelis virginiana (flowers)	Common witch hazel	S
Hippophae rhamnoides	Sea buckthorn	S
Ilex spp.	Holly	S
Lindera benzoin	Spicebush	S
Lonicera spp.	Honeysuckle	S, V
Mahonia aquifolium	Oregon grape	S
Malus spp.	Crab apple	T
Myrica pennsylvanica	Bayberry	S
Ostrya virginiana	Hophornbeam	T
Parthenocissus quinquefolia	Virginia creeper	V
Parthenocissus tricuspidata	Boston ivy	V
Phellodendron amurensis	Amur corktree	T
Ptelia trifoliata	Hoptree	T
Pyracantha spp.	Firethorn	S
Rhus aromatica	Fragrant sumac	G
Rosa spp.	Roses, most	S
Sambucus spp.	Elder	S
Shepherdia argentia	Buffalo berry	S
Sophora japonica	Pagoda tree	T
Sorbus spp.	Mountain ash	T
Staphylea trifolia	Bladdernut	S
Symphoricarpos spp.	Snowberry	S
Taxus spp.	Yew	C
Viburnum spp.	Viburnum, most	S

Plants with interesting winter bark or form

Acer griseum	Paperbark maple	T
Acer pensylvanicum	Striped maple	T
Betula nigra	River birch	T
Betula papyrifera	Paper birch	T
Betula utilis	Whitebark birch	T
Buddleja alternifolia	Fountain buddleia	S

Carpinus carolinianus	American hornbeam	T
Carya ovata	Shagbark hickory	T
Cornus alba	Tatarian dogwood	S
Cornus stolonifera	Red osier dogwood	S
Corylus avellana	European filbert	S
Cotoneaster horizontalis	Rockspray	G
Crataegus crus-galli	Cockspur hawthorn	T
Crataegus viridis	Green hawthorn	T
Euonymus alatus	Winged euonymus	S
Fagus spp.	Beech	T
Heptacodium miconioides	Chinese heptacodium	T
Hydrangea anomala ssp. *petiolaris*	Climbing hydrangea	V
Kerria japonica	Japanese kerria	S
Laburnum x *watereri*	Goldenchain tree	T
Maackia amurensis	Amur maackia	T
Ostrya virginiana	Hophornbeam	T
Parrotia persica	Persian parrotia	T
Phellodendron amurensis	Amur corktree	T
Pinus bungeana	Lacebark pine	C
Pinus densiflora	Umbrella pine	C
Pinus sylvestris	Scots pine	C
Platanus spp.	Plane tree	T
Prunus maackii	Amur chokecherry	T
Prunus sargentii	Sargent's cherry	T
Prunus tomentosa	Nanking cherry	S
Salix matsudana	Corkscrew willow	S
Sorbus aucuparia	European mountain ash	T
Syringa reticulata	Japanese tree lilac	S
Taxodium distichum	Bald cypress	C
Thuja occidentalis	White cedar	C
Tilia tomentosa	Silver linden	T
Zelkova serrata	Japanese zelkova	T

Weeping trees (often only in the cultivar)

Betula pendula	European white birch	T
Buddleja alternifolia	Fountain buddleia	S
Caragana arborescens	Siberian peashrub	S
Cercidiphyllum japonicum	Katsura tree	T
Chamaecyparis nootkatensis	Nootka false cypress	C
Fagus sylvatica	European beech	T
Larix decidua	European larch	C
Malus baccata	Siberian crab apple	T

Weeping trees (continued)

Malus hybrids	Hybrid crab apples	T
Morus alba	White mulberry	T
Picea abies	Norway spruce	C
Picea omorika	Serbian spruce	C
Pinus strobus	White pine	C
Prunus serrulata	Japanese flowering cherry	T
Robinia pseudoacacia	Black locust	T
Salix alba	White willow	T
Salix caprea	Goat willow	S
Salix pentandra	Laurel willow	T
Salix purpurea	Arctic willow	S
Sorbus aucuparia	European mountain ash	T
Tsuga canadensis	Canadian hemlock	C

Upright trees (often only in the cultivar)

Abies concolor	Silver fir	C
Acer saccharum	Sugar maple	T
Carpinus betulus	European hornbeam	T

Cryptomeria japonica	Japanese cedar	C
Ginkgo biloba	Maidenhair tree	C
Juniperus chinensis	Chinese juniper	C
Juniperus communis	Common juniper	C
Juniperus scopulorum	Rocky Mountain juniper	C
Malus baccata	Siberian crab apple	T
Malus hybrid	Hybrid crab apple	T
Metasequoia glyptostroboides	Dawn redwood	C
Picea omorika	Serbian spruce	C
Pinus cembra	Swiss stone pine	C
Pinus contorta var. *latifolia*	Lodgepole pine	C
Pseudotsuga menziesii var. *glauca*	Douglas fir	C
Pyrus calleryana	Callery pear	T
Quercus robur	English oak	T
Sorbus aucuparia	European mountain ash	T
Thuja occidentalis	White cedar	C
Tilia cordata	Little-leaf linden	T

Suggested Reading

Chapters 1 to 4

The American Horticultural Society Encyclopedia of Gardening. Christopher Brickell, ed. New York: Dorling Kindersley, 1993. In Canada this is called *Practical Guide to Gardening in Canada*. Christopher Brickell, Trevor Cole, eds. Montreal: Readers Digest, 1993. These are basically the same book and, although they cover all aspects of gardening, the step-by-step photographs of woody-plant care are well worth studying.

Modern Arboriculture. Alex L. Shigo. Durham, NH: Shigo and Trees, Associates, 1991. This book goes into the way trees grow and what happens to them when they are pruned or otherwise injured. It can change the way you think about a pruning saw.

Tree Maintenance. 6th ed. Pascal P. Pirone. New York: Oxford University Press, 1988. *Arboriculture*. Richard W. Haris. Englewood Cliffs, NJ: Prentice Hall, 1983. These two books are technical manuals for tree-care workers and they will answer all your questions on soils, nutrition, planting and the general care of woody plants.

Chapter 5

Several books listed for chapter 10 will help you with plant identification. The best ones are marked with an asterisk.

Pruning

The Complete Book of Pruning. Duncan Coombs, Peter Blackburne-Maze, Martyn Cracknell and Roger Bentley. London: Ward Lock, 1992.

A slightly more technical book but well illustrated.

The Pruning of Trees, Shrubs and Conifers. George E. Brown. Portland, OR: Timber Press, 1995. Originally published in 1972, this is one of the classic books on pruning.

Pruning Simplified. Lewis Hill. Emmaus, PA: Rodale Press, 1979. Written for the novice gardener, this book has good line drawings.

Chapter 6

Diseases and Pests of Ornamental Plants. 5th ed. Pascal P. Pirone. New York: Wiley-Interscience, 1978. Although this covers non-woody plants as well, it is the best source for control measures.

Diseases of Trees and Shrubs. Sinclair, Lyon and Johnson, 1987, and *Insects that Feed on Trees and Shrubs*, 2nd ed. Johnson and Lyon, 1988. Ithaca, NY: Cornell University Press. These are pictorial identification books with many photographs, but they may be confusing for the real novice. They don't suggest controls, but at least you will know the problem.

Handbook of Natural Insect and Disease Control. Ellis and Bradley, eds. Emmaus, PA: Rodale Press, 1992. Although this covers all plants, it does include many trees and shrubs and gives garden-friendly control measures.

Chapter 8

The Grafters Handbook. 5th ed. R.J. Garner. London: R.H.S./Cassell, 1990. I used an early edition of this enduring textbook as a student.

Plant Propagation: Principles and Practices. 5th ed. Hartmann, Kester and Davis. Englewood Cliffs, NJ: Regent/Prentice Hall, 1990. Another standard textbook that goes deeply into plant propagation.

Practical Woody Plant Propagation for Nursery Growers. Bruce Macdonald. Portland, OR: Timber Press, 1986. Everything you need to know and more from the director of the UBC Botanical Garden.

The Reference Manual of Woody Plant Propagation. Dirr and Heuser. Athens, GA: Varsity Press, 1987. A comprehensive guide to the best way to start new plants.

Chapter 9

Gardening with Groundcovers and Vines. Allen Lacy. New York: Harper Collins, 1993. A well-illustrated book about using these plants in the landscape.

The Hedge Book. Jeffrey Whitehead. Pownal, VT: Storey/Garden Way Publishing, 1991. The only book I know of that deals only with hedges.

Taylor's Guide to Ground Covers, Vines and Grasses. Boston, MA: Houghton Mifflin, 1987. Good color pictures of a wide range of plants.

See also the listings for chapter 10, Ground Covers.

Chapter 10

* = especially good for plant identification

Deciduous Trees

Flowering Crab-apples: The Genus Malus. Fr. John Fiala. Portland, OR: Timber Press, 1995. Everything you could need to know about this plant.

Landscape Plants for Eastern North America. Harrison Flint. New York: Wiley-Interscience, 1983. This useful book has good charts for features such as the seasons of interest and soil requirements. Even better are the drawings showing the size of the plant after a few years and at maturity. It does not cover as many cultivars as the *Manual of Woody Landscape Plants,* but is a useful reference.

Manual of Woody Landscape Plants. 4th ed. Michael Dirr. Champaign, IL: Stipes Publishing, 1990. I find this the best North American tree and shrub book. It contains detailed descriptions in fairly nontechnical language, and an impressive list of cultivars.

*The Random House Book of Trees. Roger Phillips. New York: Random House, 1979. This book has photographs of leaves, flowers and fruit of a wide range of species and cultivars.

A Reunion of Trees. Stephen A. Spongberg. Cambridge, MA: Harvard University Press, 1990. This book is a fascinating look at the discovery and introduction of many of our non-native trees.

*The Trees of North America. Alan Mitchell. New York: Facts on File, 1987. This is similar to *The Random House Book of Trees* but has paintings rather than photographs. It also provides better illustrations of the entire tree.

Shrubs

*The American Garden Guides—Shrubs and Vines. Written by staff members at three botanical gardens in the U.S. and Canada. New York: Pantheon Books, 1994. Worth looking at for the many color pictures, this picks out the cream of the crop, but it includes many plants for warmer zones.

Shrubs (continued)

Flowering Shrubs and Small Trees. Isabel Zucker. New York: Grove Weidenfeld, 1990. Another compendium of plants, but with more emphasis on the how-to, and good photos by Derek Fell.

Garden Shrubs and Their Histories. Alice Coats. New York: Simon and Schuster, 1992. Read this for fascinating background about the plants we grow.

Japanese Maples. 2nd ed. J.D. Vertrees. Portland, OR: Timber Press, 1987. This book is the last word on this topic.

Lilacs: The Genus Syringa. Fr. John Fiala. Portland, OR: Timber Press, 1988. This book will tell you more than you can possibly imagine about these popular plants.

Magnolias. J.M. Gardiner. Chester, CT: The Globe Pequot Press, 1989. This has wonderful pictures and full cultural details.

Roses for Canadian Gardens (in Canada) or *Hardy Roses* (in the U.S.). Robert Osborne. Toronto: Key Porter Books, 1991. This is one of the best of the numerous books on shrub roses, even though only American hardiness zones are used.

Shrubs. Roger Phillips and Martyn Rix. New York: Random House, 1989. Like their book on trees, this has excellent photographs of flowers and leaves.

The Smaller Rhododendrons. Peter Cox, 1985. *Rhododendron Portraits*. D. van Gelderen & J. van Hoey Smith, 1992. *Getting Started with Rhododendrons and Azaleas*. J. Harold Clarke, 1982. *Azaleas*. Fred Galle, 1987. All are now published by Timber Press and taken together they will be enough to enthuse anyone.

Conifers

Ornamental Conifers. Charles R. Harrison. New York: Macmillan, 1975. *Conifers*. D.M. van Gelderen and J.R.P. van Hoey Smith. Portland, OR: Timber Press, 1986. Both contain color photographs of a wide selection of conifers.

Ground Covers

Easy-care Ground Cover Plants. Donald Wyman. New York: Macmillan, 1956. An older book, frequently reprinted and still relevant. It covers more species than other books on this topic.

The Harrowsmith Gardener's Guide to Ground Covers. Jennifer Bennett, ed. Camden East, ON: Camden House, 1987. A useful small book with personal experience from gardeners across Canada.

Climbers

Clematis, the Queen of Climbers. Jim Fisk. London: Cassell, 1989. *Clematis as Companion Plants*. Barry Fretwell. London: Cassell, 1994. *Clematis*. Christopher Lloyd. Deer Park, WI: Capability Books, 1992. These three books should get you growing clematis everywhere.

Trellis. Jamie Garnock. New York: Rizzoli, 1991. *The Lattice Gardener*. William C. Mulligan. New York: Macmillan, 1995. Two books that can give you ways to incorporate arbors, archways and trellises in the garden, and have room for more plants.

Index of Common Names

The final column indicates the location of descriptions: T—deciduous trees; S—shrubs; C—conifers; G—ground covers; V—climbing vines.

Common name	Botanical name	Look under
Adam's needle	Yucca	S
Alder	Alnus	T
Almond	Prunus	S
Amur corktree	Phellodendron	T
Amur maackia	Maackia	T
Arborvitae, common	Thuja	C
Arborvitae, false	Thujopsis	C
Arborvitae, Russian	Microbiota	G
Arbutus, trailing	Epigaea	G
Arrowwood	Viburnum	S
Ash	Fraxinus	T
Aspen	Populus	T
Autumn olive	Elaeagnus	S
Azalea	Rhododendron	S
Barberry	Berberis	S
Basswood	Tilia	T
Bayberry	Myrica	S
Bearberry	Arctostaphylos	G
Beautybush	Kolkwitzia	S
Beech	Fagus	T
Beech, blue	Carpinus	T
Birch	Betula	T
Bittersweet	Celastrus	V
Black gum	Nyssa	T
Bladdernut	Staphylea	S
Bladder senna	Colutea	S
Boston ivy	Parthenocissus	V
Boxwood	Buxus	S
Broom	Cytisus	S
Buckeye	Aesculus	T, S
Buckthorn, alder	Rhamnus	S
Buckthorn, sea	Hippophae	S

Common name	Botanical name	Look under
Buffalo berry	Shepherdia	S
Bunchberry	Cornus	G
Burningbush	Euonymus	S
Bush clover	Lespedezia	S
Bush-cranberry	Viburnum	S
Butterfly bush	Buddleja	S
Butternut	Juglans	T
Buttonbush	Cephalanthus	S
Carolina allspice	Calycanthus	S
Catalpa	Catalpa	T
Cedar, Alaska	Chamaecyparis	C
Cedar, Japanese	Cryptomeria	C
Cedar, red	Juniperus	C
Cedar, white	Thuja	C
Cherry	Prunus	T, S
Cherry plum	Prunus	T
Cherry prinsepia	Prinsepia	S
Chokeberry	Aronia	S
Chokecherry	Prunus	T
Cinquefoil	Potentilla	S
Coralberry	Symphoricarpos	S
Cornelian cherry	Cornus	S
Cotoneaster	Cotoneaster	S, G
Cottonwood	Populus	T
Crab apple	Malus	T
Currant	Ribes	S
Currant, Indian	Symphoricarpos	S
Cypress, bald	Taxodium	C
Cypress, false	Chamaecyparis	C
Cypress, yellow	Chamaecyparis	C
Daphne	Daphne	S
Dawn redwood	Metasequoia	C
Deutzia	Deutzia	S
Devil's walking stick	Aralia	S
Dogwood	Cornus	T, S

Common name	Botanical name	Look under
Dutchman's pipe	*Aristolochia*	V
Dyer's greenweed	*Genista*	G
Elder	*Sambucus*	S
Elm	*Ulmus*	T
Empress tree	*Paulownia*	T
Enkianthus, redvein	*Enkianthus*	S
Euonymus	*Euonymus*	S, G
False indigo	*Amorpha*	S
False spirea	*Sorbaria*	S
Fetterbush	*Leucothoe*	S
Filbert	*Corylus*	S
Fir, Douglas	*Pseudotsuga*	C
Fir, silver	*Abies*	C
Firethorn	*Pyracantha*	S
Forsythia	*Forsythia*	S, G
Fothergilla	*Fothergilla*	S
Fringetree	*Chionanthus*	T
Goldenbells	*Forsythia*	S
Goldenchain tree	*Laburnum*	T
Goldenrain tree	*Koelruteria*	T
Hackberry	*Celtis*	T
Hawthorn	*Crataegus*	T
Hazel	*Corylus*	T, S
Heathers	*Calluna*	G
Heaths	*Erica*	G
Hemlock	*Tsuga*	C
Heptacodium, Chinese	*Heptacodium*	T
Hercules club	*Aralia*	S
Hickory	*Carya*	T
Hills of snow	*Hydrangea*	S
Holly	*Ilex*	S
Honeylocust	*Gleditsia*	T
Honeysuckle	*Lonicera*	S, V
Hophornbeam	*Ostrya*	T
Hoptree	*Ptelea*	T
Hornbeam	*Carpinus*	T
Horse chestnut	*Aesculus*	T
Hydrangea	*Hydrangea*	S, V
Indian currant	*Symphoricarpos*	S
Indigo, false	*Amorpha*	S
Ironwood	*Carpinus, Ostrya*	S, T
Ivy	*Hedera*	G
Ivy, Boston	*Parthenocissus*	V
Japanese angelica tree	*Aralia*	S
Juneberry	*Amelanchier*	S
Juniper	*Juniperus*	C, G
Katsura tree	*Cercidiphyllum*	T
Kentucky coffeetree	*Gymnocladus*	T
Kerria	*Kerria*	S
Kinnikinnick	*Arctostaphylos*	G
Kolomikta vine	*Actinidia*	V
Larch	*Larix*	C
Leatherwood	*Dirca*	S
Lilac	*Syringa*	S
Lily-of-the-valley shrub	*Pieris*	S
Linden	*Tilia*	T
Locust	*Robinia*	T
Magnolia	*Magnolia*	S
Maidenhair tree	*Ginkgo*	C
Maple	*Acer*	T, S
May-day tree	*Prunus*	T
Mock orange	*Philadelphus*	S
Mountain ash	*Sorbus*	T
Mountain laurel	*Kalmia*	S
Mulberry	*Morus*	T
Musclewood	*Carpinus*	T
Nannyberry	*Viburnum*	S
Ninebark	*Physocarpus*	S
Oak	*Quercus*	T
Oregon grape	*Mahonia*	S
Pachistima	*Paxistima*	G
Pachysandra	*Pachysandra*	G
Pagoda tree	*Sophora*	T
Parrotia	*Parrotia*	T
Pear	*Pyrus*	T
Pearlbush	*Exochorda*	S
Peashrub	*Caragana*	S
Periwinkle	*Vinca*	G
Pieris	*Pieris*	S
Pine	*Pinus*	C

Index

Main entries are in bold type.

CLIMATIC ZONE MAPS – CANADA

Lower zone numbers refer to increasingly cold areas, but there are no specific minimum-temperature limits for each zone.

Climatic Zone Maps–Canada

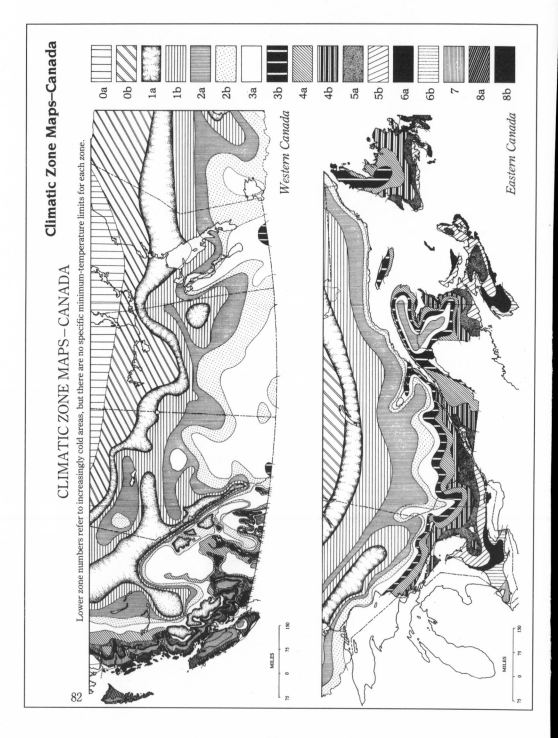

0a
0b
1a
1b
2a
2b
3a
3b
4a
4b
5a
5b
6a
6b
7
8a
8b

Western Canada

Eastern Canada

MILES
75 0   75   150

MILES
75 0   75   150

82

USDA Plant Hardiness Zone Map

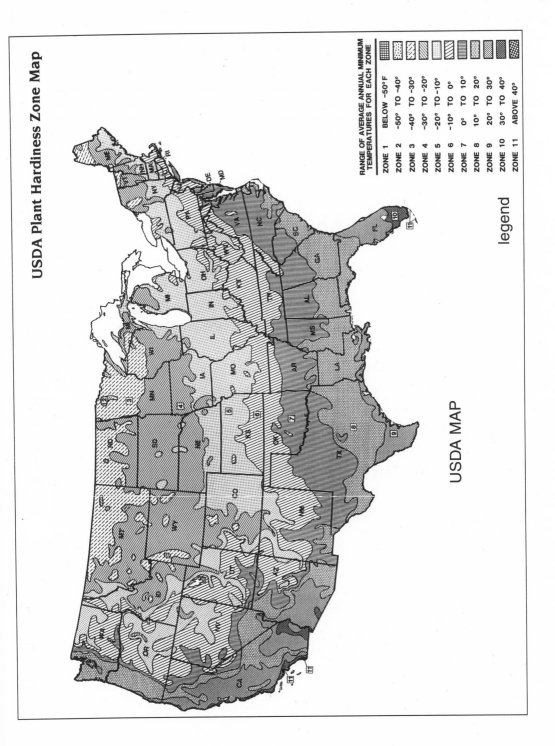

USDA MAP

legend

	RANGE OF AVERAGE ANNUAL MINIMUM TEMPERATURES FOR EACH ZONE
ZONE 1	BELOW -50°F
ZONE 2	-50° TO -40°
ZONE 3	-40° TO -30°
ZONE 4	-30° TO -20°
ZONE 5	-20° TO -10°
ZONE 6	-10° TO 0°
ZONE 7	0° TO 10°
ZONE 8	10° TO 20°
ZONE 9	20° TO 30°
ZONE 10	30° TO 40°
ZONE 11	ABOVE 40°

About the Author

Passionate about all things branched and rooted, Trevor Cole's gardening experience began at Britian's Hampton Court Palace and Kew Garden. Since moving to Canada, Cole has taught numerous home landscaping courses and worked for almost 20 years as curator of the Dominion Arboretum in Ottawa, Ontario. He was a senior consultant to Reader's Digest on several publications, including *The Illustrated Guide to Gardening in Canada* and *The Practical Guide to Gardening in Canada*. Cole has also written many Agriculture Canada publications, and is the bestselling author of *The Ontario Gardener*. He lives near Ottawa, Ontario.